"This is a powerful MUST READ resource for women to understand the process of resiliency and their resilient style in facing stressful challenges. Bravo to the author for empowering women with creative exercises and tools to strengthen their resilient style."

—**Mercedes A. McCormick, PhD, LP**, 2013 President of the American Psychological Association, Div. 52 International Psychology, and past president of the New York State Psychological Association, Division of Women's Issues

"Offering both a mirror and a roadmap to guide women to new understandings about individual thoughts, actions, and strengths, *The Resilient Woman* provides insight and the protective tools to 'woman-proof' our lives. Instead of blaming women for picking up negative ideas of how we *should* think, feel, or act, O'Gorman explains how being a woman includes the exposure to a certain amount of 'cultural trauma' and then shows women how a resilient life is generated not from what happened in our lives but by our *reactions* to those things. *The Resilient Woman* offers the tools we need to make change in our lives plus the actionable steps to help us live from our base of personal power. It's a masterpiece!"

—**Teena Cahill, PsyD**, humorist, TV and radio show host, director of Wisdom and Beyond, and author of *The Cahill Factor: Turning Adversity into Advantage*

"Exploring the individual, family, and community factors we have experienced enables us to look at ourselves in a new way. The questions raised by Dr. O'Gorman about how we think of ourselves, and the steps suggested to build a sense of resilience, are very constructive."

—**Lita Schwartz, PhD**, Distinguished Professor Emerita, Pennsylvania State University

"Unfortunately, even after half a century of feminist awareness, many smart women and girls are unable to access their power and live as fully as they would like. This book is a place to start—for women and for men who care about women and girls—to unravel the invisible forces that determine how we feel and what we're capable of doing."

—**Marsha Shenk**, pioneer in business anthropology, coach, consultant to leaders from the Fortune 50 to Solopreneurs, and founder of The BestWork® People

"While showing how our childhood influences our resiliency, Dr. O'Gorman skillfully provides insight on the wide variety of changes women experience over the years. Developing and understanding a strong resilience plays a critical role in every woman's personal and professional success."

—**Janet L. Duprey**, New York State Assemblywoman, 115th District

"Women who come to a family-law attorney are generally in pain and at a crossroads in their lives. *The Resilient Woman* offers an incredible tool to empower our clients during this period of their lives. Do not, however, mistake this book as merely a read for a person in crisis. *The Resilient Woman* explores why and how we revert to our girlhoods for so many of our emotional responses, how to analyze and overcome the results of those responses, and how to make decisions based on our adult selves."

—**Elaine Wilson, Esq.**, past president of the Foothill
(East San Diego County) Bar Association

"Look no further than *The Resilient Woman* to discover and develop your inner resilience. I could relate to so much of this book because of my own life. As author Patricia O'Gorman points out, childhood experiences have an incredible impact on resilience in adulthood, but no matter what difficult circumstance life throws at you, you too can create resilience from it. The resilience journal Dr. O'Gorman guides readers to create is an excellent exercise for every woman to use to begin the process of developing a resilient life. This is a book I recommend not just for woman; men will benefit from this information, too."

—**Erin Merryn**, *Glamour*'s Woman of the Year 2012, political activist,
and author of *Stolen Innocence* and *Living for Today*

"Wow! I wish I could have read this book twenty-five years ago. I could have spared myself decades of listening to the static of *girly thoughts* as well as participating in the self-sabotage that goes with them. Growing your self-awareness, recognizing the need for boundaries, and acquiring the confidence to take charge are critical components of a successful professional career. This is particularly true of professions that have traditionally been dominated by men. First you have to 'know what you know' and then have the faith to act accordingly. In *The Resilient Woman*, author Patricia O'Gorman offers both the background knowledge and the doable steps any woman can use to accomplish this."

—**Rebecca Lewis, Esq.**, attorney and criminal prosecutor

"Dr. O'Gorman defines 'resilient women' in a whole new light while messaging that resiliency has more to do more with one's curiosity, optimism, combatting outdated *girly* thinking, and gratitude. Her practical and warmly written book invites readers to recognize and boost their resilience as they take the journey to transform and give higher meaning to their lives. By the end of *The Resilient Woman* I was saying, 'Yes, I am!' and 'Yes, I can!'"

—**Kathryn Brohl, LMFT**, author of *Social Service
Workplace Bullying: A Betrayal of Good Intentions*

"Dr. O'Gorman's book is a practical and powerful guide for helping women develop and acknowledge their resilience. Though *girly thoughts* often undermine women's belief in their own competence, most survive life's inevitable surprises and setbacks quite well. It's now time for women to take credit for doing so. The stories of how women have tackled the toughest tests of life will be an inspiration to all."

—**Linda Sapadin, PhD**, psychologist and author of
How to Beat Procrastination in the Digital Age

"In *The Resilient Woman*, Dr. O'Gorman exposes the self-defeating ways of thinking about both self and other that women often grow up with and rely on to guide their relationships. Dr. O'Gorman provides a practical guide for the reader to reconsider these ineffective *girly thoughts* and to get in touch with and utilize strengths that underlie their resilience."

—**Thomas Lund, PsyD,** coauthor of *Narrative Solutions in Brief Therapy*

"For those trapped by social mores or personal trauma or in counterproductive thought patterns or behaviors, the author presents real stories to help understand why as well as encouragement to take charge of changing their lives for the better. While the book is purposely focused on women of all ages, most of the advice and the structured change methods offered would be helpful to men as well."

—**Michaela K. Rodeno**, CEO (retired) of St. Supery Winery in Napa Valley, CA., former VP/Marketing for Domaine Chandon, and current chairman of the board of directors of Visit Napa Valley

"*The Resilient Woman* is imbued with strength, clarity and inspiring guidance that any woman can use."

—**Maureen Healy**, author of *Growing Happy Kids*

"Dr. Patricia O'Gorman's background makes her imminently qualified to address what happens when women disregard their own needs. *The Resilient Woman* reflects her latest thinking on an issue that debilitates tens of thousands of women—a way of thinking and behaving that can literally be fatal—and shows the way to a new path of personal power. This book can save your life!"

—**Julie D. Bowden, MS**, marriage, family, and child therapist and coauthor of *Recovery: A Guide for Adult Children of Alcoholics.*

"Women so often give away their power as they go through life on autopilot, and, when a crisis hits, they scramble to unearth the wisdom and strength they always had. *The Resilient Woman* is a manual for unleashing that power and letting go of those *girly thoughts* that only get in the way of one's true self."

—**Sherry Gaba, LCSW**, speaker, cohost of *A Moment of Change* on CBS radio, and author of *The Law of Sobriety*

"This very readable book offers many of the basic tools used clinically to reverse the consequences of post-traumatic stress for women who have survived domestic abuse, street crime, war, and other kinds of institutional abuse, whether in academic or treatment centers. *The Resilient Woman* is a book I would like to be able to hand to each of my female PTSD clients to stimulate their recovery."

—**Rona M. Fields, PhD**, fellow of the American Psychological Association and author of *Against Violence Against Women*

"Patricia O'Gorman has created an in-depth yet highly accessible treatise about how women can tap into the layers of their histories and identities. Unpeeling the layers creates a step-by-step plan for creating personal degrees of sustainable agency that can be life transforming. Celebrating our weaknesses and pains as our true strengths instead of trying to manage them in the deep shadows of our psyches has the potential to reshape the meaning of wisdom from within in our homes, communities, and societies."

—**Dr. Steve Tyrell,** president, North Country Community College, Saranac Lake, NY

"As a wife, mother, grandmother, professional speaker, entertainer, and a suicide survivor, I know the desperation that can fill a woman's life . . . even when everything looks good on the outside. I urge women to read *The Resilient Woman* and take the risk of getting to know your true selves, your strong selves. You will reap tremendous benefits from reading this powerful book."

—**LaDonna Gatlin, CSP, CPAE**, author of *The Song in You*

"Patricia O'Gorman offers women a path to uncovering and accessing their natural strengths and beauty. Through recognizing their support systems and integrating their personal history, Patricia empowers women to accept, nurture, and creatively fulfill their lives. She has created an insightful, engaging dialogue that encourages positive self-reflection and growth. This is a guide to living your life with joy and confidence, a book you will read and share with your friends."

—**Robin Becker, MA**, artistic director, Robin Becker Dance

"*The Resilient Woman* brings together many effective theories on empowerment, parenting, self-esteem, self-care, and independence to provide a guidebook for woman of any age. Understanding and getting past the fear of releasing old ways of being opens the door to a future based on what really matters to you. As you discover ways to build your life from a foundation that is uniquely you own, you will release the dreams and hopes of the past that caused pain and failure.

"Applause to Dr. Patricia O'Gorman for bringing so much empowering information together into one comprehensive guidebook that every woman should have on her bookshelf."

—**Nancy Mramor, PhD**, CEO of Transformedia LLC, health and media psychologist, award-winning author, and international speaker

The Resilient Woman

Mastering the 7 Steps to Personal Power

Patricia O'Gorman, PhD

Health Communications, Inc.
Deerfield Beach, Florida

www.hcibooks.com

The names of the people in this book who have shared their experiences have been changed. This book also includes some experiences that are composites taken from a group of people who have had similar experiences. In the last case, any resemblance to specific people or specific situations is accidental.

Portions of this book originally appeared in *Dancing Backwards in High Heels* by Patricia O'Gorman and published by Hazeldon, 1994.

Library of Congress Cataloging-in-Publication Data

O'Gorman, Patricia A.
  The resilient woman : mastering the 7 steps to personal power / Patricia O'Gorman, PhD.
      pages cm
  Includes bibliographical references and index.
  ISBN 978-0-7573-1709-5 (pbk.)
  ISBN 0-7573-1709-X (pbk.)
  ISBN 978-0-7573-1710-1 (epub)
  ISBN 0-7573-1710-3 (epub)
    1. Women—Psychology.   2. Resilience (Personality trait)
3. Self-esteem in women.   I. Title.
  HQ1206.O354 2013
  646.70082--dc23
                                                                                        2012049605

Publisher: Health Communications, Inc.
          3201 S.W. 15th Street
          Deerfield Beach, FL 33442-8190

Cover design by Jane Clausen
Interior design and formatting by Lawna Patterson Oldfield

To my resilient mother, and
to the other strong women in my life.
You know who you are. I am grateful
to you for your heroism.

And to my sons, because
I just love you with
my whole heart.

Contents

Acknowledgments

T *o my family:* I'm especially grateful for my sons' love and on-going belief in me, their devotion, support, understanding, and creative ideas; Jeremy, for your ongoing checking in, and Michael, for your hard work, especially during Super Storm Sandy, which came during the final editing. And special thanks to my late father: did you ever think that telling me our family shield had a sword crossed with a pen would inspire me to be a writer? And Rob, for your love and commitment over a lifetime of joys and challenges.

To the women in my life: Thank you for your support, stories of hardship, possibility, and triumph, especially Sophie Elam and Ruth Sondheimer. You went where there was no path and left a trail, helping to plant the seed that became the concept of *girly thoughts*, and you've shaped the person I've become. And to the two Ks for your cover advice and Jane for your creative genius.

To my friends: Jane, Elie, Judy, Julie, Cynthia, Ellen, Brad, Phil, Fred, and especially Marie, for your insights into the art of dancing.

To my clients and workshop and retreat attendees: thank you for your inspiration, encouragement, and support.

To Tribal, my constant canine companion: thanks for your faithful female presence in my otherwise male-energy household. I always feel sorry for people who make the mistake of thinking you are a male because of your dominant personality—they must have missed out on knowing most of the women in my life.

To Tom: for your feedback on *Dancing Backwards in High Heels* nearly twenty years ago: a big thank-you. I heard you. And thanks also to the increasing number of researchers who are helping us understand how women act when under duress, pointing the way for how to ameliorate this.

To Peter Vegso and his staff at HCI: a heartfelt thank-you for your vision in seeing the importance of providing a guide for women to consciously develop their resilience and combat those *girly thoughts*.

To Candace Johnson: dare I say, the perfect editor? Thank you for your steady hard work, sense of humor, and playful hand in guiding and crafting this project particularly during its most convoluted of times. You are truly a joy to work with, and brilliant and insightful as well. And to Nancy Burke, my steely eyed copyeditor: you are a pleasure to have on my team.

To Barbara Bauer, the editor for *Dancing Backwards in High Heels*, for your support in taking what was then a new concept—resilience—and helping to adapt it for women.

Introduction

W*hen I wrote the original version* of this book, my twin
sons were just learning to read. One day I was dashing
around the house, and they knew I was preparing to give a talk, so
I guess they picked up on my tension. From the wisdom born of
children, they asked me if I was going to begin with a joke; "You
need to be funny," they told me earnestly. They disappeared for a
while, then a little later they proudly presented me with a joke cut
out from *Ranger Rick* and taped, with lots of tape, on to a big piece
of paper. They were in the "Why did the chicken cross the road"
stage of humor, and the joke they picked was perfect for a talk on
resilience. It went: Why couldn't the skeleton cross the road? The
punch line: It had no guts.

Many things have changed since that day. My children are now
adults; women face increasingly varied challenges; but one thing
that hasn't changed is women's lack of focus in developing and using
their resilience. So with this in mind, I began to think about revis-
ing and updating my book, *Dancing Backwards in High Heels,* with
an eye toward bringing into sharper focus the strategies for developing resilience and overcoming the obstacles we face in doing so.
What I thought would be a revision became a rewritten book and

led me to develop seven clearly defined steps for women to use in mastering their personal power.

Guts are still the essence of resilience. Resilience is about having guts—having courage born of learning from life's hard lessons and understanding how to take positive actions using this powerful inner resource. Resilience is all about learning to step into our strengths.

Buying a book on developing resilience may seem a little redundant for a twenty-first-century woman. We're all resilient, aren't we? So you may be thinking, *If I knew I needed a book on resilience, I'd know enough to not have to buy the book.* But that's not quite true either. I'm reminded of a sign I saw in my gym: *They told me to wear loose clothes. But if I had loose clothes, I wouldn't have to join.*

So what gets in the way of tapping into this part of ourselves? What keeps us from using what we know to help us bounce back when we run headlong into adversity? I finally found a simple term for this liability: *girly thoughts.* Our *girly thoughts* are those society-informed limiting thoughts and images of who we are, what we are capable of, what we are good for, how we should look, and how we should act, and they promise the rewards we will get if we are the *good girl.* They are reinforced by our families and friends and intensified by our personal experiences with trauma and we have so internalized them that we are not even aware that we are using them to define ourselves.

However, labeling these persuasive forces is not meant to trivialize either their effect on us or the seriousness with which we took them to heart. Using a lighthearted term is not meant to demean us for falling under their sway. Rather, calling them *girly thoughts* is a way of making them accessible and help us wrap our minds around this concept so we can consciously counter their incredible control over us and begin to claim our own power of self-definition.

So, what exactly is resilience? As defined by Oxford Dictionary Online, it is an ability to recover quickly from or adjust easily to misfortune or change. Resilience is something we all have to some degree, sometimes not as much as we would like, but it is in there somewhere, and it is certainly something we can *cultivate*. When we consciously focus on our strengths, our inner tempos and rhythms, we can more naturally hear our inner solutions for determining our best course of action. We find that those assets that we often take for granted form into another quality that is greater than the sum of its parts: our resilience. To begin to focus on our resilience involves:

- claiming our personal strengths, our personal battle scars if you will, that come from our tangles with life's challenges;
- learning how to *consciously* use this inner force;
- understanding how to turn up the volume of this part of ourselves and listen to our inner wisdom speaking to us; and
- embracing our ability to grow this significant capacity within us.

So it is not just a question of whether we are resilient or not, but how we optimize this quality within us—and this requires some creativity as well as vision, grit (Duckworth et al. 2012), and ownership. And our reward is an expanded sense of who we are. Just think how it would feel to walk around with a smile on your face as you think of yourself as a resilient, *gritty woman*.

Why is resilience so important for women? It is all too common for women to doubt our abilities, to see nothing extraordinary or powerful about ourselves, to be more focused on what we have to do, what's wrong with how we look, to ignore the push and pulls we feel in our bodies, to ignore our needs (including our sexual needs), and even our feelings. Yet if we stop for a moment to take a breath and consider how much we actually accomplish each day, the many roles we play, and the distances we travel, we may see quite another view of ourselves.

This other view can literally change our lives. It lifts us from the limited sense of who we are that focuses on how much we can endure to one where we realize that, despite all we have to do, we can still notice what *we* need. This awareness opens the door to allowing us to love and care for ourselves. And we can begin to do this increasingly on our own terms with the goal of leading the lives we've envisioned for ourselves. This process begins through aligning ourselves with our strengths, recognizing and owning our incredible personal power, and deciding where to use it, including (for some of us) to give to not only ourselves but also to others. Our endurance model now becomes a self-care model.

The Conscious Use of Resilience

The fact is that most of us underestimate the degree of strength and flexibility our lives require on a daily basis. We focus instead on our unfinished tasks, pushing ourselves harder while we simultaneously ignore our self-nurturing. To do what seems like the impossible task of taking care of ourselves, we need to be reminded of our own power from time to time, as my own mother—a competitive ballroom dancer in her golden years—did when she told me on more than one occasion that while Fred Astaire received top billing, "Ginger Rogers did everything that Fred Astaire did. And she just did it backwards and in high heels, and slimmed down in the process."

So even though we are most successful in life when we can achieve a balance between our two vital sources of strength—self and other—achieving this can be quite a challenge. It requires us to use all of who we are and *dares* us to be in touch with our own desires and our own needs. How to do this? *The Resilient Woman: Mastering the 7 Steps to Personal Power* offers you a comprehensive, practical, step-by-step guide to understanding your own resilience and to consciously expanding its role in everyday life through learning how to combat those *girly thoughts*. This is a process you can do at your own pace and will not take a lot of time that you don't have. I will help you learn to think differently about yourself, begin to listen to your needs and wants, start to nurture yourself, and learn very simple experiments to try out different ways of taking care of what you need within yourself and with others.

I've done this through creating simple assessments and seven steps designed for daily use. The steps in Part Two are designed to bring out the best in you—your resilience—by helping you develop strategies to build your resilience consciously. These include having you consider solutions that you used in the past that could be dusted off and used today, considering yourself in a new light as a resilient woman by challenging some of your existing attitudes about yourself, those *girly thoughts*, and learning some new skills. I will do this through:

- Helping you use your natural qualities, such as curiosity and creativity,
- Showing you how to make space within your life to perfect the art of really listening to yourself instead of all the external messages that bombard you,

- Guiding you in setting *helpful* boundaries,
- Encouraging you to free yourself to take risks while
  thinking positively, and
- Helping you learn how to develop the gift of
  gratitude in your life, and experiencing the
  joy that comes from living in the safety of
  the life you have created.

You will find that your resilience can be built and expanded through taking control of your thinking and your actions, which you will be guided in doing by the seven steps provided in the third part of this book. Of course to do this does require that you consciously challenge those *girly thoughts*, your less-than-helpful negative inner dialogue, but I will show you how! Each chapter will guide you in creating your very own Resilience Plan, and through writing a personalized Resilience Journal you will develop a complete set of action steps that are specific to you.

So join me on a journey, a quest if you will, into the very best that is in you. Come to know who you really are, how strong you truly are, how proud you can be of what you've made of the challenges life has served up to you. Discover your very own resilience.

PART ONE

Warming Up: Detecting and Challenging *Girly Thoughts*

The emotional, sexual, and psychological stereotyping of females begin when the doctor says, "It's a girl."

—Shirley Chisholm, first African American woman elected to Congress and first major-party African American candidate for president of the United States

As you warm up and begin to *stretch* your idea of who you are and what you are capable of doing, you'll notice, access, and further develop your resilience. In doing so, you'll create a new mind-set for your capacities, one that you can use immediately and consciously as you go through your day to decrease your anxiety, and even your anger, and increase your effectiveness in managing the challenges before you.

In Part I we'll explore the secret weapon in dealing with life's stressors: your resilience. You'll learn that this concept doesn't just apply to those who have experienced major trauma, but is a quality that we all utilize, often without being aware of it. And you'll learn what gøøets in the way of your effectively using this persuasive inner resource: the societal pressure we all feel in our *girly thoughts*.

ONE

Recognizing Resilience: Our Secret Weapon

IT'S FUN TO BE A WOMAN. IT'S FUN TO FLIRT AND
WEAR MAKEUP AND HAVE BOOBS.

—*Eva Mendez*

I*t is fun to be feminine,* and it's also fun to be strong. That's where our resilience comes in. Resilience? What does resilience have to do with me? I hear this question often from friends and the women I counsel. My answer is always the same: *Everything.*

Resilience is a concept that has been evolving slowly and that is only now beginning to receive widespread attention. In psychological and sociological literature, *resilience* is used to describe a dynamic, responsive quality developed by people who lead normal, fulfilling lives despite having been subjected to trauma in all of its various forms (Chareny 2004). This trauma can result from a disruptive early home life or from the chaos of battle, or rape, or bullying on the job, but, in every case, it puts those who were subjected to it at high risk for developing personal and social problems. People are labeled resilient because they possess the ability to recover from the adversity they have experienced while they retain a positive self-image and view of the world (O'Gorman and Diaz 2012).

As a result of such clinical definitions, resilience is frequently thought of as a quality belonging only to those who have survived great hardship. Yet all healthy people have endured hardships such as illness, divorce, challenges at work or with family, and they develop resilience, too. Just as the body has the resilience to protect itself from disease and heal after injury, so the mind has psychological resilience. In the body, a certain amount of exposure to disease immunizes us against future illness; we build antibodies and our bodies become more resistant to that same disease or illness. With regular exercise, our bodies become stronger, more flexible, and ready to respond to challenge and stress. Likewise, a certain amount of stress strengthens our psychological resilience and increases our ability to handle greater and greater challenges. But this is not to say that all stress is good. And certainly I am not endorsing the euphemism that "what doesn't kill you makes you stronger." Too much stress can overwhelm our resilience, at least temporarily, as we will see in Chapter 4.

Psychological resilience draws on all aspects of the self: emotion, intellect, spirit, and sexuality. As individuals, we develop our own means of coping with life, our own unique point of view. The exact nature and form of our resilience are as unique as our personality, but, as you will see, our resilience does tend to fall into certain clearly defined patterns. How we experience our resilience and how it manifests itself depend upon who we are and what we have experienced in our lives.

We have all heard of women who have tackled a major challenge and won against overwhelming odds. Real-life examples include political activist Aung San Suu Kyi of Myanmar, and Kris Carr, cancer survivor, activist, and blogger on *Crazy, Sexy, Wellness Revolution*. Fictional heroines such as Katniss Everdeen in *The Hunger Games*, *The Good Wife's* Alicia Florrick, and Beatrix Kiddo in *Kill Bill* are examples, too. We have heard of the courage many people show in the face of death, disease, war, or tragedy. We have seen time and time again how members of entire communities pick up their lives and begin again in the aftermath of catastrophes such as tornadoes, hurricanes, fires, or floods. These are all examples of and testimony to our capacity to develop resilience.

Yet each of us demonstrates resilience in small ways, too: when we reach for our cell to support a friend, when we identify our needs and ask our partner to meet them, or we find the courage to end a destructive relationship or make a new beginning, when we take a deep breath as we regroup and counter negative thoughts, and when we try again when things don't go as planned. In drawing upon our strengths, we draw on our resilience. We may express it in any number of ways—through our initiative, empathy, insight, creativity, good humor, ability to set boundaries and form relationships, or sheer tenacity (Wolin and Wolin 1993). We each develop our own style and source of power—whatever allows us to face the challenge and prevail.

Thus, all women have the potential to master the art of resilience. We all share a special ability to take charge of our lives and find for ourselves the meaning, richness, connections, and purpose we seek—and still nurture ourselves, even if it is often much easier for us to determine what others need instead of focusing on our own needs. So taking charge of our own lives involves some extra focus and attention to access the power to know what we need, the vision to overcome the obstacles to our self-care that arise, and the strength to act on that knowledge. When we need to make a decision on what is right for us, our resilience is there to guide us. If we permit it—if we invite this part of us to come forward in our thinking, into our consciousness—our resilience can inform and shape our actions and responses to allow us to be the women we want to be.

A Life-Altering Definition

Uncovering the ability to recognize and begin to flex your own muscle, to see yourself and your life in new ways—to identify and recognize the resilience you already have and how to cultivate it—can truly change your life. Let's break this down, for this definition of resilience can be life altering.

The power to know what you need—yes, what *you* need from a partner; what your body needs (from rest, exercise, and nourishment to sexual satisfaction); what you need from a supervisor or coworker instead of what everyone else needs, not what needs to be fixed/accomplished/achieved. This is the power to understand yourself, rather than going through life unsure, confused, and feeling removed from your "real" self.

The vision to overcome the obstacles to your self-care, which means having the perspective to see the *big* picture concerning the obstacles that arise when you try to focus on yourself, and learning to develop solutions to overcome these obstacles.

The strength and courage to act on that knowledge as an activist in your own life, taking care of your own needs, your own desires, your very own wants. And when necessary, to have the courage to act on your needs. Remember, having courage is not the absence of fear but is acting in spite of the fear. Yes, this does involve making yourself a priority, but throughout this book I'll show you how and why this isn't as difficult as it may seem at the outset. Developing a plan (whether that plan involves taking baby steps or making huge shifts) and taking action are the final legs of this important triangle, because in the final analysis, resilience is more than just insight, or wisdom, or "blue-skying." Resilience is getting it done!

Our Conscious Use of Resilience

Interestingly, becoming conscious of our strengths makes us stronger. Our resilience increases as we recognize the magnitude of what we have already accomplished and survived. Our past victories help us to believe we can meet the challenges that lie ahead; we come to believe we can do as much and more again. This represents a new, more positive, even dynamic, view of how people can live a successful, satisfying life and replaces the myopic focus on obstacles and problems by widening the perspective to look past the problems. We become stronger when we focus on solutions with ourselves—the creator of what works for us—at the center.

Women and Resilience

I believe the specific issues confronted by women in the process of discovering their resilience are different from those experienced by men; our society makes this discovery of inner strength a more daunting process for women than it does for men, resulting in many women compartmentalizing their strengths, much like men are criticized for doing with their feelings. Women have traditionally derived strength and identity through their connectedness and relationships with others, rather than knowledge of themselves. This affects so much about us, from our sense of well-being to our sexuality to our career choices. We are often other-directed, observant of the people around us, particularly of those who share our lives. At the same time, to access our resilience we must learn to listen to the inner messages and signals of our resilient self. And to add an extra challenge to this process, to do so we must learn to actively confront the many damaging messages from society—*girly thoughts*, those less-than-helpful ideas that are so pervasive as to actually create negative inner dialogue—that get in the way of women listening to their own needs and desires. Our *girly thoughts* pull us away from thinking of our needs and focus us on how we are not enough in the eyes of others. And to make matters even worse, these *girly thoughts* also result in our often-harsh judgment of *other* women, which perpetuates the power of this destructive force and reinforces the cycle of negativity.

Resilience is a quality inherent to all human beings, male and female. Yet I have addressed this book specifically to women because we, more than men, are particularly vulnerable to losing touch with our personal power, particularly when we are in intimate relationships, particularly when we feel needed. The combination of self-expectations and other-directedness can lead many women to assume primary responsibility for the care of others while setting aside their need to care for themselves, often with results that are pervasive and affect all aspects of their lives from their sexuality to their weight to how tired they feel. Another word for this is *codependency*, a concept we will explore throughout the book.

We have all certainly seen this other-directedness played out: women who fall for a man who they see as "full of potential," so they begin sacrificing themselves for him, only to be disappointed when after all the sacrifice, he doesn't achieve what they feel he could; women who convince themselves that getting married will magically fix the relationship; women who get involved with someone who is already seriously involved with someone else and hope they will be the chosen one; women who try to please their partner sexually but are not in touch with their own sexual needs; working women who become mothers, and/or care for ill or elderly family members, and focus on caretaking to the exclusion of their own needs; women who are independent in the workplace but come home and appear to shrink and lose their bearings, afraid they will lose their partner if they assert themselves.

And add a little—or a lot—of trauma to the equation, and, instead of looking to themselves and their loved ones for reinforcement of their self-worth, women are forced to look to the greater society for this important human need. This misdirection leads to the situation many women find themselves in: their self-worth is held hostage by a society that blames women for the many challenges they face.

Girly Thoughts in Action

Perhaps *girly thoughts* can be seen as a way women sabotage themselves, but, if so, we are getting a lot of help. It is remarkable how so little has changed in how women are treated in some ways. Consider that the practice of advertising jobs according to sex, with professional jobs for men only, ended in the early 1960s, as did the practice of legally paying women less than men for the same work. But we know how well that law worked: women are still paid 77 cents to every dollar a man makes for the same job (Coy and Dwoskin 2012). Some female commentators feel that in some ways, things are actually more challenging for women now that the excuses are no longer overt: for example, the excuse used to be "We don't hire women because we don't have ladies rooms." Statements like that allowed women to see the source of their rejection as outside of them, but those overt excuses have become more covert: women are told they are not as qualified as their male counterparts, which women often interpret as meaning they are somehow personally deficient (Whitman 2012). The road is still steep ahead of us.

Women have a tendency to internalize those society-informed limiting thoughts and images of who we are, what we are capable of, what we are good for, how we should look, and how we should act, and we unconsciously act them out with other women, perpetuating their force. They are reinforced by our families and friends and intensified by our personal experiences with trauma. I discussed this idea with a friend of mine, Dr. Tom Lund, a fellow psychologist, who gave me the idea to label these ideas—society's way of teaching women to hold the blame for what goes wrong in relationships and in lives—our *girly thoughts* (O'Gorman 2009). These messages have a persuasive appeal. One of the implicit promises of *girly thoughts* is that if we are *good girls* and do what we are supposed to do and feel as we are supposed to feel, we will be taken care of and life will go as we need it to.

Given that these messages have a societal origin, *girly thoughts* are much more difficult to challenge: they exist in the images that surround us, and we feel them in the very air we breathe. *Girly thoughts* crowd us out as we try to know ourselves and our needs, including our sexual needs. And they let us know how we will be judged if we do not measure up to the ideal. These thoughts are often reinforced by family dynamics and intensified by trauma that may further disempower women.

And fighting *girly thoughts* is tricky. Makeup and perfume are marketed to us, designed to bring out our inner qualities in a particularly alluring way; so, too, are clothes (which change every season) that are must-haves if we want to look current and fashionable; and we are encouraged to sculpt a body like the ones we see in magazines, but in many photos those bodies are digitally enhanced, and, quite frankly, there is no one who quite has the proportions that are considered ideal—just think of Barbie dolls.

The messages we receive are rather appalling. In an analysis of magazines, psychologists Terri Conley and Laura Ramsey found women depicted as "flawless, passive." We may not like this, and we spend much emotional cache trying to tune these messages out, but we live in a society where news was made when a magazine that is popular with teenage girls agreed to stop Photoshopping the girls it featured to improve their desirability, but not to do the same for models and celebrities—a modest gain. This editorial change began with the efforts of a fourteen-year-old eighth grader who blogged that the girls in the magazine just don't look like the girls in her school (Pesta 2012). And this issue goes beyond the United States. The European Women's Lobby (2012) found that research suggests the most effective messages are those received without conscious recognition, speaking to the power of visual/digital advertising so common in all of our media, which frequently utilize digitally enhanced images of women's bodies to sell products. The result is that worldwide, only 2 percent of women feel they are beautiful.

The problem is exacerbated by the very way women are considered by employers and lawmakers. Recent examples include statements made by two well-educated and influential elected officials, one from each political party, who felt comfortable making outrageous comments that blamed and marginalized women. Missouri

Representative Todd Akin commented that women's bodies are able to prevent pregnancies if they are victims of "a legitimate rape" (Slater 2012). And New York State Assemblyman Vito Lopez required "that women not wear bras to work . . . requested that they wear short skirts and high heels . . . gave them money for jewelry . . . urged them to break up with their boyfriends," and paid off women who had accused him of sexually harassing them (Dolnick and Hakim 2012).

While these are admittedly extreme examples, research on women confronting such images (Good, Moss-Racusin, and Sanchez 2012) underscores how complicated a process this is for women, for women derive a sense of value by how close they can come to an *ideal* while at the same time understanding that ideal is a fantasy. It is a classic double bind that cannot be won. We see models starving themselves to death as they can never be thin enough, women shopping themselves into bankruptcy in order to have the new favored spring or fall color with the right length pants and the correct tightness of their skirt, and most women are exhausted by their efforts to be "enough," even while doubting that they can ever be adequate.

Now, this is not to say that we shouldn't have fun, dress up, wear high heels and makeup, perfume, and the latest styles. But we shouldn't place our self-worth on how close we can come to an artificial model in doing this. Dressing up should be fun, not oppressive; it should not be yet another indicator of how inferior we are.

Internalizing these *girly thoughts* profoundly affects us, and this internalization causes spiraling problems. On a simple level, we become very conflicted about how to dress. We want to enjoy our bodies, enjoy new styles, but then feel uncomfortable with the unwanted attention doing this may attract from strangers—men making lurid comments, other women being catty. These reactions cause us to feel that somehow we have done something wrong. Over time we dial down our sexuality, and, unfortunately, our sexual feelings, because of course *good girls* are not sexual, as we try to fit in more, be less obvious, and attract less unwanted attention so we can be taken more seriously in the areas that we deem important. "Few men have to deal with being seen as a sexual object, or being lusted after and not listened to, as they try to pitch a product idea," a client recently lamented to me. This balancing act takes a great deal of energy and work, often at the cost of our resilience, as we become more attuned to how others see us and less in touch with what we want to accomplish with our own power.

When we let our *girly thoughts* rule, we create a vicious cycle—how we are not good enough, how if we try harder, maybe we can be deserving—but what we become is more anxious and worried, which can lead to, for example, further fixation on keeping our partner—even if we are no longer attracted to that person, even if being with him or her doesn't make us feel good. Our feeling of well-being is undermined, causing us to feel less connected to ourselves, less sexual, as we try, for example, to preserve a relationship that isn't working—because we have convinced ourselves that we need it—rather than focusing on what it is right for us, knowing we can handle the consequences.

And buying into our *girly thoughts* flies in the face of what research is documenting in terms of women's needs. The key to women enjoying their sexuality at every age and stage of life is connectedness to their partners and their feelings of well-being (Cawood and Bancroft 2009). Our *girly thoughts* undermine this, for they take us outside ourselves and force us to see ourselves only through the eyes of others, and this leads us to critical self-judgment.

So, what are we to do? Begin by knowing that we already do a daily dance of resilience. For many of us, this is a quiet dance to discordant music blasted in from the outside. But through learning to really listen to the beat of our strengths, needs, and desires in a more conscious, rewarding, and even fun flow, we can change that dance to a celebration of our mastery of resilience.

Your Resilience Journal: Are You Ruled by Your *Girly Thoughts?*

You've just learned about *girly* thoughts; it can be a little scary to consider you might be ruled by something that you've just been made aware of. So take a moment to see if you have *girly thoughts* and if they have been influencing you without your awareness of them.

- Do you feel your worth comes from your looks and not from who you are?
- Are you critical of your body shape or size?
- Do you feel the key to getting what you need and deserve is to be close to perfect?
- When you encounter misfortune, do you blame yourself by saying, "I'm not (fill in the blank) so I deserve this"?
- Do you ever blame other women's misfortunes (such as an unfaithful partner) on their weight, clothes, or age?
- Do you dread growing older because you will no longer be seen as attractive?

- Do you feel you will be less desirable to a partner if you are successful?
- Are you reluctant to voice your opinion in your work? In your personal relationships?
- Do you personalize conflicts by thinking that you have done something to cause the problem rather than considering that the other person might have a role in what is occurring?
- Do you feel that if you are a *good girl* that you will be rewarded by life working out as you wish it to?

If you answered "yes" to several of these questions, you need to consider that your *girly thoughts* may be more influential than you have considered. If so, take a moment or two in your own time to complete the next exercise. You can answer these either all at once or as the answers occur to you. Write out the answers in a journal—a nice, bound, hard copy, or on your phone or computer, or anywhere you can begin to compile your thoughts on your resilience. As you continue through the parts of this book, you'll have opportunities to continue journaling, and, when you've completed your Resiliency Journal, you'll have a roadmap to your new, more resilient self!

What's in Your *Girly Thoughts*?

It is a good idea now to see just what your brand of *girly thoughts* are, because to begin to combat them, you need to consciously understand what they are saying to you. Answer each of the following questions in your journal, and be sure to leave several lines between each answer in case you want to come back at a later time to one or several of these questions.

- What worries do you have with your dress or your body that make you feel "less than?" What image of yourself comes to mind that fills you with anxiety or disgust? What thoughts keep nagging at you, making you feel inferior?
- What do you want to do but feel you can't do because you are a woman?
- What perceived personal failing allows you to expect or excuse the poor behavior of others?
- What societal expectations do you try to live up to so that you will be rewarded?

Now that you've begun to scope out your *girly thoughts*, you can begin to consider how you want to begin an inner dialogue with this potent and less-than-helpful inner force, as you'll see other women do in the next chapter.

TWO

Everyday Heroism:
Losing the Victim Mentality

WOMEN ARE IN LEAGUE WITH EACH OTHER, A SECRET
CONSPIRACY OF HEARTS AND PHEROMONES

—*Camille Paglia*

W*hen I think of resilient women,* I often think of Zoe, a friend
from early in my career. Zoe was beautiful, wise beyond her
years, comfortable in being sexual and handling the responses she
received, and a font of information on dating. I admired her exuber-
ance and her uncanny ability to land on her feet no matter what the
situation—particularly when it involved guys. I was stunned when
she broke off what looked to be a permanent relationship with a very
good-looking guy because "he just wasn't meeting my needs."

Zoe explained that she had learned to set limits on how much she
gave.

Otherwise I find myself giving and giving, sacrificing what I need while secretly expecting him to change. I realized as a kid that, if my needs were going to be met, I had to figure out how to arrange this. I had enough chaos as a kid. My father was absent and my mother had lots of boyfriends, which gave me lots of examples of what not to do in relationships. I learned I had to depend upon myself, not on Prince Charming or my mother. Seeing my mother's struggles freed me up to focus more on what I needed so as not to be like her; she spent so much energy desperately trying to hold onto whatever guy she was with no matter what it cost her emotionally.

I was intrigued by Zoe's stories. Her determination, self-assuredness, and warm humor came through despite the pain of what she described. I soon realized that while Zoe was unusual, she was not unique. Many people have this quality of confidence and inner knowing. Like all of us, they struggle with life's challenges—setbacks, negative thoughts, transitions, loss—but whatever problems they encounter, they refuse to be overwhelmed or beaten down.

As a psychologist, my curiosity was piqued: What was this ability, this inner strength that enables people to weather life's challenges and consistently come out on top? Over the years, I've come to identify that quality as resilience. I've also come to see that resilience is a universal trait.

Unfortunately, many women have never consciously accessed their resilience and remain cut off from actively developing and intentionally utilizing this part of themselves. As a therapist and seminar leader specializing in women's issues, I've seen hundreds of women in this situation. They come to counseling or seminars seeking an essential piece that is missing from their lives. They may be successful women who are desperately putting enormous energy into meeting a partner and not paying attention to their own feelings, desires, or needs; driven, successful, yet dissatisfied career women who do not have the time or energy for a meaningful relationship in their lives; working women who are caring for children and aging parents they love, yet who feel overwhelmed and understimulated and are not finding the time to care for themselves; women who are afraid to embrace their sexuality; or young women who are terrified of stepping into life without the parental support they resent. Many of these women inexplicably find themselves battling a sense of isolation and loneliness that pervades their lives, or trying to match up to standards that seem beyond their ability and that leave them feeling *less than.*

In some cases, these women are facing a difficult transition, such as a divorce, job loss, a move, marriage, new motherhood, a health crisis, or aging, and they feel unequal to those demands. Others are survivors of childhood trauma who at times find their energies so focused on the past and the resultant pain that they have little energy available to meet the challenges of their adult lives. Or they are trying to figure out how to be successful in life and are relying on the images of successful women portrayed to them in the media to guide them, while at the same time, trying to be the *good girl* so they will be given what they deserve. All these women feel powerless and somehow blame themselves for not being able to "do it all," for not being happier, more fulfilled, more at peace with the lives they lead. They often experience a restlessness, a frustration they cannot define. They seek more control over their lives and the means to make the changes they need to bring about a satisfying balance.

The essential piece we all seek is the conscious use of our resilience. So what gets in the way of accessing resilience? One of the obstacles is our *girly thoughts*.

Girly Thoughts = Antiresilience

Although the term is new, the research on the dynamics behind *girly thoughts* is not. In 1970 Broverman's research found that "healthy women, as opposed to healthy men, were considered to be more submissive, less adventurous, more easily influenced, less aggressive, less competitive, more excitable in minor crises, more emotional, more conceited about appearance, less objective and disliking of math and science" (Cekelis 1998). This is the image of the *good girl* that we, and our mothers before us, were raised with.

Have things changed in the last forty-plus years? One would hope so. And indeed many things have. Today more young women attend college, and girls have full access to sports in school. But as much as things have changed on the outside, the *girly thoughts* our mothers and grandmothers were raised with are still prevalent in our very own thinking (Gere and Helwig 2012). This results in women being in a double bind; at workshops, retreats, and in my clinical work, I frequently hear statements that can be summed up like this: Women fear that if they are all they want to be—and can be—they may not be desirable. And if they make themselves desirable, then they may have to sacrifice other important parts of who they are.

Laura recently spoke to me about this.

My father took away my childhood with his rages and need to control. My ex-husband took away my early adulthood with his alcoholism and threatened to take away my children in court, but I'll be darned if my current partner is going to take away my independence. If this is going to work, it has to work with me being able to hold onto what I need. I'm just worried that if we live together, I'll get anxious about keeping him and I'll cave.

How do we women feel about this double bind? Frequently angry. But instead of expressing this anger, women internalize their anger, and this leads to the development of depression, which is essentially anger at another turned inward (Jack 2012). The anger women feel at the unrealistic demands placed on them by society become internalized, and, instead of realizing their problems are a result of their partner, their boss, or society, they come to believe the problem they are having is their own fault. Self-blaming, internal messages like "I'm no good," or "I'm worthless"—in other words, *girly thoughts*— are triggered by a variety of challenges, such as implied judgments, criticism, and rejection.

The struggle for women is that these thoughts are so common that we frequently are not aware of them. We don't even realize that we are thinking them, for they have become so much a part of how we see ourselves, how we see other women, how we reason, and where we determine the problem to be, which is most often within ourselves. These thoughts may include:

If only I was more beautiful . . . blonder . . . younger . . . had whiter teeth . . . lost weight . . . had bigger breasts . . . a smaller ass . . . was into kinkier sex . . . didn't have bags under my eyes . . . wasn't so tired all the time because of the kids . . . was a more fun woman.

Then he wouldn't have . . . yelled at me . . . quit his job . . . left me . . . cheated on me . . . started drugging again . . . not

promoted me . . . lied to me . . . fired me . . . ignored me . . .
just watched TV instead of talking to me . . . ignored what I need
sexually . . .

When we do think thoughts like these, our inner wisdom is *not*
speaking. These are society's messages, often combined with the negative messages of our family of origin. The problem for us is that we
believe them, as Charlene did when she found out her husband was
having another affair . . . just as she was about to move to join him in
the new community where he had finally found work.

I felt I was falling off a cliff. I thought I was going to die. I
didn't know how I would ever make it through. And of course I
blamed myself. I felt like such an idiot, like such a loser to have
believed him. I quit my job, said good-bye to everyone in my
community, to follow him to a new state. I couldn't even begin
to be angry with him; I was in such shock, trying to figure out
what I had done to cause this and wondering how I could have
prevented it.

Trauma—A Source of Our *Girly Thoughts*

We come to embrace our *girly thoughts* honestly. For many of us,
they are a logical outgrowth of the traumas we experienced, whether
that was the big trauma of childhood abuse or the subtler trauma
of sexual harassment at work. Our *girly thoughts* reinforce the societal messages that bombard us, and we erroneously believe them, for
they offer a way to help us make sense of what is happening to us;
others use these constructs as a further justification for their own
poor actions: a woman is supposed to (fill in the blank). They offer

a causation that implies a solution of sorts by requiring a change on our part that may not be possible, but which does provide at least a direction that gives us the illusion of control . . . control we do not really possess. Twenty years after the fact, Caitlin shares her internalization of her own trauma.

> I really did believe that the sexual abuse I experienced with my neighbor, beginning when I was ten, was somehow my fault. After all, he told me that "I made him do it." And he said it often enough that I began to believe him. That's part of why I never told anyone; I felt so guilty. So I learned to turn off the sexual part of myself, later finding pills and booze were a good way to numb myself, and ended up being called "The Ice Queen" in college.

Codependency: Girly Thoughts *in Action*

A tip-off that we are thinking *girly thoughts* is when we link what we believe to be a personal deficit to the painful action of another, letting the other off the hook as responsible for our pain and taking responsibility for their actions! *I'm not loveable or he wouldn't have cheated on me,* or *I'm undesirable because I'm overweight,* we think, or we reach erroneous conclusions, like *I must stop putting pressure on him for sex because I'm too old for that anyway,* or *I'm a bad mother because I couldn't control my children's genetic inheritance that led to addiction,* instead of realizing that their addiction may not be about us. Or we use the reasoning offered by our *girly thoughts* to blame a friend, a coworker, a celebrity for the ills that have befallen them.

When we think *girly thoughts,* we are blaming ourselves—and blaming ourselves keeps us stuck trying to control things we cannot control and feeling responsible for someone else's choices. And when we believe these *girly thoughts,* we set the stage for moving into another whole realm—developing codependency, which is not taking care of ourselves but taking care of others in the hope that they will eventually take care of us, perhaps by rescuing us. We need to lose the victim mentality because it keeps us stuck in our *girly thoughts.*

Girly thoughts and the resulting codependency can have other results, too. If we are healthy enough, they can also make us angry— angry because they are a trap! Angry because they make us victims. But since anger is often a difficult emotion for women to show (who wants to be labeled a b#*&ch?), some of us have a tendency to medicate our anger through eating, drinking, drugs, or exercising too much. The way out? We need to develop resilient thinking so we can move on, take charge of what is in our control, and protect ourselves in the process.

Let's return to Charlene and see how she made this shift in thinking.

> This was the man I loved. We were actively trying to have a family together. His job moved him to this wonderful area of the country, perfect for raising a family. This was to be our new beginning, a time for us, a time when he wasn't going to be pursuing other women. He promised. When I finally moved there and found a job, I was devastated to learn that all the weekends that I couldn't come—because of a snowstorm or a family obligation— he was spending with her. All the time he had no cell phone service, all the late nights that he was "working hard," he was really playing hard.

What did I do? I did what I had been trained to do—I blamed myself. Every time I saw him, I felt such love; he was so kind, so sorry, that I blamed myself even more. I felt bad for any small urge to be angry, finding reasons within me for why he betrayed me. With the stress of moving and looking for a job, I had been eating badly and gaining weight. To save money, I had not bought new clothes or had my hair done regularly. I didn't feel good about myself, and I was so focused on moving as quickly as I could. I realize now that my *girly thoughts* kept me from holding him accountable for what he had done and kept me as "the responsible party."

Resilience Is Living Life from the Inside Out

When we think *girly thoughts,* we are actually defining ourselves *externally,* based on the opinions of others, such as a man we love, rather than defining ourselves *internally,* based on who we know ourselves to be and how we are feeling.

Girly thoughts are clearly not okay. They are expensive to use emotionally. Seeing ourselves from a one-down position that an external view demands is a sure sign that we are disempowering ourselves. This is the opposite of using our resilience. This is basing our self-worth on what a committee of others thinks of us; this is a dangerous thing to do.

After attending my self-parenting retreat, Charlene began to see herself differently. She looked at herself not from the outside in, but from the inside out.

I looked in the mirror from the inside out and saw the tremendous love I am capable of feeling. I realized that there is nothing wrong in loving another or in being willing to make changes in one's life for someone you love. I have the capacity to do this, and this is actually an admirable quality. I stopped feeling that I was deficient. I am now beginning to put myself first, making decisions based upon what I need, not just what he needs, which is changing the dynamics in my relationship with my husband. I feel stronger than I was, more resilient. And this shift in me, I realize, is only just beginning.

Everyday Heroism

My goal is to help women understand their own resilient qualities. I help them develop a vocabulary of their unique personal strengths and show them that they already rely upon their resilience unconsciously and can learn to develop it further . . . and this comes as a surprise for many of them.

I help these women acknowledge their extensive accomplishments by asking them to consider the myriad tasks they routinely perform for home and family, employer, friends, and even themselves. Through appreciation for their everyday struggles, they can begin to see how much they rely on their resilience on a daily basis. Each small task they handle so expertly every day seems commonplace, manageable, and perhaps of little consequence. But when all of these demands are considered together, they take on a new dimension, an *everyday heroism*.

Cultivating a Resilient Voice

Our resilient voice is the opposite of our society-driven *girly thoughts*, and it speaks to us continuously throughout our day. We may come to know of our resilience in many ways: intuitive reasoning, a spontaneous action that saves the day, a new feeling, an insight that points us in a new direction or validates dimly perceived feelings. We may have relied on our resilience, this "sixth sense," many times and not even have been aware of it. Yet when we do become aware of it, we can learn to use its counsel to help us decide what is right for us. Learning to use resilience is a matter of learning to listen to ourselves. How we do this, and how we speak to ourselves, can vary between women and even within ourselves at different times of our lives.

Elka felt her resilience as a longing.

> I live in the bush in Australia. I've never been part of any artistic group. My husband discouraged me, telling me I didn't have the "voice." But I felt such a yearning inside. I listened to the "voice" of my need, applied, and was accepted to be part of this worldwide virtual creative effort, much to his amazement and my delight.

Kathy experienced her "voice" as something she found herself *not* choosing. At age thirty-nine, Kathy realized she hadn't listened to that "little voice."

> I should have known that I was picking up on something. After all, I dated my husband for nine years and never agreed to marry him. And then the trip to Vegas, a couple too many drinks, and we were married in a cute little chapel, with no friends, no family, and no celebration. And now on our third anniversary, I realize that this is a big mistake. That little voice has become stronger and much louder, and now I'm listening.

The Simplicity of Resilience

This attention to ourselves and to our countless daily successes—large and small—reveals the tangible benefits of our resilience. We begin to see the simplicity, the ease that our resilience affords us as a blueprint, an inner structure around which we can gather and organize our strengths. We can then use this blueprint to make the important changes we need in our lives. When we learn to trust ourselves, we can move forward more confidently with a new acceptance of who we are.

Tanya, a bright twenty-nine-year-old research fellow, decided her shyness would be a liability in her career goal to become a professor. To overcome her shyness, she insisted on forcing herself into situations that would "snap me out of it. You know, to be like other women, more social, even though my girlfriends kept saying I was just fine the way I was." The result was that she was often nervous and uncomfortable, but still shy. The more she struggled to change this, the more ineffectual she felt. Her discomfort increased as job interviews were scheduled. When she feared her lab work would suffer, she sought counseling.

As we talked about her childhood and adolescence, Tanya told me that she had been happiest during those periods in which she had arranged her life to accommodate her shyness rather than trying to overcome it. In high school she had a few close friends but avoided large gatherings. At college she worked as a research assistant rather than as a waitress or store clerk.

Like many people, Tanya took for granted the wise choices she had made so easily and naturally earlier in her life. Now, in a new setting she no longer trusted herself but tried to impose unrealistic expectations she believed she *should* fulfill. Reminded of her earlier self-understanding, Tanya decided to once again trust her instincts to make the best decisions. As she returned to complete her postdoctoral fellowship with a new interest in demonstrating her personal strengths, Tanya was amazed at how quickly her shyness became insignificant. She began to take charge of her life and factor her shyness into her decision making. No longer at the mercy of her shyness, Tanya once again excelled.

When we know who we are and hold realistic expectations for ourselves, we can take pride in our assets rather than fighting with ourselves. We stop squandering energy on *should* and *have to* and begin to accomplish our true goals. When we are assured of our personal strengths, we can more readily accept our personal challenges.

The Luxury of Learning Who We Are

One challenge of adulthood is to recognize our individuality: what makes us the unique people we are. In this, our resilience can serve as a valuable guide. It enables us to examine what qualities are our own and what qualities such as *girly thoughts* we have borrowed inappropriately from others.

To accomplish this, we need first to become aware of our personal style of resilience. Once we are aware of that, we can make it more balanced, more consistently present in all areas of our lives, and use it on a daily basis as well as in times of stress and crisis. To do this, we begin by observing the situations in which we claim our power and those in which we yield it.

Before the birth of her twins, Virginia worked part-time at a grammar school as the volunteer coordinator for school events. Everyone she worked with admired her flexibility, good humor, and ability to keep everyone working together. If it needed doing, they all knew they could count on Virginia. Once her daughters were born, however, Virginia became another person.

> I now had a second-grader and infants. I was exhausted. The house was in a perpetual state of chaos. Not that my husband didn't try to help. He watched the kids almost all day Saturday when I did the shopping and cleaning. But he worked during the week. I told myself it was unfair to ask him to do more when he came home at night.

In exploring her predicament, it became clear that Virginia, who was so competent at work where she easily delegated responsibilities and kept everyone on track, was unable to translate these skills from work to home. Once her twins were born, she put aside her professional flexibility and took on sole responsibility for her home and children. Her model in this, she explained, was her mother; Virginia wanted to be for her husband and daughters all her mother had been for her when she was growing up.

> We can't afford a nanny or a maid. Even with five children, my mother always had the house spotless and everything in order. And she had time for me and my boy talk. That's what a mother should be. I said to myself, *I guess I'm stuck.*
>
> When I heard myself say that, I cringed. I'd never been stuck in my life. I refuse to be beaten! That's when I hit on the idea of beginning a mothers' support and play group. It took quite a bit of e-mailing and scheduling, but I'm a pro at that. Besides the larger group that meets twice a month, three of us have organized a housework routine: one watches the kids and the other two pair up and clean house.
>
> This was my salvation. For one thing, I'm not struggling to live up to unattainable standards. I still don't know how my mother

managed it, but now I know she was the exception, not the rule. So I can let that hurdle go. Second, I like people; friends are important to me. I get more done, not less, when I have a friend to talk to.

When we are true to who we are, true to our personal strengths and priorities and our own needs and unique gifts, we often find new energy and confidence. We are better able to meet our challenges and overcome them.

Madelyn, the oldest daughter in a family of four children, was always the strong one in the family. She acted as a second mother to her siblings, and she continued this role into adulthood. When her mother became ill and then died, Madelyn was there to take charge of her invalid father by moving him, cleaning out their family house, and settling her mother's affairs—this in addition to her full-time job and a family of her own. A year after her mother's death, Madelyn came into therapy to understand why she felt so distanced from her life.

> With all I have to do, I don't have time to get caught up in feeling sorry for myself. I feel like an impostor, like I'm just going through the motions. Everything is the same in my life on the outside, but somehow I'm missing on the inside. All I do is work and manage one crisis after another. My husband asks me what's wrong, but I can't tell him. I don't know.

Like many women, Madelyn identified strongly with her role as nurturer and family caretaker. She was constantly giving to others at the expense of her own needs. Eventually, women like Madelyn find themselves asking silently, *What about me?* They struggle with their guilt about feeling this way. In an effort to still the inner voice that reminds them of their own neediness, they may resort to compulsive spending, overeating, alcohol or other drug abuse, or other self-destructive behaviors. Madelyn just totally shut down emotionally, distancing herself from her family and girlfriends.

In therapy, Madelyn began to understand the tremendous pressure she had been under by taking on more and more without stopping to consider how it was affecting her. "I just kept taking care of what needed to be done." She came to understand that to keep giving she needed to receive, that taking time for herself to speak to friends or have dinner with her husband would not compromise her ability to give to others but would deepen it instead. And she realized that she needed to stop and honor her own grief about her mother's death and put some limits on how much she was taking on. In fact, she deserved to be able to do so.

Balancing Caring for Others with Caring for Ourselves

Madelyn came to realize that the same skills that allowed her to run her home and nurture her family could also allow her to organize activities to nurture herself. She could get back in touch with her own needs and feel a connection to herself and her life as an individual again and still be the *good girl* she was raised to be; in fact, she could be an improved version of this image of herself. It is important for women to realize that the traditionally feminine role of nurturer can indeed give them a source of strength and identity; they must also realize that if there isn't balance, this nurturing can rob them of their ability to care for themselves. This is when caretaking moves into codependency—caring for others to the exclusion of caring for oneself and hoping they, or someone, will care for you. This is when women feel trapped and overpowered and needing to be rescued, rather than enhanced and empowered, by their caregiving role.

To own our power is to allow ourselves to derive benefit from who we truly are; our desires and needs are important parts of our identity. This means we need to acknowledge our everyday heroic acts and our traditional sources of strength as we practice more consciously and deliberately utilizing our own personal strength—our resilience.

Through this new self-awareness, a fuller image of our self emerges. We discover more power, clarity, and determination to care for ourselves. By accessing our resilience, we can discover the fulfillment that we so deserve. Those who have faced trauma can find healing as they continue to expand their resiliencies, acquiring new pride and acceptance in place of shame and guilt. Our resilience is our most powerful tool in our ability not only to survive but to thrive.

The Role of Resilience in Our Lives

To learn of our resilience is to learn to listen inward. Here we find a new acceptance and no longer need to live up to external standards or the *shoulds* dictated to us by the expectations of others in our *girly thoughts*. We begin to feel rewarded by what we are doing for ourselves and in our lives. We are learning to come from the inside out based upon our needs as opposed to the outside in, which is listening to what others expect of us. Such acceptance fosters our self-esteem. Our outlook becomes more confident and more optimistic. We begin each day living in our own skin, feeling we can accomplish what we need and resuming control over our lives through the active use of *conscious resilience.*

We can learn to realize our own potential, to know and nurture ourselves, and to create and follow our own blueprint to achieve self-fulfillment. As we claim our personal power, we can use it to find more meaning and balance in life.

This is a large undertaking, because it encompasses so many parts of ourselves, parts that we are uncomfortable with and have judgments about, parts we may even hold shame about concerning past, present, and future. We need to understand the impact of our families on our development as women, including the rules we were given, the interactions, and even the traumas we experienced, and the meanings we attached to them. Then we need to look beyond our families to the larger context of society and human history and the lessons we have learned about being women; we need to examine how many of these lessons may have been translated into *our girly thoughts*.

In our individualistic, competitive society, we are taught to look outside ourselves for recognition, value, and purpose. We are inundated with conflicting messages about what we as women should do and be. We may stop listening to ourselves and hear only those outside messages. Unaware of our need to be true to ourselves, we may struggle fruitlessly to fulfill unrealistic or ill-suited roles and lifestyles and pay a huge emotional price in the process. Rather than drawing on our own unique strengths and talents, we may judge ourselves against popular role models or struggle against external standards of body shape and size, accomplishment, or success rather than trusting our own inner values. As a result of how far we fall from those external standards, we may blame ourselves for everything that isn't going as we wish in our lives and in the lives of those we care about. For these reasons, the lessons we've learned from society, our *girly thoughts,* have a direct bearing on the development of our resilience as women.

Now that we have begun to *out* those *girly thoughts* by identifying and labeling them, and you have begun to understand the hows and whys behind them, you are ready to take the steps that will allow you to own and utilize the inner power of your conscious resilience. You will then be able to relish in living in this part of who you are, fighting those *girly-thought* forces, and enjoying life on a whole new level.

The journey we'll make together promises more poise and greater self-assurance as you realize that you actually know more about the *steps to take* than you give yourself credit for, and can have more fun and deeper joy by grounding yourself in who you are: a resilient woman.

Your Resilience Journal: Do You Use Your Resilience?

Take a moment to ask yourself whether you agree or disagree with the following statements. Write a few sentences about the answers in your journal, and work at your own pace. Make this a pleasurable experience as you get to know more about you.

- I consciously use my resilience, my own inner wisdom.
- I'm able to hear, and to challenge, my very own *girly thoughts.*
- I am able to accomplish the tasks I decide are important, and still keep myself as a priority, making room in my life for my own needs and desires.
- I can let myself, and others, see the best that is in me.
- And when I am in love with another I continue to love myself; I never feel someone is my "better half."
- I can learn from crises, whether those from the past or those facing me in the present, allowing me to be motivated from within and not reactive to what is outside of me.

- I am creative, flexible and able to develop new solutions to existing problems, and resurrect solutions from the past to help me face current challenges.
- I accept that some circumstances can't be changed; this helps me focus on the circumstances I can affect, allowing me to say NO as a complete sentence.
- I accept the constant changes within my own body, understanding that I am more than how I may feel or look at any one moment.
- I have an inner optimism, feel pride in myself, and do not make excuses for my strengths; in fact I'm curious about myself and my capacities.
- I can choose good people/safe people to be in my life, which this allows me to not take personally the nonsense of others.
- I realize I can learn from the misfortunes I've experienced and even feel impressed by the "me" that has been shaped by those misfortunes, which have taught me peace, and gratitude for the riches and blessings in my life.

If you agree with all or most of these statements, you probably already use your resilience on a regular basis, and Part II can help you make this a more conscious process as you learn to expand your repertoire. If you disagree with all or most of these statements, Part II will help you learn more about developing and expanding this important inner strength—and congratulations on deciding to embrace this idea!

PART TWO

Start Dancing: Develop a Resilient Mind-Set

There are short cuts to happiness,
and dancing is one of them.

—Vicki Baum

In Part II, we will further explore the concepts of identifying and understanding how your resilience functions in you. At the end of each of the next four chapters, you will take a simple assessment that will help you determine how resilient you need to be, guide you in identifying your own resilience style, and assist you in understanding to what extent you still unconsciously use your childhood resilience beliefs. I recommend taking these assessments initially to clarify your current resilience as you plan to more consciously develop it, and again during major life transitions to aid you in keeping focused on using your resilience in a conscious way.

THREE

Your Outside Supports— Protective Factors

EVERY TIME I CLOSE THE DOOR ON REALITY

IT COMES IN THROUGH THE WINDOWS.

—*Jennifer Unlimited*

esilience is a reality that may be difficult to wrap your mind
around, but it is a part of you nevertheless. Oxford Dictionary
Online defines resilience this way:

a. Elasticity; the power of resuming an original shape or position after compression, bending, etc.

b. The quality or fact of being able to recover quickly or easily
from, or resist being affected by, a misfortune, shock, illness, etc.; robustness; adaptability.

However you define resilience, it is a vital part of who you are *today*. Before we get to the assessment quiz that will help you identify your personal protective factors, let's take a look at what other influences impact your use of resilience.

You and Your Resilience: Embracing Who You Are

Whether you have paid attention to this part of yourself or not, your resilience forms an important part of who you are. And whether you take resilience for granted or you actively try to run from it, your resilience remains there as a steady guiding force that helps you navigate the sometimes-treacherous waters of life and the perplexing currents of your own needs. Even when your resilience surprises or even frightens you due to the ferocity of this part of yourself, it is an important part of your being, and making it more conscious will allow you to draw upon this part of you, use it to your full advantage, and even come to enjoy it.

Getting Through Life's Assaults

We tend to notice our resilience more when we are under assault. We have all had that feeling of trying to get through one thing when several more appear on the horizon, each commanding our attention, each coming down the chute aimed directly at us. Yes, this is a moment to push aside our *girly thoughts* and consciously use our resilience. But what else in our life can assist us? Remember, resilience is a dynamic process between what is challenging us and demanding our attention, our skills in dealing with it, and the elements in our life that can literally *protect* us from the intensity of the demands heading toward us.

This chapter focuses on those elements that protect us. Whether we are talking about friends, health, age, religious beliefs, community supports, family, or economic supports, *protective factors* provide support for us that can make life meaningful and rewarding and have the potential to blunt the intensity of the likely impact of negative events on us.

Before you take the first assessment, let's focus on what protective factors are and their relationship to the development of resilience. The equation below illustrates the way our *girly thoughts* influence the potential impact of a negative event on our lives.

**Negative event + interpretations viewed
through the lens of our *girly thoughts* – power
of protective factors = how resilient you need to be**

In other words, the impact of any negative event is intensified by the direct influence of our *girly thoughts*. That impact is lessened by the power of our protective factors, as we will see in the stories that follow.

We will end this chapter with an assessment that will determine the level of protective factors you have in your life, and then you will be able to determine how resilient you need to be. Now don't be concerned if you determine that you have few protective factors. Many highly resilient women are those who had to learn to rely just on themselves because there was little else in their life to buffer the negative events surrounding them. Other women who have more protective factors can afford to be less resilient, as they have more cushioning in their environment that helps absorb the blows that life tends to deliver.

First, let's look at two stories that illustrate the importance of protective factors.

Many Protective Factors and Minimal *Girly Thoughts* Can Reduce Pain

Sophia had many protective factors to assist her and buffet the pain and humiliation she felt when life dealt her a very cruel blow. She came from a loving two-parent family with some financial resources, had a strong belief in God, and grew up in a supportive community in Michigan with several good friends. Her parents sent her to a good college and then law school, helped set her up in an apartment when she graduated, and still paid for her cell phone. She was therefore educated, emotionally secure, financially stable, and had supportive relationships.

Sophia always felt independent, a trait in which she prided herself. She wanted to make partner in her firm, and she worked incredibly long hours. Secretly, Sophia felt the reason she perhaps pushed herself so hard was perhaps a compensation for feeling that she was not the greatest looking woman in the world. Short, or petite as she likes to call herself, big-boned, she worked out, ate well, and was often described as solid, healthy, and wholesome. As she didn't comfortably fit into *how* women should look, she decided early in her life that she wouldn't be held accountable to this measure of who she was. As a result, she didn't focus on *girly thoughts* about her looks.

Sophia signed up for an online dating service and met Marty, a businessman who lived in Washington State and traveled extensively. She fell in love. Even though Marty's work hours were long and his travel schedule extensive, they managed to stay in touch through e-mails, calls, and the very occasional visit. But she always felt he was there for her; through work crises and problems with her parents' declining health, he always offered a sympathetic ear, a supportive e-mail, and even a sweet card.

Sophia decided to propose to Marty, and, as part of her surprise, to tell him that she had passed the bar in Washington State and was active in pursuing a transfer within her company to their office in Seattle. When she told him, she could have sworn there were tears of joy in his eyes.

Just two weeks later, Marty was killed in a climbing accident. Sophia learned of this through a news account and was devastated. But she rallied and found out where the funeral was, thinking that the saving grace in this horrible turn of events would be that she would finally meet Marty's mother and four brothers, who she had heard so much about. Together, she and her new almost-family could grieve.

When she arrived at the funeral home, she asked for Marty's mother and was introduced to his father . . . who, Marty had told her, had died when he was six. *Maybe he is a stepfather?* Sophia thought, *but Marty looks so much like him.* She felt disoriented, and for a moment she wondered if she had the wrong room. Then she glanced at the coffin, and there was Marty.

But he wasn't alone. Apparently Sophia wasn't the only fiancée to show up. Sobbing uncontrollably over Marty's body was a very young, slender, beautiful woman who was reaching into the casket trying to kiss him. As Sophie tried to make sense of this, another gorgeous woman, clearly older than she and Marty, arrived. The second woman shoved the first woman aside and threw herself on Marty. A pushing, screaming match began as Sophia listened in horror to the two women yelling that they had each been engaged to him.

Now in a state of shock, Sophia mumbled to Marty's father, "I thought I was engaged to him." His father shrugged and said, "Marty got around."

As her shock passed, Sophia found herself getting angry. Angry at Marty, and angry at herself for believing everything he'd said. But she found the silver lining in her crisis, and her resilience emerged in her gratitude. Sophia realized how grateful she suddenly was that she hadn't left her family behind and moved to Seattle before this all came out. "Then I *really* would have been pissed," she mused.

Few Protective Factors and Plenty of *Girly Thoughts* Make for a Hard Fall

Melissa, a young, attractive woman, was thirty-five when she divorced. Her marriage obviously had some serious issues, so she wasn't entirely unhappy when she and Jake decided to end it. *Better do it now while I'm still young enough to meet someone else,* she thought.

But moving on became difficult for Melissa, and she began to drink to ease her anxiety. She had never completed college because she became pregnant in her junior year and dropped out of school to work as a secretary, which she continued to do after her divorce. She and Jake sold their home at a loss, since neither one could afford it on a single income. But Melissa was able to find a small apartment in the same school district so her sons could continue attending the same high school. Jake had a higher salary than Melissa did, so he rented another house; although it was much smaller than the one they previously owned, their two teenage sons soon decided to move into their father's home. Jake asked Melissa for child support. She was devastated both emotionally and financially. She began to do the bar scene looking for her next husband, one with even more money than Jake brought in.

Melissa then began to drink heavily; she was copying a coping strategy she learned from her mother and had sworn as a child to never repeat. She gained weight, which just increased her feelings of self-loathing and growing feelings of unattractiveness. She soon lost her job and her apartment; this left her with no choice but to move in with her sister and her family and live on their living room couch.

Melissa's downward spiral was dramatic. Her divorce and the resulting financial pressure were partly to blame, but so were the lack of supports in her life. Melissa had few protective factors: she hadn't completed college, she had few job skills (and lacked an understanding employer), and all of these conspired with the *girly thoughts* she had in her head.

Major life crises, few protective factors, and measuring her self-worth by external standards, her *girly thoughts,* meant that to successfully weather these events, Melissa needed to be very resilient. Unfortunately, she either hadn't developed these skills or she was so overwhelmed when her children moved out, and by her problem drinking, that she couldn't access them.

Origins of Resilience and Protective Factors

Protective factors and resilience are connected and form a balance of sorts, like a seesaw. The more protective factors we have, the less we may need to develop resilience, and *girly thoughts* tip our inner seesaw. The origins of all three lie in our childhood.

We carry our first lessons in resilience from our childhood with us into adulthood as we try to make sense of the world and find our place within it. We experiment with different ways of having our needs and desires met. We see how the adults in our lives, especially our parents, prioritize what is important, how they take care of themselves and us, and how they solve problems. We witness daily the manner in which they express love, face failure, and meet challenges.

As children, we were practical. We came to conclusions concerning what worked best for us, gave us the attention we needed, and brought us rewards or helped us avoid pain. We learned the behaviors our parents reinforced and the behaviors they discouraged. We came to understand the consequences and efficiency of our actions by trial and error. Meaning and social considerations came later. Through this understanding, we began to develop our own coping style.

The quest of every child is to find a positive self-image. We wanted to see ourselves as acceptable, pleasing, powerful, competent, and influential beings worthy of love and regard. Our innate programming propelled us toward mastery in physical, mental, and social development where we learned what was expected of us, as little girls, by our family and by the greater society in which we lived. If our homes were warm and nurturing, our parents and other adults helped us achieve these positive goals and reinforced our efforts toward them. We learned to trust ourselves because our parents trusted us first. We learned to love ourselves through their love of us. Children from such families internalize the insight, compassion, and self-regard they experience from loving caretakers.

I recently watched as a small girl of five came running to her mother, crying, on the first day of soccer practice.

"I can't do it!" she cried. "It's too hard."

Her mother scanned the crowd of parents, aware that her daughter was the only child who was giving up just as she had begun.

"It's all right, Elyssa," her mother said calmly. "It may seem hard right now, but I know you can do it. You're a good, fast runner. You can do fine."

Minutes later, Elyssa once more came crying to her mother's side. Again her mother reassured her, "You can do it. I know you can. Yes, it is hard, but you've done other hard things, and you can do this. Remember swimming? It seemed hard at first, too, but after a while it was your favorite. It might be the same with soccer, but you need to try."

Head bowed, Elyssa returned once more to the field, first moving slowly, then running. In a few minutes she had taken her place among the other girls and boys, obviously enjoying herself and delighting in her speed and skill as a runner.

Elyssa's mother is a powerful woman, I thought; *she is such a good teacher*. Later I wondered whether, if I had told her my thoughts, she would have dismissed the idea, saying, "Oh, well, I was just doing my job," or "I'm not powerful; I was just helping my daughter." She would probably not see, as I did, that such everyday responses of a mother to her child represent vital lessons in resilience, the value of which extends far beyond simply learning a new skill or overcoming fear of new situations. In these simple interactions, Elyssa's mother taught her daughter several important lessons about herself and her abilities.

First, her mother reassured Elyssa that she could do well in this new sport. It might seem hard, but she could handle difficult moments. Her mother's reminder that she had faced other new situations and mastered other skills helped Elyssa remember these successes and draw confidence from them.

Elyssa's mother acknowledged and validated her daughter's feeling of being overwhelmed even while she encouraged Elyssa to remember that she had other qualities on which she could concentrate instead, such as her skill as a runner. She reminded her daughter that she was larger than the part that felt overwhelmed. Her mother helped Elyssa see herself from a different perspective and discover new options. Rather than acting on the first choice that came to her—to give up—Elyssa could choose another response—to try again. By not insisting that Elyssa return to practice but giving her the choice, her mother reinforced her daughter's sense of control over the situation. In later years, Elyssa will likely be able to draw upon her various resilient qualities in meeting life's challenges.

A Difficult Childhood

Not all children are as fortunate as Elyssa, however. Instead, their childhood experiences are stressful or abusive. They have no one to provide the consistent guidance and support other children receive. Yet many disadvantaged and high-risk children learn these lessons as well as or better than their luckier counterparts. In many respects, it is a paradox: on the one hand, children from disadvantaged homes are vulnerable to their parents' inadequate nurturing, while on the other, they are challenged to learn to care for themselves, to learn to self-parent. To a degree, the more stress on the child, the more necessity and opportunity exist for the child to compensate through experimentation; the child learns to act on his or her own behalf and develops new avenues for learning and support. The need to be self-sufficient often leads to high levels of functioning in such individuals (Levine 2012; Tough 2012).

When I think of resilience in this context, I am reminded of Susan, a classmate of mine. Her father was a violent alcoholic who would periodically come to school intoxicated to yell at her or the principal or our teacher for some real or imagined wrong. Sometimes there were bruises on Susan's face and legs, which we all pretended not to see. She had a younger sister and brother for whom she was often responsible.

None of this stopped her from being the top student in our class academically, or from dressing in a most distinctive manner. When her mother came home from work, Susan walked to the library to do her homework—after she had straightened the house and cooked dinner. Sometimes Susan went to a friend's house to do homework. Later, as I got to know her, she came to mine.

I asked Susan once how she managed to do all she did. She told me how desperately she wanted to get out of her family's lifestyle, and she knew school was her only chance. She said she felt different from the rest of her family because she saw herself as a survivor. She concentrated on fulfilling this self-image. As years passed, I heard news of Susan: of the advanced degrees she earned and her career as a state legislator, and her somewhat quirky dress. Susan's clear vision and determination were all part of her resilience.

It is important to stress that there is a limit to the positive outcomes of such a challenge on young children. In their need to achieve competence in certain areas, children are often forced to neglect other areas of development, such as the ability to form lasting relationships and express needs. Without protective factors that can allow children to moderate hard-won coping strategies, they are at risk of developing an unbalanced style of resilience.

The Role of Trauma in Forming *Girly Thoughts*

Providing a sound balance of protection and independence is difficult enough for a healthy family, but for a family experiencing chronic or extraordinary problems, the task of providing this balance for children can become a strain on an already overburdened family.

It is important to remember that all families have problems. Typical families work productively to find solutions, obtaining outside help if necessary. Even during difficult times, they will continue to provide needed love and support for their members. In fact, working through manageable problems is a positive lesson that serves to bolster a family's strengths. A struggling family, by contrast, may be overwhelmed and even disintegrate in the face of difficulties.

For children, change and its resultant stress are a normal part of life: the first day of school, a theater tryout, or the first night away from home. Such distress may be uncomfortable, but often it propels us to new learning. The frustration of reaching for objects we could not yet grasp led us to stand and then to walk. It is part of developing a larger understanding of the world and gives us experience in responding to stresses and distressful events in life. We learn that most upsetting events are temporary and soon lose their importance. We learn to keep our disappointments in perspective and go on. These are valuable lessons that we can draw from in the future.

Trauma is very different from distress. Trauma is an abnormal life experience. Within a family, it might include sexual or physical abuse, or neglect; the death of a parent or sibling; abuse against the mother; extreme poverty; divorce; alcoholism; addiction; incarcerated or mentally ill parents; or intense fighting between family members (Felitti et al. 1998). Disaster outside the family, such as racism, a natural catastrophe, war, or tragedy, can be a source of trauma also. And there are other sources of trauma just beginning to be understood: trauma that comes from children being reared in families doling out stories of terror, torture, and humiliation from the past along with the child's milk, which is known as intergenerational trauma. And trauma in families where children lie awake at night and worry for a parent's safety because of gang warfare, or when a parent's profession is combat-related, which is secondary trauma (O'Gorman and Diaz 2012).

When a child experiences trauma, she may develop painful feelings about herself that are likely to be long lasting and resurface in adolescence and adulthood. These feelings do not disappear when the trauma is over but may form a basis of her negative feelings about herself, perhaps of worthlessness, unlovability, helplessness, or shame. In fact, they can form the basis of believing and embracing the *girly thoughts* that abound in our culture, for *girly thoughts* explain, first the girl and then to the woman, why life is so difficult for her, and that it is *her fault*.

This is such a double-edged sword for women. Not only are there many challenges for women simply by virtue of the fact that they are women, but we also blame women as if they personally created this.

What We Needed:
Protection and Independence

Children need many things from their parents and other caregivers. Of these, protection and independence are particularly significant in the development of resilience. A child must have appropriate measures of each, although they can be conflicting and confusing at times, even overwhelming, for parents and child alike.

The conflict between protection and independence is evident in the two-year-old who wants to do it herself, yet cries if her mother walks out of the room. It is equally present in the adolescent who complains that she is too restricted or not allowed to make her own decisions but angrily demands her mother drive her to the mall. The two needs represent a vital dynamic that shapes who we are, both as children and adults. Much depends on our ability to successfully achieve a healthy balance between them.

Protection

All children need protection. Learning safe behavior is a lifelong process. But how is that protection to be given? The answer to this can make all the difference.

Imagine a one-year-old child coming into a room that has been childproofed. The child is able to explore without restrictions, to learn about the room and the objects in it, and about herself in relationship to them. The child can move independently and rove about as she wishes. If the room isn't childproofed, being held by her mother or being placed in a playpen will protect her. She would be equally safe but restricted and not free to be stimulated in the same way.

The degree to which a child should be protected is a constant consideration for parents. While it may be true that the "burned hand teaches best," parents must decide what is an acceptable risk and what is not. A mother must let her child learn to walk on her own and accept the many falls and tears along the way. Yet other situations are not so clear-cut, and, as the child grows, these situations become more and more a matter of individual judgment.

Learning how to protect herself is important for the child because, as soon as she begins to move around in her environment, she receives specific instructions that clearly imply that the world is not always safe. These range from warnings about safety hazards—a hot stove or busy street—to rules for her social behavior, such as how to dress, not taking candy from strangers, or not letting anyone touch her in a certain way.

Parents can teach these lessons in various ways. Unfortunately, many parents instill a sense of fear or shame as a way to teach their children appropriate behavior. For a healthy balance, children need to learn to protect themselves, not out of fear, but out of respect for themselves and their bodies so they can demand that others respect them also.

I was at a mall during the holiday season one year and had an opportunity to observe two mother-daughter interactions. In the first instance, a frustrated mother, her arms full of packages, yanked her four-year-old daughter's coat in an effort to move the dawdling girl along. Her daughter yelled at her, "Stop it! You're hurting me!" The mother stopped. Still frustrated, but also visibly upset, she said, "I'm sorry, I didn't mean to hurt you, but we have to get going!"

Shortly after this I observed another mother and daughter. Again the mother, burdened by too many packages, was trying to make her way through the crowds with her five-year-old daughter. The girl stopped at a toy counter to look at the dolls. Her mother turned angrily to her and smacked her across her back. The girl didn't say anything. She hung her head and followed her mother out of the store. This interaction led me to suspect a very different relationship between mother and daughter. Here the child was being raised to believe that being hit was acceptable, and her hanging head seemed to say that she knew she was to blame.

These mother-daughter pairs had much in common. Both girls were well dressed and well groomed. Both had the attention of their mother in this very busy mall. But the quality of their attention varied greatly. The first girl received a yank from her mother, but also her mother's acknowledgment that this was wrong behavior. This four-year-old felt entitled to articulate her feelings and to stand up for herself, even against her mother. The second girl had learned to not stand up to her mother. She learned it was acceptable for parents to hit children and that it was her fault if she were hit. I thought about what very different lessons each mother taught her daughter about self-protection and her right to be treated with respect.

Independence

While children need protection, they have an equal need for independence from family and home and an ever-increasing desire for it. Independence means moving away from parents and out of their protection. Many parents find it difficult to accept that, as their daughter matures, they become increasingly less central to her accomplishments and developing sense of self as peers and the subtle messages of the greater society take hold. While this is the birthplace of *girly thoughts*, it is important that parents support and facilitate a girl's desire to act for herself and make her own decisions.

A child growing up with a good sense of independence has developed this due to her parent's trust that she is ready to go forth in the world. Whether independence means spending her first night at a friend's house or cooking her first meal, a girl nurtured to become independent feels her family's support, even if she cries at her friend's house and needs to come home, even if her first meal is inedible. Her self-esteem grows a little more with each success as she gradually prepares to assume responsibility for her actions and their consequences.

Or if the child has trauma in her childhood, she learns independence as a resilient survival skill, a result of understanding the need to set clear boundaries around those personal challenges she sees others experiencing. Her growing independence is a result of her need to survive amid somewhat hostile inputs. The reinforcement for her actions comes internally as she builds an understanding of what works and what doesn't in her world.

Achieving a Balance

A good balance between decreasing protection and increasing independence is very important to a girl's healthy development. One who is overprotected and not allowed to make mistakes may conclude that she is incompetent, or that she can only have what she wants if others obtain it for her. As an adult, she is liable to have an underdeveloped resilience. She will continue to look for protection from others, such as her spouse, her boss, a more experienced coworker, or a friend.

Appropriate independence is also very different from too much independence. While it is true that some children are able to cope with too much independence and go on to assume a stellar resilience, they do so at a cost to their inner well-being. More often, girls who are given little protection and too much independence develop feelings of shame when they confront situations for which they are unequipped. Unable to judge how much is appropriate for themselves at that age, they believe they are to blame when they are asked to do too much or when they need more adult help. This often sets the stage for overwhelmed resilience. Or a child may develop a self-contained, brittle, resilience style, feeling that she must keep achieving because that is all of who she is and she has no other choice. (Resilience styles will be explained in greater detail in the next chapter.)

Many years ago, I counseled a mother and daughter during the girl's spring break from an exclusive boarding school. They came to see me about the intense arguments they were having about how much money the daughter, Star, would receive each month when she went to spend the summer by herself in New York City. Star was only fourteen years old. When I expressed my amazement that such a young girl would be allowed to live on her own in New York City, her mother hastened to assure me that Star would be subletting a friend's apartment in a very fashionable part of Manhattan and that her daughter was looking forward to beginning her modeling career. "We have family in the city, so if anything happens, Star will have people to call."

"Where will you be?" I asked the mother.

"I'll be in Europe with my fiancé."

It was clear that the arguing was not about money but about the fact that Star was terrified about being on her own in the city, even though she was loathe to admit to it. She found it easier to sabotage the whole plan by getting her mother angry than to admit she couldn't handle so much freedom. I helped them reach a compromise: Star agreed to stay with relatives and not sublet an apartment. The money issue evaporated.

Situations such as Star's can put a girl at risk of developing a paradoxical resilience. Unable to ask for help or to admit that what is expected of her is more than she can master, she may compartmentalize her skills and develop strengths in certain areas, such as in her career, while remaining overwhelmed and unable to access her resilience in other areas of her life. For example, she may have a difficult time in seeing her strengths outside of a work environment. If Star were to pursue modeling, her looks may become so important that she could feel that her beauty was the only reason she had value. She would then need support in understanding how to express her needs and how to nurture herself in many different ways so she didn't focus so much of her identity on one aspect of herself.

Of Roots and Wings

As our resilience forms and develops under the influences of these early years, the stages through which we pass enable us to formulate two formidable components of our resilience: a knowledge of who we are—our *roots*—and a widening capacity to reach beyond our immediate situation to the wider world—our *wings*.

Our roots comprise the deep sense of self that arises from our interactions with the world, the responses we receive from our environment, and our increasing ability to obtain what we need. Even as infants, when we felt distress and needed comfort, our developing resilience allowed us to explore our bodies and to keep searching until we found our mouth and our thumb so that we could suck and soothe ourselves.

Our rootedness is our belief in that self, our determination to overcome whatever is placed in our path to get to where we need to go. This began with the long, determined process it took to learn our earliest skills—to sit, to crawl, to walk—and includes the mastery of every ability we now exercise in our everyday lives.

Our rootedness, then, is our identity, which grows slowly over the years and results in our self-concept, what we know about ourselves. It is through this knowledge that we assess our strengths, weaknesses, and emerging capabilities. This is the part of us that contains our beliefs about who we are and retains our personal values, and as such can be profoundly influenced by the societal messages surrounding us and wend their way into our *girly thoughts*.

Annalee was born in Korea and adopted by American parents when she was six months old. Her birth mother had decided on adoption because she knew that as the daughter of a young Korean factory worker and an African American serviceman, Annalee would be afforded more opportunities in the United States.

Annalee's adoptive parents, a middle-class couple of Swedish and Finnish descent, lived in Nebraska. They loved their little daughter with the passion known only to those who have had to search for a child to love.

"My parents saw themselves as a family now connected to Korea and the black community in America," said Annalee. "They made it a point to learn about Korea and to speak to me about it, so that the country of my birth was meaningful to me. My adoptive father had also been in the armed services, so he was able to talk about what life was probably like for my birth father."

As a family, they became involved in cultural events that allowed them all to celebrate her heritage and theirs. This allowed Annalee to build a special sense of identity in which she took pride, and her pride later sustained her in dealing with the racism of the American culture.

Annalee also grew up hearing stories of how she was a sweet but determined baby, how she would focus her attention on a goal and keep on trying until she achieved it. Whether she was tying her shoe or learning to read, her concentration was exemplary. As she grew older, the pride she'd developed in herself led her to be proud of her academic ability.

I grew up knowing I was different from most kids around me, but as I got older, I liked my specialness. I realized that I had relatives in three countries who spoke languages other than English. So I began to study languages in elementary school. I gave up trying to be just like the other kids. I realized there was nothing I could do that would ever make me like them, so I decided to be the most me I could be.

This was a long, hard struggle. I remember when I was about to have a solo in my third-grade Christmas show. I overheard two of my classmates saying "brown-skinned girls with slanty eyes can't sing." I just dissolved into tears and slumped to the floor. My mother wandered backstage and found me. She looked at me and held me. She always seemed to understand my pain, and she was pretty good at teaching me to fight back.

After I finished a good hard cry she said, "Let's go show them how truly ignorant they are." I belted out "Santa Claus Is Coming to Town" as it had never been sung before!

Today Annalee attends college on a scholarship and is majoring in art and Asian studies. "I'm happy that I know and like who I am. I enjoy playing up my individuality."

Our roots give us a valuable connection to our past and the positive experiences that helped to make us who we are. Here, in our roots, are the bumps we encountered that set us on a new direction, the molds we used only to recast later on. Here is the past that exerts its influence on our present.

Our Wings

Our wings provide us with another aspect of our resilience that is very different from our roots. While our rootedness stems from the depths of our being, our wings enable us to extend our vision beyond our experience to reach out into the world. Our wings allow us to use our fantasies for practical purposes, to move beyond the limits we feel placed upon us.

We were developing our wings when we spent our time as children in imaginary play, coloring, playing house, and writing stories or reading of other worlds, of princesses in distress and happy endings. We met people with other lives and imagined ourselves to be them. It was through such dreaming that we began to know more about the world, to sense our own desires for the future. We learned a bit about what life had to offer, and we began to glimpse what we wanted for ourselves. We even used our wings to help shape the life we wanted to have.

Julia was born into a working-class family of five children. Her father was a fireman and a chronic gambler who lost most of his paycheck each month. Her mother, unable to get by on her husband's earnings, was dependent on her own family for food and small loans. Even as a young child, Julia saw how indebted her mother was to her grandmother.

"With that kind of power over my mother, my grandmother exacted a heavy price in the form of obedience to her every whim," said Julia. "I never wanted to be so beholden to someone else."

She vowed as a young child not to get married, not to be poor, not to be so helplessly trapped as her mother was. Julia began to dream of other lives. She fell in love with movies and television and the different characters she saw there.

I spent hours fantasizing about the people and the lives they lived. I remember I drove my family crazy trying to speak like the characters so I could lose my Bronx accent. My brothers told me I was showing off. But my playacting allowed me to imagine that my life could be different and better than my parents'.

I was always told I was such a curious child. Maybe I was just nosy, but I wanted to know how people got to where I saw them in life. I always felt that life wasn't something that happened to you, it was something that you went out and found.

Early on, Julia used her natural inquisitiveness and interest in people to find out how she could make her life into what she intuitively knew she wanted. Today Julia is in an executive training program in personnel for a large hotel chain. Her natural inquisitiveness and eagerness to go out and learn about people has paid off.

As adults, our wings still allow us to imagine a different life, to continue to dream, just as we did as little girls. Our dreams and fantasies are a central part of who we are. Sometimes we share our dreams with friends or family and invite their assistance in making these dreams become reality. Sometimes we keep our dreams private and use them to help us develop a clearer image of who we are and what we can become.

Reconciling Our Past

In childhood and adolescence, we are often unaware of the quality of our upbringing or the full meaning of our early influences. Our attention is so focused on the challenges of new discovery and development just ahead of us that we don't take time to look back. We may not recognize the unique blend of our parents' strengths and shortcomings and how they affected our ability to develop our roots and wings. We may not consider the impact of how young girls were portrayed in the stories we read or in the movies we saw.

In later years, however, we begin to see the significance of these influences. Sometimes the consequences of the ways in which our parents protected us or gave us their permission to grow may not be evident until we are parents ourselves, and we're making the same decisions for our children. We may experience the same difficulty as our parents did in achieving a healthy balance. Or we may need to live apart from our family for some time before we recognize how deep our roots or how wide our wings have grown.

In developing our resilience, we can begin to discover the benefits and failings of the past. We can draw on past strengths to make us stronger, or work through past traumas to make us more of who we want to be.

Protective Factors: The Key to Resilience

The ability to handle distress and trauma varies from one person to the next. Certain protective factors may provide us with shielding to handle these situations so we may recover more easily from their negative effects. Such factors include our unique attributes, our family environment, and the influence of the larger community.

Personal Attributes

Certain qualities in one's physical and psychological makeup can form the basis of early resilience. For example, Susan's initiative in finding ways to complete her homework, as well as her reliance on her own capabilities to build a better life for herself, arose from an inner sense of self she established early in life. This independent self-image allowed her to conceive of a different way of living than the one her family showed her. As a result, she was able to create a healthy distance between herself and the trauma of her father's alcoholism and her resultant chaotic home.

Family Environment

Our personal traits do not exist in a vacuum but in the context of our family, which can contribute significantly to the development of our resilience or thwart it. Protective factors associated with families include family cohesiveness and the positive attention we receive from our parents, siblings, and other family members. The amount of structure and limit setting provided in the home, especially during adolescence, are also variables.

While a family cannot protect a child completely from circumstances beyond its control, parents can reduce the damaging effects of even trauma. Lessons a family can teach can allow a child to learn how to distance from the pain of trauma, and this plays a crucial role in determining how those circumstances ultimately affect the child's later life.

My friend Isabelle grew up in a displaced persons camp, one of hundreds of camps set up throughout Europe after World War II. Here homeless, war-torn families were reunited and struggled to reestablish their lives in the midst of chaos, poverty, and illness. When Isabelle talks of her childhood, she remembers her life in the camps as a time when she learned from her mother a sense of personal power.

For example, by the age of five, Isabelle had learned to bargain for bread and get it at a price the family could afford. Survival skills, she explained, were well rewarded by her mother, and young Isabelle felt pride in her accomplishments despite the stressful circumstances. These early achievements laid the foundation for subsequent successes in her life. As an adult today, Isabelle is a competent woman with both a rewarding family life and fulfilling professional career.

Ruth grew up in similar circumstances. She, however, looks back in horror at her life in the displaced persons camp. Ruth remembers the confusion, deprivation, and scant provisions. She remembers that her mother would curse her for being born, saying how much easier it would have been to feed a family of two rather than three. Ruth grew up feeling unwanted and as if there were nothing she could do to make life better. The lesson of her childhood was learning to endure—endure her mother's rages, the poverty, and her own fears. Ruth grew up feeling she was less worthy than other children.

As an adult, Ruth continues to perceive herself this way. She faces life with determination but little spirit or self-esteem. She has worked for a large corporation since her graduation from college and has moved up the corporate ladder in carefully defined steps. But she is unhappy. She feels empty and has been unable to find fulfillment in a series of marriages. Her sadness is, in part, the pain of the familiar, the sense of despair and inadequacy she has carried with her all these years. It is also the pain of her own lack of vision that life could be different.

Community Environment

Just as the family can foster resilience and a child's healthy self-esteem, so the community can serve an important function in protecting a child. Children benefit from dependable caretakers, supportive role models, and other social support from the community as a whole.

Inez grew up in a poor family in Arizona. Her family was from Mexico and spoke Spanish at home. Inez taught herself English, first on the streets and later at school. Her father was disabled and her mother did domestic work. Because she was the oldest child, for most of her childhood Inez functioned as the person in charge during her mother's absence.

The brief exceptions were two weeks every summer when I was sent to the church-sponsored summer camp. When family friends told my mother about the camp, she at once made arrangements for me to go. I remember telling my mother that I didn't want to go, but she insisted that I have the chance to be a child, if only for a little while.

I worried about my father and the rest of the kids. The first week I was pretty tense, but after that I began to relax and just be a kid. I'd play and swim. I remember the sense of freedom I had. There were meals I didn't have to cook, friends I could just play with, and new things to learn, like ceramics. The counselors were wonderful. Every summer for seven years, I fell in love with my group leader. Some of them kept in touch with me over the years. Everything about camp made me feel special.

For Inez, summer camp was a different world, a place where she could try on new roles and new ways of being. Her mother realized the value of exposure to different people and different lifestyles; these allowed Inez to dream. The lasting bond with adults in authority who she knew on a first-name basis became the model on which Inez eventually built her own life. Today, she is a teacher in the neighborhood where she grew up. To all who know her, she is a walking success story.

Each woman develops her resilience to a different degree, depending on her unique experiences and the presence of risk and protective factors in her life. Even in the same family, siblings discover different ways of coping with their situation. Some women, for a variety of reasons, have underdeveloped resilience; an imbalance between opportunity and protective factors has not allowed them as yet to develop their natural resilience. Others regularly rely on their resilience to meet daily challenges. I frequently find that even people unaware of their resilience can nevertheless identify elements in their childhood from which they drew special strength and meaning.

Specialized Community and Cultural Supports

In an effort to create a culture change, to redirect our *girly thoughts* in a more positive direction, many groups are actively working to change the way young girls absorb cultural messages about their abilities and potential. The introduction of federal funding through Title IX in 1972 to support sports for girls has resulted in not only opportunities for sports development for girls in the schools but also has resulted in many community-led organizations with outstanding results. Film festivals like the Tucker Film Festival at the University of Minnesota show independent films about girls and sports from around the world, helping to challenge established stereotypes here and abroad. Organizations from Girls Action Foundation in Canada to retooled efforts in the Girl Scouts of America support girls and work to expand their image of what is possible for them. Many media-oriented organizations are developing to help expand the horizons for young girls. Engineeryourlife.org is one example of an organization that educates girls about nontraditional female occupations, and it has received national recognition.

Yet even with this multifaceted approach, raising a generation of women who value themselves and ignore *girly thoughts* has proven to be an uphill battle because the pervasiveness of negativity of how girls and women feel about themselves continues.

Getting to Know Yourself

Here begins the interactive portion of acknowledging and cultivating your resilience. You'll begin a journal so you can play with these concepts and give yourself the time and space to consider how they apply to you in the development of your resilience. Now is the time to think about what will work best for you—typing on your computer and smart phone, or writing longhand in a bound journal. There is no right or wrong way to go forward. Some of you will find it works best to write in quick bursts; others will want to make space to think this through. But if you find you don't have the time to do this leisurely, at least find a time to do it quickly and then go back and review it later. The important commitment you are making to yourself is to begin to play with these ideas and see what they spark in you.

✦

This first assessment will help you understand what parts of your life have been literally *protective* of your development, of who you have grown to be.

Assessment One: Determining Your Own Protective Factors and Outside Supports

The peace and stability of a nation
depend upon the proper relationships
established in the home.
—Jade Snow Wong

Take a moment to ask yourself the following questions, then write out your answers. Leave some empty space between your initial response and the next question, in case you want to come back and elaborate later on some of your answers.

Which of the following protective factors, if any, were true of your experience as you were growing up? What other positive circumstances had a lasting effect on your life? In your journal, make a list of the factors that apply to your upbringing, and write sentences or bullets to describe how you feel they impacted you.

Individual Factors

- good health
- good problem-solving and communication skills
- good self-esteem
- sense of control in your life
- achievement orientation
- flexibility
- sense of humor
- optimism
- intelligence
- curiosity
- empathy
- interest in other people
- interest in novel situations
- other important qualities

Family Factors

- strong family ties
- warm, caring, and supportive family environment
- close, positive relationship with parent(s)
- nurturing extended family
- positive family stories
- predictable, positive family rituals and routines
- clear boundaries or limits
- structure and consistency

Community Factors

- positive school experiences
- positive religious affiliation
- close relationship(s) with other caring adults
- supportive role models
- structured group opportunities (Y, camp, youth groups, sports teams)
- consistent child care

Think back to your childhood. Which of these protective factors (or their equivalent) are present in your life today?

Our childhood puts certain influences in play that shape our attachments, our roots, and our needs for independence. We respond to them; we grow because of them; they help to form us. If we are well protected, we have one view of the world and need to do less on our own. If we have fewer protective factors, there is more of a requirement for us to develop more resilience if we are to be successful in life. Such is the powerful early influence of our protective factors, an influence that continues throughout our life and shapes the patterns of resilience we develop.

FOUR

How You Use
Your Resilience Today:
Your Resilience Patterns

IF YOU CAN'T BE A GOOD EXAMPLE, THEN YOU'LL
JUST HAVE TO BE A HORRIBLE WARNING.

—*Catherine*

*I*n *the previous chapter,* you began to see how your early experiences in protection and independence shaped the resilience
you have today. Determining how you use that resilience today is
the next step in the process of understanding how to consciously
develop and strengthen it.

Resilience Styles

Every woman has developed her natural resilience to a greater or
lesser degree. Many of us compartmentalize our resilience by putting
it in boxes of different sizes rather than integrating it as a resource

77

we use consciously across all parts of our life, and this makes it less readily accessible, As a result, as you first become conscious of your own resilient qualities, it is important to recognize the extent to which you already draw on these strengths and the areas in which you do so. The ways you presently use your resilience depend on the challenges and reinforcements you experienced in childhood, adolescence, and early adulthood, as well as the ways you have come to understand those experiences; in other words, you need to determine the patterns that work for you and how to apply them to the challenges you currently face.

I have found it useful to think in terms of six different styles of resilience when talking about their application for personal development. It is important to keep in mind that the following categories are not value judgments, nor do they indicate your potential or need for change. These are only general characterizations, descriptions if you will, of the ways in which a woman tends to use her resilience now, today. Based on the circumstances to which that same woman responds tomorrow, these styles can change. However, within each resilience style there is also an implicit opportunity for growth, based not just on how you are dealing with challenges now before you but how you would rather be dealing with those challenges.

An overview of resilience styles also shows that the development and use of resilience is a far more nuanced process than many consider. Resilience is not an "on or off" quality; you're either resilient or you're not. Resilience is a dynamic quality that builds on past experience and uses it to address the challenge in front of you today.

Let's look at each of these styles in greater depth.

Paradoxical Resilience

Some women use their resilience in particular areas of their lives but not in others; this is the definition of paradoxical resilience. This can result in women feeling they are at war with themselves, for they hold themselves so differently in various areas of their life.

Many women are successful at work, where they hold positions of responsibility and are skilled at making choices. They feel pride, even a sense of accomplishment, in this part of their life. Yet these same women are utterly different in their personal lives. Although they are decisive at work, they are unable to make decisions at home. While they are assertive on the job, they may even allow themselves to be subjected to abuse at home. They are unable to apply the same skills that gain them promotions at work to their personal relationships, needs, or preferences.

Other women with paradoxical resilience manage a home, juggle the needs of children and spouse, participate in community events, and serve in positions of responsibility in volunteer organizations, yet these women feel they cannot compete in the professional world. They see their skills as an expression of the love they have for their family, religion, or community rather than also a reflection of their personal resources.

Both groups of women have allowed their *girly thoughts* to dominate an important part of their lives, but not all of their lives. They need to explore their individual strengths and skills to see how they can be applied in other areas of their lives. In doing so, they can own their personal strengths and talents and begin to define themselves on the basis of who they are inside, not just by their capacity to perform specific roles in particular settings.

Davina feels she lives two lives. Professionally, she is a resourceful and competent accounts executive with an advertising firm. At twenty-eight, she has already risen in the company and is told she is being groomed for bigger and better opportunities. She is known for her energy, her ability to win new accounts, and her attention to detail. She looks and acts the part of a young, successful career woman.

At home she lives with Ron, a thirty-two-year-old student. In her honest moments, Davina knows Ron will never finish college. But she spends her time trying to make him happy—a useless effort, she knows, although she doesn't dare to let her frustration show for she is desperately afraid that he will leave her. Being alone is the worst fate imaginable for her.

To see her at home is to see someone very different from the vital young woman she is at work. At home, she is anxious, unsure of herself. She is afraid that if she is assertive, Ron will feel threatened and leave her.

Davina says, "My parents are upset that I'm living with Ron and constantly criticizing him, and their disapproval only forces me to defend him. They wanted something better for me, they say. They are caring people who always encouraged me, while simultaneously undermining me. For example, I'd study long hours to get A's. My parents were proud of my grades but criticized me for working too hard for them. They always told me I was beautiful, but no boyfriend was quite right for me. They thought I made poor choices."

Davina's childhood was a series of contradictions, so it is no wonder that she reflects this by the unevenness of her growth. At work, she feels she can ask, even demand, what she needs and wants. She advocates for herself. But at home these same tasks and skills seem alien to her.

Women who use their resilience paradoxically actually are very resilient; it is just that they confine the use of their resilience often only to one area. The task for these women is to explore ways to apply their strengths more evenly in their lives. Owning their resilience will cause them to confront the self-defeating beliefs they learned in childhood about women's competence, and capabilities—their *girly thoughts*. As they free themselves of these ideas, they can begin to develop a new self-image based on realistic information about who they really are.

Stellar Resilience

Women who have withstood extraordinary circumstances and survived great challenges often develop stellar resilience. Their competence, security, and self-fulfillment belie the chaos, tragedy, or hardship they experienced in their early lives. As adults, they may have achieved a happy home life despite an unhappy childhood. They may have money and security despite impoverished beginnings. They may seem happy and at peace with the world, despite having suffered terrible tragedy.

Despite their obvious success, however, the feeling that even now they are not "normal" or capable of living an ordinary life because their lives in the past were abnormal haunts many women of stellar resilience. They are plagued with the idea that they have no way to create a normal life for themselves or their family because they have never experienced an average home or upbringing. As a result, inwardly they may feel damaged, scarred, different, or even tainted.

Many women of stellar resilience feel they have paid a high price for their survival. When they look at themselves in the context of their family of origin, for example, they often feel separated, uncomfortable, and perhaps angry. They may experience "survivor's guilt" for having survived and thrived when others they love have not. They often feel they exist in limbo between their present accomplishments, which they can't quite own, and their past, which they are still struggling to fully overcome.

Their *girly thoughts* may serve to undermine them further by causing them to question their strength and their sense of purpose. They look at the message behind their *girly thoughts* and see what they think "normal" looks like; although when they try to achieve this "normal," it still feels elusive.

Their sense of self contains not only the positive values of their childhood but also their knowledge of their ability to withstand and master pain. But with this mastery comes the realization that the other shoe may drop, so they live on guard and always dreading the next major challenge. They become hypervigilant, wary of intimacy and allowing themselves to be free sexually. And this awareness may compromise their vision of the future; they need to learn to move beyond the anticipation and mastery of pain, and learn to use their energies to develop a more enjoyable present. Instead of constantly worrying about surviving the next disaster, they need to learn to anticipate pleasurable outcomes.

Maria is a woman of stellar resilience. She is a social worker and is recognized as a leading authority on child abuse. She is married, has two boys and a girl, and considers herself successful in her life. When viewed from the outside, her life is ideal: a two-career family, a nice house in Hoboken, New Jersey, and healthy children who do well in school. But Maria is plagued by the idea that all she has created is a sham.

Maria was one of three children. Her father worked hard to provide a good home, but he died young of a heart attack. Maria's oldest brother was killed walking home from school one day in an apparent random shooting. Her mother had a terrible time coping with her losses, and the children were sent to live with relatives for a time; Maria went to live with an aunt who owned a small convenience store. She was required to come home after school every day to work behind the counter and sweep up after hours. Maria discovered she enjoyed dealing with customers and that they in turn liked her. Despite her grief, she began to realize how well she got along with others, including teachers, and later, employers and clients.

Maria and her siblings returned to live with their mother shortly before her mother's remarriage.

My stepfather disliked us, and our home became unbearable. Life was a nightmare of disorder and cruelty. My brother became an addict. Eventually he was thrown out of the house to live on the streets. My sister did somewhat better—she got pregnant and lived with her child's father. Both my siblings remained in Newark in the old neighborhood. Both are now married to blue-collar workers, are raising large families, and, like our mother, struggle to make ends meet.

My siblings see their lives as defined by their childhood. Not me. My early responsibilities at the convenience store taught me that I had other options in life. In high school I found a job and worked hard to prove myself. Somehow, though, it's too easy to say that hard work and education alone allowed me to escape. I think there was some strength in my chaotic family that allowed me to survive the poverty and abuse and be able to use it in my adult life. I saw I could work hard and achieve something. When I did, people saw me in a new way. I could be more than that poor kid without a dad. So in my work I reach out to try to make the system work for other poor kids. Yes, I work long hours, don't see my husband or my own kids as much as I'd like, and I endure the craziness of the "system," but I'm driven. There has to be a better way, and I am determined to find a way of making the changes necessary to make it work for the kids.

Maria also benefited from her relationship with her sister.

After our mother remarried, life was hell. We both vowed to leave as soon as possible and create a better life for ourselves. Together we daydreamed and blue-skied about what our life would be like. I think that the support we gave each other allowed us both to see beyond our childhood reality, and having seen what we wanted, we were both freed to go after it. The only difference between our dreams was that my sister was going to marry someone to take care or her. I was going to do it on my own.

My sister is taken care of. She hasn't left the old neighborhood, but she seems to be doing just fine. I have left and feel like an alien when I return. Now that I am out, I do not know where I belong. People look at me as if I'm a freak. I feel accomplished but not connected. I have been able to deal with the past abuse by my stepfather, but it has been difficult to find a new relationship with him. Yes, I can lecture, I can write, but I still struggle with my feelings—about my father and my brother, how our family was torn apart, and my sense that there is nowhere that I belong, and no one who can quite understand me.

Many women of stellar resilience feel a need to give back and often enter the helping fields: nursing, teaching, social work, medicine, and psychology. Or they may turn their considerable energy to humanitarian causes, such as world peace, environmental preservation, or the protection of children. As a result, they are vulnerable to giving too much of themselves, sacrificing their energy and identity in helping others, denying their own needs (sexually and otherwise), and developing codependency. Women can expand their identity to include important factors in the present that can help further shape them, such as their ability to connect to others, to commit to a cause, to be empathetic. In this way, they use their considerable resilience to integrate their past and present. They need to retain enough of their resources for themselves and enjoy the rare luxury of nurturing themselves as they nurture others. This can be their gift to themselves: the ability to enjoy what they often unselfishly give to others—a sense that life can be different and hold positive rewards.

Overwhelmed Resilience

Women who have been overly challenged and survived their traumatic childhood by accepting the blows and threats of others, unable to find a way to fend them off, may have survived the trauma, but only by paying a great price for their survival: the sacrifice of their self-esteem and positive self-image. Their resilience is overwhelmed by reliving past traumas, and sometimes by the re-creation of those same traumas in the present.

Rather than learning to see adversity as a challenge or an adventure, they have attempted to control the challenges in their life by viewing themselves as the cause of the difficulties they encounter, and this puts them at great risk for developing codependency, which is caring for others but not caring for themselves. They think of their need for comfort and understanding, for a loving sexual embrace, with distain and shame. They are, after all, in some way responsible for what has befallen them—or so they believe.

Using our resilience enables us to discover and draw on inner strengths, retain optimism, and reach out for help and support. In contrast, shame can make us wish that we were never born or that we could simply disappear. The overwhelmed woman may feel helpless and withdraw from situations; hopelessness may pervade her life. Where resilience finds safe ways to express feelings, shame often results in unexpressed feelings. Where strong resilience provides an identity that announces, "I can face this problem," shame whispers, "I am the problem."

Sometimes women face an overwhelming crisis that inundates their resources for dealing with it. In this scenario, a woman's considerable resilience is simply overwhelmed by the cascade of events surrounding her. She loses access to her strength because her focus is simply on surviving the horrific blow that life has delivered her.

Girly thoughts can offer the illusion of comfort; they certainly point us in a clear direction, but a direction that is not likely to help us resolve what is before us. So when we are overwhelmed, our *girly thoughts* may cause us to blame ourselves for our predicament, creating even more of a hole for us to dig out of.

The task before us is to remember our strengths, wisdom, and worthiness. For women raised with trauma, this is often a long and arduous process that takes us back to the origins of our pain and making conscious the conclusions we reached in childhood about the world and ourselves. As adults, the painful conclusions that helped to make survival possible can still be honored, for they did work, but now they can also be built upon and challenged, and new, more appropriate and nurturing beliefs can be developed.

Women facing trauma head-on need to remember that this incredible pain is temporary and it will pass. They need to remember that they can resurrect and use their resilience skills (even though they may not feel accessible) to deal with this major catastrophe, just as they had dealt with lesser challenges in the past.

Glenda was in a solid recovery from her drug abuse when her husband and oldest daughter were killed by a drunk driver. She is in a downward spiral. "Yes, I've known hardship. I've known pain. And I've known escape by trying to snort it up my nose and use pills to end the pain. But now I can't get out of bed. All I keep thinking of is how good it would feel to go away and be high. And I want to kill the person who did this."

As a teenager, Glenda began sneaking pills as a way of coping with a very emotionally removed and self-centered father, a mother who kept falling apart, and an older brother who was sexually abusive. She dealt pills and cocaine in college but has been clean now for many years. "Yes, I was named after the 'good witch' in *The Wizard of OZ*," she says. "But I don't feel very good now. I feel broken, numb, back at square one. And no, I'm not speaking to anyone in the program, not even those I sponsor in NA [Narcotics Anonymous]."

Glenda's resilience has been overwhelmed. Glenda is emotionally shut down, angry, and walking through life feeling that her own needs for comfort are wrong. "What right do I have for a hug when my daughter and husband will never feel anything ever again?" Rather than resilience, she feels shame and self-hatred, and unworthy of the nurturing and love she so readily gives to others. She does not believe she deserves to ask others for comfort or to have her own needs met. These are the beliefs she needs to challenge now.

But healing again is very possible, whenever it begins. And it can change how a person feels in the world and how she sees her pathway in it. This can be a long and challenging process, but the potential gain far outweighs the pain. With time and support, a woman whose resilience has been overwhelmed can learn to thaw emotionally and allow her strengths to again take their place in her life. The challenge: Women whose resilience is overwhelmed must first reflect on how they have used their resilience in the past; they need to recall the solutions to problems they have utilized in the past, even if they do not feel those solutions can be used now. As they begin to recall their well-developed survival skills—even if they feel those skills are not accessible at the present time—they can remind themselves that what they are experiencing now is temporary.

Self-Contained Resilience

Some women have had to be so resilient for so long that the positive aspects of resilience have become exaggerated. These women learned early in life to distrust others, and so believe they can only rely on themselves. As a result, they become isolated and unable to reach out. They spend their time and energy shoring up their defenses, ready for the next major task, the next attack. They are so fearful of being vulnerable that they can never feel safe enough to let down their guard, and their resilience becomes brittle. They act more like an island unto themselves. *Girly thoughts* are not a concern for them, as they are self-directed and compulsively self-reliant.

A woman of self-contained resilience can be very successful by external standards. She can look great, meet deadlines, negotiate, and get the job done. She develops certain skills to perfection but tends to neglect her emotional needs in other areas in her life. On the inside, she may even be a stranger to herself. Relationships often end with her partner saying she was too closed off or that she would not let allow herself to be loved.

Carla is a bright, attractive banker who works for a major bank that specializes in international finance. At forty-eight, she became a vice president. She works hard and puts in long hours, both of which have paid off with career success.

On the surface, Carla is friendly and exudes competence. In fact, her competence defines her. She works at this part of herself morning, noon, and night. It is the only part she knows. She socializes for work, but not on a personal level. "I feel that I either lost the art of friendship or perhaps never developed it," Carla muses. "I know that I frequently disappoint my family by being so unavailable. I am always late, only spending a little time with them, or I decline invitations outright."

Carla's childhood appeared stable. Her mother was a teacher, and her father was a moderately successful businessman. Carla grew up in a suburb of Memphis in a home that her parents still own. But the outward stability was deceptive. Carla explained:

> My mother is what psychologists call narcissistic; everything has to be for and about her. I was able to give this a name when I noticed my mother playing with her grandchildren. She kept dancing around saying, "Look at me! Look at me!" Her only way of engaging them was by having them pay attention to her.
>
> My father was known as the problem in the family. His moods would alternate between depression and rage, the latter directed

verbally at my mother, who he constantly tried to please and never could.

My younger sister, Nina, was the preferred daughter. As the older sibling, I was always encouraged to give in to her because I was supposed to be too mature to act out my feelings.

Carla soon learned that her feelings did not count for much in her family, but her ability to handle difficult situations did. This is what she has carried with her into adult life.

Carla has not had the opportunity to branch out and develop other parts of herself. When asked about her personal goals, she is quick to quip, "Men? I can understand why a man needs a woman; I just can't understand why a woman needs a man. My biological clock? It stopped working a long time ago."

Carla was able to keep her life in perfect order until recently, when she was diagnosed with cancer. Now, she has had to begin to confront the feelings she had previously ignored. She is beginning to see that she will need to give up her inflexibility to weather this new reality in her life. She wants to explore more of her personal side and has already begun to use her resilience to grow and nurture other parts of her being.

The tasks that lie before women of self-contained resilience involve using their well-developed resilience to explore other parts of themselves. Just as their insight and well-honed skills have been developed to bolster an air of competence in their lives, they need to learn to relax and to trust that others will meet their needs as they experiment with being more vulnerable. In doing this, their isolation will subside, leading to a richer and ultimately more rewarding life, and a evolution of their resilience style. The challenge: Women utilize their self-contained resilience to challenge themselves to develop flexibility and vulnerability—almost as if these are additional tasks to be accomplished. In the process, they will discover that their security is not really compromised by being connected to others.

Underdeveloped Resilience

Women who were raised by overly protective or permissive parents and were sheltered from dealing with the challenges of life frequently have underdeveloped resilience. A woman with underdeveloped resilience may appear entitled; when someone else (often her parents or her partner) continually runs interference for the consequences of the decisions she makes, she always questions her decisions, seeks approval for her choices, and lacks the adaptability to handle life's challenges. Our society has moved from the teacher being right to the student being right; children are treated as a luxury because tired parents may indulge them instead of guiding them. Through no fault of their own, these children are a product of the evolution of our society (Wolf 2002), and they grow up to have underdeveloped resilience.

If a child has been protected and not allowed to make decisions, she might appear to be passive, tentative, or inexperienced in owning her power to make choices. Women of underdeveloped resilience resemble children who have not learned to anticipate their own needs or to make their own way. These women have in some ways taken on their *girly thoughts* without even considering that those thoughts contain something to be challenged. They *are* their *girly thoughts*.

Most often, women who have been so overprotected that they have little sense of the world or of themselves are the ones who have not developed their resilience. They have been taught to depend on others to take care of them or make the important decisions for them. As a result, they never see themselves as complete. If a woman relies on a partner as her "better half," she may always feel anxious that her partner will leave . . . and, if that does happen, a woman with underdeveloped resilience may feel that she has lost an essential part of her own identity.

This was the case for Sally. "I guess I had gone through my life without making a decision for myself," she said. "I never had to, until my divorce. Before that, I did everything by the rules. The sad thing is, the rules didn't protect me from this pain."

Sally grew up as the second of four girls in rural South Carolina in a rigidly religious family. "My parents raised us with the knowledge that they and God had the answers to our problems," she said. "I grew up to depend on my parents to solve whatever trouble came my way. They were loving, kind, and gentle people. We had a simple life and never lacked anything. I went to a fundamentalist college that stepped in where my parents left off in taking care of me and my decisions."

In college Sally met a young man, and they married.

I always looked to my husband to provide the framework for my life. I always felt at a loss when he wasn't home. I did everything I could to please him. I quit school when we married to let him be the provider. I let him make all the decisions.

So three children later and while I was pregnant with our fourth, I was stunned when he said he was leaving me for someone else. I couldn't even imagine how he had met someone else, but it turned out she was someone at work he'd been seeing for several years. All that overtime he was "required" to do turned out to be her.

I was devastated. Nothing in my life had prepared me for this. If I had been alone, I might have killed myself, but I couldn't do that to my children. I just had to find another way. With all the stress I was under, I even considered an abortion but had a miscarriage in my fourth month, which I blame on my husband. Suddenly I realized that I had to get myself together in a way that I never had to before. I had to earn a living; I had to provide a family life for my children. I had to survive.

Sally needs to develop her resilience. In her present, difficult situation, she is fortunate to have warm and loving support from her family and others in her church, but she still has much to do alone. She is hurt and bewildered, but she is using this part of herself to grow, to challenge old beliefs, and to take the next step.

"It's pretty hard right now; the kids and I have to learn how to do everything differently. But hard as it is, there is some part of me that loves it, too. I feel good doing things for my family and for myself. I like the feeling of accomplishment. For the first time in my life, I'm beginning to know what self-sufficiency means."

Or a second possible avenue to underdeveloped resilience is addiction: these women became addicted in their teens, or earlier, and never really grew up. Going through these developmentally important years under the influence of drugs or alcohol and not developing emotionally can result in the need to make up for lost time when they finally go into recovery. This becomes particularly important if they also have children, who emotionally may be more mature than they are.

Serena, who had been an addict for years, left rehab and came home with a vengeance. She was finally going to be a mother to her three teenagers. The only problem was that the teenagers had been taking care of her, their home, themselves, and each other for a long time. They didn't need someone coming in and making a bunch of rules that didn't make any sense—even if that someone was their own mother. They were the resilient ones. She was the one who had to learn to grow and develop more skills, which she was able to do thanks to a parenting program in her outpatient substance-abuse treatment program.

The task facing any woman with such underdeveloped resilience is to begin to experiment with being independent. To do this, she must find safe situations with ample support for taking risks. Small initial steps are in order, such as dressing to please herself and changing the way she organizes her time. With the support of girlfriends and others she can also begin taking risks, and when she sees what happens as she makes choices, she will begin to nurture her own inner resilience. The challenge: Women with less than optimal resilience can begin to consciously use their current skills to expand their resilience base. In this way, they learn to actively make their own decisions and to comfortably take responsibility for their actions.

Balanced Resilience

There are many pathways to achieving balanced resilience. For many women, this is a product of learning to take care of themselves despite the challenges, sometimes major ones, they have faced in their lives, or perhaps because of them. They have learned to be balanced as a result of hard work on themselves, and it has paid off.

They have learned to listen to and to honor their own needs and desires, from their careers to friendships and family to the somewhat forbidden area of sexuality. They've also learned to care for the other parts of their lives that require attention, they have learned to balance their needs against their responsibilities, and they've become better able to deal with both. This is the goal of the quest to connect with the self and to be able to be in balance within one's life.

Balanced resilience can also be found in women who have led reasonably happy lives without major loss or trauma. Often raised in families that offered protection and guidance, women of balanced resilience have had less need to draw consciously on their inner resilience. Their challenges have been the normal transitions of growing up and learning to cope with life. They tend to bring their strengths to bear equally in all areas of their lives.

Women who have learned to develop balanced resilience have learned how to take the best that society offers and reject the rest. They even have fun with their *girly thoughts* and enjoy dressing up and playing with products, but on their terms, and they laugh at the absurdity of what they believed in the past. The key is that they are not ruled by these thoughts. The thoughts are conscious, and women with balanced resilience are able to see them for what they are.

The task of a woman with balanced resilience is to learn more about her resilience and to use this part of herself to enhance her development. Life is full of challenges, from doing well in school, surviving adolescence, and separating from one's family, to finding a partner, building a family, establishing a career, and learning to deal with growing older. Facing these challenges with the assistance and guidance of our resilience allows us to accomplish these transitions less painfully and to perceive them as rewarding, even as adventures.

These life crises are used as opportunities to grow and flourish, and to discover deeper meaning in life.

Peggy, who grew up with six brothers and sisters, has always described herself as "the girl next door."

> I grew up on a ranch. We were all taught to love the land. Each of us had jobs to do for the family. Family life revolved around the needs of us kids, the cattle, and the ranch. We were comfortable, but by no means wealthy. The feeling that there was enough for everyone was much more important than material wealth.
>
> Our mother typified this by saying, "What kids need is love." So even when we went through years of drought or when money was tight, we knew that our parents loved us and that we would get through these problems together. Our roots were firmly established in our family and in the earth we all loved.

When Peggy speaks of her childhood, she smiles. After growing up in Missoula, Montana, she graduated from high school, went to junior college, and married at twenty-one. She gave birth to her first child at age twenty-three.

> I loved being a mother. When I had to, I went to work part-time. The boys got jobs to help pay for their school expenses. Then my husband, Al, was laid off, so I went to work full-time in a supermarket. To my surprise, I was steadily advanced and am now a manager. Al was able to find another line of work. The boys married and settled nearby. We were set.
>
> Until recently, that is. Al is being transferred out of state away from the boys and their families. Now I'm at a crisis point. I've managed other transitions in life, but this one doesn't seem fair.

I love being a mother and grandmother. It was bad enough to go to work full-time when the boys were still in school, but now we'll be fourteen hundred miles away. Yes, I know we need to go, but it hurts. And to tell you the truth, at my age I'm afraid to move and start over in a new community. My grandson Jeb tells me I'll just have to sprout wings so I can come back often. But I think he really has a point. I need a new way to take care of myself, a new way to see myself to accomplish this move.

Like most women of balanced resilience, Peggy's personal power has been largely unconscious. Not given to introspection, Peggy has taken for granted her ability to cope with life's demands. Peggy's resilience has been a natural outgrowth of her life, a comfortable part of who she was. Life has challenged her, but not beyond what she felt equipped to handle.

Now that she is confronting a major challenge, she needs to draw upon her flexibility, her personal power, to make this major transition. To accomplish this with the same equanimity that she has had at other transition points, she needs to be more conscious of her own ability to withstand change and make the best of it. By discovering her resilience and using it to counsel and guide her through this difficult time, Peggy can change this challenge into a new possibility for internal growth and development.

Being balanced in our resilience can take many forms; it can even result in taking some of life's challenges by choice, and this challenge can lead to growth in new and even exciting ways.

Assessment Two: Your Own Resilience Profile

If you risk nothing, then you risk everything.

—Geena Davis

The six basic patterns of resilience are designed as general descriptions only. In reality, our personal style of resilience and the areas in which we experience satisfaction or problems are more complex than the categories represented here. Most individuals find that they have the characteristics of two or more categories, but that one comes closest to describing the way they currently use their resilience in their lives. These categories prove to be a useful way to define areas of strength, areas of challenge, and areas for growth.

Your *resilience profile* allows you to see the ways in which your resilience presently functions in your life. What are your strengths? What areas can be improved? How can you apply your personal power to new areas of your life? The short assessments on the following pages will highlight the areas in which you have already completed the most amount of work and allow you to see areas on which you may want to concentrate. The purpose of the assessment is not to tell you what to do, but to point out some options for furthering the development of your resilience and using it more consciously.

These short assessments are designed to help you determine your style of resilience. Use your curiosity to see what resiliency styles you are using. You can sit down and go through these questions quickly, or do a couple at a time and think about them between your journaling opportunities.

Answer the ten italicized questions under each type of resilience with a yes or no. Each question is further explained with examples, and you may want to further elaborate your answers in your journal entries.

Paradoxical Resilience

To determine if you use your resilience paradoxically, ask yourself the following questions:

1. **Do you use your strengths and personal power in only one part of your life?** For example, do you limit the use of some of your capacities only to work or only to your family; that is, are you decisive at work but not at home? Do you find you have more confidence at work than at home? Or that you have more confidence at home than at work?

2. **Do you feel you are two people, or have two selves, because you deal with challenges in different spheres of your life so differently?** For example, are you competent when dealing with personal decisions at work, but not at home? Do you feel that you have a home demeanor and a work demeanor that are in contrast to each other—that is, assertive in one place and passive in the other?

3. **Do you fear being your best—that is, using your strengths and resourcefulness in your personal life?** For example, are you afraid that a loved one will leave you if he or she sees how capable you are? Do you fear that you must appear to be weak and "less than" if you are to keep a partner in your life?

4. **Do you fear being your best—that is, using your strengths and resourcefulness in your work life?** For example, do you fear that others will compete with you if they see your abilities? Do you fear that others will be angry with you if you are more forthcoming? Do you fear that being more competent at work could prove to be a burden and overwhelm you?

5. **Do you feel burdened by somehow being more capable or competent or resourceful than others?** For example, do you fear that this

will single you out as needing to perform better than others? Do
you fear that more will be expected of you? Do you fear that somehow you will make yourself work harder if you own your
competency?

6. **Are you afraid that your personal powers will drive others away
from you, particularly those you need, because you won't be seen
as both strong and needy?** For example, are you concerned that
you cannot be competent and have needs, that you must choose
one or the other? Are you concerned that your capacities will prove
to be frightening to your friends or others whose opinions are
important to you?

7. **Do you believe that luck determines many of your successes?** For
example, do you feel that outcomes are not really within your control? Do you believe that luck plays a large part in achieving them,
and does this belief stop you from feeling pride in yourself?

8. **If you work hard on something, is it difficult for you to take credit
for its success because you fear this may single you out and not
be acceptable or feminine?** For example, do you feel you need to
attribute success to others rather than owning it for yourself? Is it
difficult to see your own personal power in making something
happen?

9. **Do you worry about not having the ability to accomplish today
tasks that you have accomplished successfully in the past?** For
example, do you lack confidence in yourself? Does this result in
your becoming anxious or feeling dread as you approach a new
task or challenge?

10. **Do you feel that you must appear weak, or less than you are, to
have people love you or be close to you?** For example, do you fear
your strength will scare others away? Do you fear that you must be

alone with your strengths, capacities, and desires because they will be unappreciated by another?

Total "Yes" answers (0–10) under Paradoxical Resilience_____

Stellar Resilience

To determine your degree of stellar resilience, ask yourself:

1. **Have you encountered tragedy or formidable barriers in your life?** For example, have you ever been sexually, physically, or verbally abused? Have you lost a parent, close relative, child, or friend? Have you lost a limb or the functioning of a part of your body? Have you previously had or do you now have a serious illness?

2. **Have you often wondered how you survived while others around you did not do nearly as well as you?** For example, did you have a sibling who became mentally ill, addicted, or incarcerated? Did your friends get into difficulty with the law, use drugs, drink excessively, turn to prostitution, or drop out of school? Did family members struggle with addiction, depression, poverty, or disabilities?

3. **Are you actively working to create a better life than the one that you had as a child?** For example, do you try to make sure that there is enough good food to eat? If you experienced violence as a child, do you work to ensure a safe environment? If you experienced abuse, do you work to create a loving environment? If your childhood home was chaotic, do you strive to create an orderly and consistent environment?

4. **Do you struggle with the feeling that you do not know what a "normal" lifestyle is because you never experienced what "normal" people have? Do you see other women who are more *girly* as having more normal lives?** For example, do you feel at a loss as to how to

conduct your life because you have so little guidance from your childhood? Do you feel that you get by in life by the seat of your pants, or that you can fail as easily as succeed because everyone else knows something that you don't? Do you feel you really don't know the ground rules? Do you feel you do not know how others live, how they manage, or how they have avoided the pain that you know all too well?

5. **Do you feel that you have to guard yourself and those you care about by constantly surveying your environment to see what potential threat may be coming near?** For example, do you feel you have a normal life now, but that it is very vulnerable to disappearing? Do you fear being found out or rejected if others learn of your past? Do you feel that your lifestyle now is beyond what you dreamed of as a child but that it may be taken away from you?

6. **Do you feel you are not entitled to feel good or to come first if doing so means that someone you care for must come second?** For example, do you take care of everyone else before you take care of yourself? Are you so sensitive to the needs of others that you forget that you have needs as well?

7. **Do you feel that your life is successful?** For example, are you proud of what you have accomplished in spite of the stresses you encountered? Do you feel that you have fashioned a life that suits you and makes sense for you? Have you accomplished some of the goals that you set for yourself?

8. **Do you feel a need to help others because you understand what it is to suffer?** For example, have you chosen a career in which your primary responsibility is the well-being of others, such as in teaching, medicine, law enforcement, or counseling? Do you volunteer your time to help others in need?

9. **Do you, or did you, see yourself as wanting to save the world or one very special part of it?** For example, do you acutely feel the pain and suffering in the world and want to make it stop? Do you become angry, agitated, sad, hopeless, or depressed when hearing the news? Do you just avoid the news all together?

10. **Do you see yourself as a survivor?** For example, are you conscious of having made it through a difficult past and feel that you possess the ability to do this in your life? Do you think of yourself as essentially tough—either on the outside or inside?

*Total "Yes" answers (0–10) under Stellar Resilience*_____

Overwhelmed Resilience

To determine if your resilience is overwhelmed, ask yourself:

1. **Do you feel you can't rally your resources to deal with the crises in front of you?** For example, do you feel undone or overwhelmed that you can't face this crisis? Are you exhausted, depleted? Do you feel like you need to eat, drink, or drug away your feelings?

2. **Do you focus on your pain, going over and over again the same awful reliving of what has happened?** For example, do you feel trapped by your memories? Do you feel scarred or tainted by the experiences you had as a child and as an adult? Are you unable to stop thinking of them? Are your memories waking you up? Consuming your thinking?

3. **Do you ever "wish you weren't here" as a solution to new or existing problems?** For example, do you wish you could disappear in stressful moments? Do you wish the earth could swallow you and you would be gone?

4. **Do you have little or no access to your personal power?** For example, is it difficult to make decisions? Do you find it hard to know what it is that you need to do to take care of yourself? Do you feel more acted upon than active in your life?

5. **Do you deny or not know what you need?** For example, when someone asks what you need, do you draw a blank or switch the question to see what it is that they need? Does it feel almost impossible to reach this part of you?

6. **Do you feel shame when you think of your own neediness?** For example, is it shameful, alien even, to be seen as so needy? Are needs all right for others but not for you? Do you wish that you did not have any needs?

7. **Do you have periods of hating yourself?** For example, have you wished you had never been born? Have you ever wished to hurt yourself as a punishment? Did you feel your birth was a mistake, one that you have paid for ever since?

8. **Do you focus on caring for others as a way of avoiding caring for yourself?** For example, is it easier to see what others need than what you need? Does caring for others allow you to feel that at least you know how to do something right? Is caring for others the closest that you come to experiencing caring at all?

9. **Do you feel trapped by the past and unable to move beyond it?** For example, do you feel defined by your childhood experiences and unable as an adult to redefine yourself? If you feel you were a victim as a child, does this equate to being a victim as an adult? For example, do you feel "less than" others because of these experiences? Do you hold your present relationships hostage to your past? Do you fear you will be rejected if others know of what you have endured?

10. **Do you feel that if you could be more pleasing to others that they would rescue you?** In blaming yourself for the pain you are in, do you see as a solution your being sweeter, more compliant, less a risk taker as a way that this pain could have been averted?

   Total "Yes" answers (0–10) under Overwhelmed Resilience_____

Self-Contained Resilience

To determine if you use your resilience in a self-contained way, ask yourself:

1. **As a child, did you feel that you could only depend on yourself?** For example, did you feel that your only chance of survival was to not rely on someone else? Were you frequently disappointed by the adults around you?

2. **Was mastery of any threat the most important aspect of dealing with it—more important, for example, than being comforted?** For example, were you uncomfortable in allowing others to see that you were afraid as a child? Did you feel that you had to deal with problems alone? Did you focus your energies on conquering those issues in your life that were the most frightening?

3. **Do you still depend primarily or only on yourself?** Do you have problems trusting others? For example, do you keep an eye on those close to you to see if they are about to disappoint you? Do you feel that you must be ever vigilant?

4. **Are you impatient with others when their way of handling tasks differs from yours?** For example, do you find yourself critical of others, particularly those you are closest to? When others say that you are critical, does this come as a surprise to you because you only have their best interests at heart?

5. **Do work and other commitments keep you from being available to friends and family?** For example, do you find yourself frequently late or declining fun invitations because of work commitments? Do you feel your work is close to being mastered if only you do this one next thing? Do you find yourself disappointing those you are the closest to? Does your work serve to isolate you?

6. **When you are upset, do you find yourself turning to your areas of competence to distract you from your feelings, perhaps because you don't want to "act like a girl?"** For example, do you find that you throw yourself into work when you are upset? Is it shameful to feel vulnerable? Does work provide an emotional comfort? If everything else seems to be going poorly, do you feel at least you can control your work?

7. **Do you feel that if you "could" do something you "should" do it?** For example, do you find that you rely only on your competency to determine how you will approach something that needs to be done? Do you find that even if you do not want to do something, you do it anyway?

8. **Do you fail to factor in your desire to accomplish tasks along with your ability to do them?** For example, do you find that you do not listen to how you feel or how motivated you are in approaching a task, seeking merely to get it over with, whatever the personal cost? Do you fear being labeled "lazy" if you postpone something that needs attention?

9. **Are you more comfortable with your competent self rather than your needy self?** For example, do you find yourself spending more time trying to shine through accomplishments than trying to determine what you need and taking care of this part of you? Is it more comfortable to perform and earn what you need than to ask for it?

10. **Are you more comfortable producing something than feeling your feelings?** For example, do you switch into production mode when you are upset—pull out some paperwork, clean the house, start a new project, even bake a cake? Do you feel that figuring out what you need to do for yourself takes too much time from your work?

    *Total "Yes" answers (0–10) under Self-Contained Resilience*_____

Underdeveloped Resilience

To determine your degree of underdeveloped resilience, ask yourself the following questions:

1. **Do you feel that you were overprotected or indulged as a child?** For example, did you feel smothered as a child? In looking back on your childhood, do you feel it was stifling or suffocating? Were you sheltered from taking responsibility for the consequences of your actions? Were your wants too readily given into?

2. **Were you rarely given opportunities as a child to make decisions for yourself, instead being treated as a delicate girl?** For example, were you given a set of rules to which you adhered that kept you from learning how to think for yourself? Were you discouraged from learning how the world was? Did you learn to see it through the lens of how *girls* were supposed to think?

3. **Was your dependence on others cultivated?** For example, were you constantly told that only your parents knew what was best for you? Were you made fearful of being on your own? Were you made to feel that you were incompetent to be on your own? Do you look for a partner who knows what is right for you?

4. **Is it difficult for you to plan and set goals for yourself?** For example, do you find it difficult to determine if an action is in your best

interest? Is it hard for you to foresee consequences when they affect you? Are you shy about asking others to help you? Do you have problems rallying your resources?

5. **Do you depend now on someone else to make you whole?** For example, do you feel that your worth is tied to your caring for others? Do you fear that if a loved one leaves, you will be less than you are now? Do you think of your loved one as your "better half"?

6. **Do you find little opportunity in your life to experiment with independence?** For example, do you find yourself hiding behind the opinions of another, fearful of expressing your own? Do you devalue your own life experiences? Are you so afraid of being wrong or incompetent that you fear acting? Does this make you so angry that you verbally lash out at others?

7. **Do you feel unequipped to take care of yourself?** For example, do you feel you know very little of what you need or how to go about having these needs met? Do you feel that others know more of what you need than you do? Do you expect others to know you so well that you do not need to speak up for yourself?

8. **Do you feel that others know more of the answers in life than you do?** For example, do you more readily turn to another for advice than seek your own counsel? Do you usually discount your opinion if someone else has a stronger opinion?

9. **Do you feel you function less as your own best friend than you would like to?** For example, are you more critical of yourself than you are of others? Are you frequently nicer to others than you are to yourself? Do you more readily make excuses for someone else than you do for yourself?

10. **Do you have difficulty thinking and acting as you would wish?** For example, do you feel that you must still meet an external

standard? Do you watch your actions to make sure that you are behaving correctly? Do you worry excessively about what others will think?

Total "Yes" answers (0–10) under Underdeveloped Resilience_____

Balanced Resilience

To determine your degree of balanced resilience, ask yourself:

1. **Do you know your major strengths?** Can you list what skills you use to be successful in different areas of your life? Do you use your strengths both at work and at home?

2. **Do you tend to focus on your strengths without needing to apologize for them—that is, do you reject your *girly thoughts* so you are not back taking the power of your actions?** For example, do you like the parts of you that are strong? Are you proud of these aspects? Do you make time for them, by showing your skills at work, for example? Do you make time for hobbies—that is, if you like being active, do you make time for working out, yoga, or sports? Or if you enjoy reading, do you make time to read?

3. **Do you feel you can set limits on others that allow your needs to be satisfied?** For example, is it okay to come first? Can you delay your child's, spouse's, or coworkers' requests so you can complete what you are doing that is important to you?

4. **Do you feel you can see the shortcomings of others as about them and not take the poor actions of others personally?** For example, can you ignore the rude statements made by a loved one who is having a bad day? Can you let his or her comments be a manifestation of frustration and not a comment on his or her feelings about you?

5. **Do you feel gratitude for the positive things in your life?** For example, do you stop to smell the flowers, notice the positive events and scenes amid a hectic day, or take a moment to smile at even your own misstep?

6. **Do you feel you can make your own luck, at least some of the time?** That is, do you feel you have enough power, control, and influence in your own life to make things happen the way that you wish for them to occur?

7. **Do you focus on presenting the best that is in you?** For example, are you aware of what is the *best* in you? How you want to be seen by the important people in your life? Do you put effort into being seen in that way?

8. **Do you use the information your family taught you in your daily life?** For example, do you draw upon the lessons you learned as a child even if you have had to reinterpret them as an adult? Do you feel a positive connection between the past and the present?

9. **Do you like yourself, or better yet, love yourself?** For example, when you think of yourself, do you smile? Do you take care of yourself? Do you treat yourself the way you would treat a good friend? Do you make demands on yourself that are possible for you to meet? Do you treat yourself with respect, allowing yourself to say no to tasks that you are too tired to do or tasks that are unappealing?

10. **Do you use your resourcefulness and flexibility to accomplish your goals in life?** For example, do you allow yourself to be creative on your own behalf in meeting your needs? Do you reserve enough energy to allow yourself to be successful in achieving those objectives that are important to you, even if they are important only to you? Do you allow yourself to see the big picture, and give yourself the permission to develop new solutions to existing problems?

*Total "Yes" answers (0–10) under Balanced Resilience*_____

Scoring Your Personal Profile

For each category, tally the number of positive responses.

- 7 to 10 "Yes" responses in a single category indicate a *significant way* you use your resilience.
- 4 to 6 "Yes" responses in a single category indicate a *moderate way* you use your resilience.
- 0 to 3 "Yes" responses in a single category indicate a *minor way* you use your resilience.

How to Use Your Resilience Profile

You can expect to find a major or moderate reading in more than one category. This resulting profile indicates your progression in the development of your resilience—where you began and where you are now. It can also highlight areas in which you may want to concentrate in the future. For example, you may find that you have most of the characteristics of stellar resilience because you have achieved many personal goals against great odds and have a need to help others overcome the difficulties you experienced, but in some ways you are somewhat too self-reliant and isolated, two common traits of those of self-contained resilience. This would indicate that you have been able to move beyond the earlier coping styles you used when you felt that you needed to do everything yourself to a style that reflects your pride in knowing that you have survived and can now more freely interact with others. Further, you may see that you are reluctant to exercise your competence in certain areas, a sign of paradoxical resilience. You may decide that your occasional isolation is fine but want to develop your resilience in all, not just some, areas of your life. You will want to concentrate on the growth tasks of the paradoxically resilient.

Or you may find that your resilience can be described as balanced but that you experience shame concerning certain issues. This allows you to know that you have worked through being overwhelmed. You may choose to work on shame as a way of elevating and integrating your overall pattern of resilience. Or you may find your resilience is basically balanced, but, because of some childhood traumas, you have some stellar qualities. You may decide to use your resilience to explore more of your childhood and understand its impact on your adult life.

Experience has taught me that no matter the degree of resilience you have already developed, you can learn to recognize it more consciously and use it more effectively to get what you need and want. Remember, your resilience profile is composed of the coping skills you have developed to date. It highlights the struggles you have encountered in your life, describes how you have made sense of these, and can point you in a new direction of growth as you consolidate the gains you have made. When you learn to recognize your resilience, you can incorporate its guidance into your everyday life and know that it will aid you in times of greater stress and trial.

For more about resilience styles, visit http://patriciaogorman.com.

FIVE

Roots of Resilience: Why It Is Difficult to Access Your Strengths

You never know how strong you are until being strong is the only choice you have.

—*Author Unknown*

Now that we understand how we approach resilience, we need to understand why we have needed to develop resilience in the first place. It may come as a surprise to learn that, even as children, our need was to protect ourselves. In this chapter, we will look at how this process began, with the goal of being able to more consciously develop this skill as we move forward.

Protecting Your Inner Child

Each of us has a vulnerable core, a part of us that ran headlong into the world, unafraid, curious, confident, and able to master incredible skills and feats. But at other times, that inner core was terribly wounded and afraid. We call this our *inner child* (Oliver-Diaz and O'Gorman 1988). This inner child resides in each of us as part of our remembered past. Our inner wonder and childlike curiosity combined with remembered pain is a powerful driving force in each of our lives.

While we each need to hold and protect our inner child, the vulnerable core that in childhood experienced the pain of disappointments and traumas that were very real, we also need to keep this young, vulnerable part of who we are from being the decision-maker in our adult life, particularly when we are in situations full of conflict and anxiety. This is a tall order. By learning to gently hold this past pain, we can use those early hard-earned lessons now to help us face the new challenges before us. We can use our growing resilience to do this by developing the adult tools that help us make sense of what happened to us and to those we loved in the past. Our resilience can also serve to protect us from the overwhelming feelings that our remembered pain can sometimes generate by helping us develop helpful boundaries between the past and the present. Developing boundaries is crucial when we relate to moments of crisis.

By turning to our inner child for guidance (and essentially putting our inner six-year-old in charge of asking for a raise, confronting our boyfriend about who he is texting, or telling our parents we cannot come over for another dinner this week), we further burden ourselves in a moment when we are already feeling tense and unsure. Doing this is problematic in two ways: First, young children are usually not successful in asking for a raise, so putting our inner child in charge is a setup for whatever we are doing to fail. Second, putting our inner child in charge of an emotionally laden encounter can also reawaken pain we felt at three, six, or ten years of age, which can rekindle earlier traumas and the pains that have been sealed over.

And yet, this is what so many women do. In such moments, they may lead through the reasoning of their inner child instead of using their adult resilience and problem-solving skills. They fall back on understanding only through early emotion instead of taking a moment to think through what is happening. As a result, they feel even more unsure and vulnerable, and maybe out of control. Combine this scenario with harsh *girly thoughts,* and it is no wonder that many women struggle to feel competent.

Your Inner Child's Role in Your Adult Life

Your inner child can provide depth in your adult life. Your memories of the past can offer a richness, a texture to your daily living by giving it meaning and substance beyond the immediacy of your current experience. But this is very different than having your past, your inner child, as the decision-maker in your adult present.

Part of the process in developing resilience is making conscious the beliefs of childhood and liberating yourself to see the world now as an adult; the world today is more complex and nuanced than you experienced it as a child. This process can allow you to support the part of you that experienced the pain of the past while you simultaneously realize that you do not need to be governed by those beliefs today as an adult. You can keep your inner child alive and can speak to this part of you—but your inner child no longer needs to be fully in charge of your life.

As we age, we hope our understanding of how to motivate ourselves and others, influence the world around us, and stake our own place within it grows as well. Our adult resilience helps us accomplish this, while also teaching us how to protect our vulnerable self, our inner child. The confusing part is that until we develop the *conscious* use of our resilience, we may default to the reasoning used by our inner child, even when we are not aware we are doing so.

Transforming Your Vulnerable Side

Recognizing and working with your vulnerable side can be a valuable tool in the development of your resilience, for it is often within your vulnerability (epitomized by your inner child) that the stresses that contribute to the development of your resilience are seen most clearly. You can see what forces have helped to shape your resilience and then more consciously use those forces to help address other issues in this part of yourself, as we will see with Rennie.

Rennie was terribly jealous of the attention her husband, Ted, paid to other women at any time, but it was particularly appalling for her when they went to parties. There, she would be racked by feelings of betrayal, self-pity, rage, and humiliation. When they went home after the party, Rennie would hurl accusations at Ted, which led to horrendous fights. Afterward she would be repentant and beg his forgiveness, but her rages over time took their toll on the marriage.

"I just couldn't seem to make myself stop. It was like I was possessed and out to destroy Ted and our relationship," said Rennie. Eventually it felt easier to not be together, and they separated.

After their split, Rennie's jealousy began to diminish. It felt less dangerous to consider the feelings that led to their separation. Gradually Rennie understood that her jealousy of Ted was more about her feeling anxious in public situations than about Ted's behavior. She realized that when she went to a party, she needed a special type of attention and reassurance from her partner to help her overcome her fear. Much of her anger at Ted came from her feeling that she could not ask him for the support she needed.

In trying to be independent and live up to her own expectations, Rennie held fast to the notion that self-reliance meant that she should not ask for what she needed. Rather than admit her own vulnerability, she found it easier to accuse Ted of wrongdoing. Yet it was her own unacknowledged sense of helplessness that caused her rages.

Rennie began to look for this neediness in other situations.

> I saw patterns of behavior I'd never noticed. In fact, there were many occasions when I felt anxious, and each time I covered this anxiety with other emotions that I could externalize. Once I was aware of this pattern, my anxiety became less unpredictable and easier to control. I realized I had been overprotected in my childhood, my resilience in this area was definitely underdeveloped, and now was an opportunity to change this.
>
> It was as if knowing what it was and when it occurred took away the sense that it was larger than life. I realized that my rages had more to do with me and my ability to handle my anxiety than with Ted's behavior. I could make different choices as to how to deal with my feelings.

It is in the process of identifying these less acceptable aspects of self and in making peace with them that we find our own voice. In this way, our vulnerable side is a valuable ally. It can tell us what is ours and ours alone—a vision, a point of view derived from our own way. It is not apart from our life, a separate being, but integral to it. Until we learn the lessons of our vulnerable side, we live with less than we are and could be.

Assessment Three: How Resilient Did You Need to Be as a Child?

Be your authentic self, that way
you have no competition.
—Author Unknown

Who you are has to do in part with how resilient you needed to be as a child. Take a moment to think about the following questions and then write out your answers in your journal. Leave some empty space between your initial response and the next question in case you want to come back and elaborate later on some of your answers. Remember to do this at your pace, whatever your pace is for this day or week.

Give yourself some time to relax and think about the following questions. Picture your inner child. Gently take her hand, pull her into your lap, make it comfortable to have a conversation with this part of who you are. Now ask the part of you that knows what is right for you, your resilient voice, to also join you. Ask your inner child and inner resilient voice to help you answer these questions. Take your time and go back and forth between these two important parts of who you are. If specific memories come up, write these down as well. Invite them in; treat these memories as an old friend who has come for a visit.

- Safety:
  - Did your parents understand what you needed to feel safe?
  - Did they readily provide this, or were they angered or overwhelmed by your needs?
  - What did you learn from this about how to take care of yourself?

- Independence:
  - Were your needs for independence understood? Or was too much expected of you too early, leaving you feeling that you needed to do things by yourself?
  - When independent action is needed today, are you usually ready for it? Or do you feel overwhelmed or not capable?
  - Do you enjoy a sense of accomplishment from your efforts, or do they always seem insufficient or ineffective? Or are they too much and too isolating?
- Expectations of being a girl:
  - Were you encouraged to be a *good girl?*
  - How did this translate into how resilient you needed to be, and which areas of your life you could use your resilience in? For example, were you taught that sex was bad, and *good girls* shouldn't feel those feelings?
  - How did the understanding of what was expected of you become your *girly thoughts?*

Spend time with your inner child, and what you will soon learn to know as the voice of your resilience. Ask about these areas and how they influence your life as an adult today. Note these thoughts in your journal.

Assessment Four: Accessing the Beliefs of Your Inner Child

Where there is great love there are always miracles.
—Willa Cather

Learning to love yourself is the gift of the conscious development of resilience. Because so much of who you are today is rooted in the child you once were, it is important to understand how this part of you still functions today. Take your time when taking this assessment; don't push yourself if you begin to feel anxious or uncertain—remember, your inner child exists within you at many levels, at many ages, in many ways, from verbal to nonverbal body memories. Find a moment when you can be sweet to yourself. Invite in your inner child.

Beliefs in Childhood

Now jot down the beliefs you had in childhood. Everyone has key ages that were important to them (they will be different for each of us), and answer the following questions for each significant age that comes to mind. Remember, you can do this all at once or a little at a time.

When you were a child:

- What did you believe you were capable of doing?
- What did you believe you were entitled to?
- How did you believe you should be loved?
- How were you a good little girl?

If any of these beliefs changed at different ages, note this as well. Now ask yourself:

- Which childhood beliefs do you still use?
- Which of these beliefs create conflict in your adult life?

For more about inner-child work, including meditations, visit http://patriciaogorman.com.

SIX

Understanding Your Family Legacy: Your Roots and Wings

A SINGLE ACT OF KINDNESS THROWS ROOTS OUT
IN ALL DIRECTIONS.
—*Amelia Earhart*

NO BIRD SOARS TOO HIGH, IF (S)HE SOARS WITH (HER) OWN WINGS.
—*William Blake*

W*e've explored the importance* of your inner child, about how you saw the world and how you need to protect this part of who you are. Now we'll begin to explore boundaries by coming to understand the profound influence your family had on you in terms of how you developed resilience.

We receive nourishment for our growing resilience, our roots and our wings, from many sources. These include our personal encounters with the world, as well as what we learn from others, especially our family. Among our most important lessons are those our relatives teach us about life, about ourselves, and about how to make our way in the world. These lessons define our family's values, ingrained beliefs, attitudes, and lifestyle, and they help us develop our understanding of which boundaries are good for us, and which are not. A family's main teaching vehicle is its stories. Yes, those tales told at Thanksgiving, at family reunions, and shared with our partner and our friends, and they have more impact on us than we might think.

Our Family's Tales

Virtually every family has its well-worn tales. These stories involve parents, grandparents, and assorted relatives, both real and fictionalized. They speak of how our relatives set out to meet their destiny and describe what they encountered along the way. In anecdotes and yarns, we learn of the rogues and scoundrels, the heroes and the saints that abound in each family.

These stories teach us what life is all about; we learn that life is hard or fun, unfair or not to be taken too seriously. As young children listening to these tales, we form our vision of the future. If this vision is positive, we have permission to soar, to equal or better past triumphs. If the vision is negative, we may feel our options are limited, or we may experience more difficulty separating from our family, and our boundaries with others may be more challenged.

Stories frequently function as parables or fables, offering conclusions and morals. We learn by example about good choices and the consequences of not following rules or traditions. We learn what constitutes success, how to deal with failure, and how dreams can come true. Sometimes these are tales that tell us what ancestors learned or what they wished they had done.

Life Rafts

The eminent psychologist Bruno Bettelheim spoke of family stories as potential life rafts passed down from one generation to the next (1988). Indeed, some stories buoy us above our current circumstances and allow us to glimpse the strength, courage, tenacity, or cleverness used by our ancestors to overcome adversity. The significance of these stories lies not in their facts, but in the messages or meanings they convey. In our darkest moments, such stories remind us that others have traveled this way before us, confronting trials as great as those we now face. We are not as alone as we thought.

A friend told me a story concerning her ancestor Yung Mee. This ancestor was married to a rice farmer in South Korea more than two hundred years ago. Yung Mee's husband was the oldest son in his family, and, as his wife, her responsibility was to observe the Lunar New Year. This ritual involves preparing special foods and arranging them in a particular order for a family feast. The whole family then gathers and hopes the spirits of their departed relatives will join them in the feast.

One year it seemed unlikely that Yung Mee would be able to keep this holiday. She had just given birth to twins and was still recuperating as the day approached. Nevertheless, she issued the invitation for all to attend. Her husband's family arrived, concerned that this most important holiday would not be properly observed. Instead they found the delicious feast perfectly arranged. When asked how she had done this, Yung Mee demurely smiled. It was said that her deceased in-laws themselves had come to help her prepare the feast. She was not alone.

"As a little girl, hearing this story," my friend said, "I was very literal. I wanted to know just how Yung Mee had done this. Who had really helped her? Even I knew one woman couldn't have accomplished this alone. My grandmother smiled at my insistence. That was the point of the story, Grandmother told me. We don't know. We cannot know—just as we cannot always know how we will accomplish what seems to be impossible for us, but, when we are determined, we can make great things happen. The story of Yung Mee tells us to go ahead anyway, for we will find a way."

The importance for the family repeating this tale is the message that miracles are possible when one does what is right. The degree of literal truth in this story does not matter. This tale and others like it supported this family during the horrors of the Korean War and their later immigration to America. Yung Mee's faith and resolution when called upon to do the impossible made the family's hardships bearable and somehow understandable. "Remember Yung Mee," they would say, meaning "miracles are possible."

Handed down from generation to generation, these stories define us as a family and give us a sense of identity, our roots. Our family's teaching stories tell us how women will be rewarded, how people in our family are supposed to act, and the values to be upheld: family first; the importance of money, honesty, and hard work; the importance of protecting the women; individual freedom; asking for support. They spell out our family's beliefs: when things get difficult, you need to try harder; women are usually wrong; stay with what you know. When taken together, these themes make up the characteristics that define our family as special and unique. These narratives are subtly shaped by each generation's viewpoint and often refashioned from one telling to the next, adapted to take into consideration the current challenges facing us.

Our Own Legacy

Through our family's stories, we can discover personal meanings that bear on our developing resilience. Our family's oral history enables us to develop a sense of who we are, a sense of connectedness with others that can allow us to feel less isolated, more empowered, and better able to meet the challenges that lie before us. These stories allow us to say, "I come from a family of immigrants, risk-takers, adventurers, hard workers, farmers, or professionals." This identity can feed our resilience by reinforcing our roots.

"I come from a family with strong women and a clear sense of right and wrong," Michelle, a woman who had learned to develop balanced resilience, told me.

> My mother was deeply religious, and the solace she received from her faith carried us through many difficult times. My mother taught Bible studies in our church. My love of Bible study taught me to love school and made me realize that learning was what I did best.
>
> I grew up in poverty on a farm in rural Alabama. None of my kinfolk went to school beyond sixth grade. But I had a dream, and I knew I came from a family that makes dreams a reality. There was my great-great-grandfather, a freed slave, who wanted to own some land. He worked hard, very hard, for years until he could buy a few acres. My grandmother, too, wanted something impossible. She wanted to play the organ. Our family tells how she would come up with all sorts of ways of making small amounts of money, which she saved to pay for her lessons.
>
> So I wanted to be a teacher. I wanted to complete high school and go to college. I've made that dream come true. Like my forebearers, I, too, developed a plan and worked hard until I achieved my goal.

Through our family's oral history we, like Michelle, can develop an understanding of who we are and the forces that formed our beliefs. They define our strengths as they give us roots.

Stories can also fill us with visions beyond our daily life. They nourish our wings, our dreams for ourselves. Even when we look at our circumstances and see only chaos and pain in our immediate surroundings, stories can tell us of larger vistas and new possibilities. Tricia, now a successful professional who moved from paradoxical resilience to balanced, told me of her childhood.

When I was a girl, living in a home characterized by violence, abuse, and alcoholism, I blamed my mother for many things that were wrong with my life. I saw her weakness, her confusion, anger, and self-centeredness. I've since come to see that, vulnerable, and, at times, overwhelmed as she was, my mother in fact gave me many gifts of value, although I did not consciously recognize them as such at the time.

Those gifts were my mother's stories. She would tell us tales, largely fanciful, of the heroic exploits of our relatives who challenged life as they saw it and created change. My favorite story is one she told me in response to my asking about our heritage. In actuality, my mother is Ukrainian and my father Irish, but, instead of telling me this, she told me that we were related to Cherokee Indians. She created a legend of a great-great-grandfather who came to America, married a Cherokee, and took her back to Ukraine.

I was only eight years old. I believed this story and felt connected to the Cherokee, a heritage that was more available and more positive than my troubled immediate family. I began to think of myself as Cherokee. I would braid my hair, wear headbands, and run like the wind. I felt proud, strong. I felt a part of something larger than myself from which I could draw strength. It fed my deepest conviction that I was different, special in a way that my day-to-day life belied, and that one day I would live up to this great promise.

Today Tricia recognizes those stories as the gifts they were. "It was as though on some level my mother realized that she could not do much to change what was happening within my family, but she gave me what she could," said Tricia. By encouraging her daughter's use of fantasy, Tricia's mother gave her permission to dream. This allowed Tricia to look past the immediate confusion and pain and envision how different life could be.

> It didn't matter that these stories of my ancestry had no basis in historical fact. On some level I knew they contained an important truth. They told me I was unique, that I had inner, untried qualities I could learn to draw on. In that respect, they were absolutely true.
>
> Looking back, I'm not sure how much my mother herself recognized this inner meaning, but it may be that she did. For my own part, I am amazed that my eight-year-old self could understand this aspect of my mother's stories and instinctively derive such strength from it.

Tricia's resilience was in evidence even then, allowing her to see the light and nurturing aspects of an otherwise dark childhood. Through this recognition, Tricia has been able to make peace with her mother and come to terms with her past, and become balanced in her approach for how to use her strengths.

"Best of all," she said, "this understanding has enabled me to be the mother I want to be to my children."

Stories About Us

Of all the stories we hear from our family, the most essential to our early identity are those about ourselves. Their unspoken meanings and the ways in which they are told give us evidence of how we were viewed as a child. If our family jokingly speaks of our insatiable appetite and how quickly we grew, it implies that we were loved and that we challenged our family even as an infant. We may find these same themes repeated in later stories about ourselves: how we challenged our teachers, how we read earlier than others in our class, or how we asked questions that were difficult to answer. These stories form images that help us establish an identity and can help us feel good about ourselves.

Yet if the same story of our appetite is told to emphasize how demanding we were, how selfish and disrespectful we were of other's needs, or how we were never satisfied even as a breast-feeding infant, it gives us a very different feeling about ourselves. We learn that we were difficult, abnormal, and somewhat out of control. We were a problem for our parents. A story told in this manner has the potential to produce shame. Stories with this theme told throughout childhood can make us feel bad about ourselves, especially if the theme reverberates with other stories of our being difficult or being a burden to caretakers.

The effects of such a characterization may continue to be detrimental even as we grow to adulthood. These stories may be a way for family members to shame us, detract from our adult status, and keep us in a familiar, one-down role. Our present identity within the family may tie us to events long past—mistakes, for example, that we are powerless to rectify. If we let them, stories can serve to keep us small and dependent and lead us to think poorly of ourselves. These constitute the dark legacies we may need to change.

Family Roots of Our *Girly Thoughts*

Our family's tales about female relatives hold a special importance for us as women. They reveal the strategies, successful and otherwise, employed by the women in our family as they struggled with many of the same issues we face today. As such, they form the basis of our family's take on *girly thoughts*. We depend on these to teach us about being a woman: our role in society, our relationships, our sexuality. Our family legends influence the formation of female traditions and expectations and give us a roadmap for the way women in this family should act; they define what the future may hold for us.

From her earliest years, Melissa heard about the beauty of the women of her family and how they used their beauty to their advantage. Her great-aunt Sarah used her beauty to circumvent family rules she felt were oppressive. Sarah's very religious Jewish family became enraged when she expressed her desire to model hats. Undaunted, Sarah argued that the money she earned could be used to put her older brother through medical school. She won her argument, and Sarah became the first woman in the family to work outside the home.

Sarah's action created a tradition that encouraged women in her family to participate in more public forums and break out of the traditional mold for women. As a result, when her great-niece, Melissa, went to college she pursued another revolutionary career choice: acting. With the inner confidence she derived from her great-aunt that challenge is possible, and the self-confidence that she had from winning beauty competitions as a child, she starred in several college productions and earned walk-ons in some TV shows.

Stories may also serve to define the relationships a woman will have with her husband, her children, and other family members. What does it mean to be a good wife? A good daughter? A good mother? These roles vary from family to family. Some families are matriarchies, where women dominate their quiet husbands. In other families, the women serve their husbands in long-suffering silence. In some families, the women are considered the smart and savvy ones; in others, women are foolish and frail.

My friend Hanna told me one of her favorite family tales:

One story I heard throughout my life was about my great-great-grandmother Verity. She lived in England and had the misfortune to be married to an alcoholic seaman. My grandfather would sign on to a ship, take the money, get drunk, and miss the sailing date. Each time he did, Verity, who worked as a cook for a middle-class family, would become enraged. She'd yell at him, sometimes beat him, and always threaten to throw him out.

Well, one time he signed on to a ship and swore on the family Bible that he would make it this time, that nothing could keep him from his obligation. But the usual happened. He went out to celebrate, got drunk, and fell asleep on a street corner. He was afraid to go home to his wife, so he stayed away. Only when he read of the disastrous sinking of the *Titanic,* the ship he was scheduled to sail on, did he dare to venture home. Grandmother Verity, who had thought him dead, was so happy to see him that she never yelled at him again.

The assumption behind this story was that Grandma Verity saw the error of her ways and mended them. In my family, this tale has always been taken as meaning. *Never push your man; you could lose him.* In the back of my mind I've always heard the warning, *No husband will be perfect; settle for one that's "good enough."*

Although all the women in my family learned this lesson, we dealt with it in different ways. My mother picked a man who was so stubborn, she seemed to have no influence on him; my grandmother treated my grandfather so tentatively, she seemed afraid that he would break. I, on the other hand, seem to be afraid to commit myself to a man, knowing I'll have to live with "good enough."

Recognizing a story's implied message and its effect on us is the first step to understanding the value these stories have for us. It can free us from our *girly thoughts* to choose the legacy that fosters our resilience and to set aside the lessons that detract from it. My friend, already in the process of addressing her fear of commitment in relationships, began to understand why this story was one of her favorites, as it was indicative of the beliefs with which she had been raised. Knowing that the source of her fear was drummed into her head from childhood, she began to consciously refute this "truth" by asking out someone she thought was very interesting and beginning to meditate daily to deal with her anxiety.

It is not easy being a woman; understanding the messages your mother received and had to understand and transcend or embrace can build some empathy on your part, but the riches contained in these traditions are not limited to knowledge of how to conduct ourselves within our family or how to establish a better relationship with our mother. These messages about how to be a *good girl* also serve another function: they prepare us to receive and take to heart society's messages that become lodged in our *girly thoughts*. As the role of women in our society continues to be redefined, our family legacy often holds the wisdom of how our ancestors managed change, and it may hold the key for what will work for us. As we look within for solutions to the problems and difficulties in our lives, our family history, and, specifically, the stories of the mothers and women in our family may contain clues that will point us in the right direction.

Finding Our Own Way

Discovering personal meaning in family stories is necessary if we are to move past our family's interpretations of events and find our own definitions. As we develop resilience and independence from others' ways, we will find our stories change, too. We can aid this natural evolution through consciously choosing the stories we tell and then consciously choosing the meanings we ascribe to them. Through these stories, we define for others what we see as the important images of our family. Through retelling our favorite stories, we can keep alive the memory of an important person or time, or message, in our lives. We can select the legacy we choose to live by and pass on to our children.

"My mother-in-law died before my daughter Rainey was born," said Lori. "She and I were very close, and it was a great sorrow for me that she didn't live to see her granddaughter. She was a doctor, a breast surgeon, at a time when that was much less common than now. So I take down the family photo albums from time to time, and we look at the pictures and talk about our family. Rainey is curious about her grandmother. I tell her all the stories I can remember about her courage, her dedication, and her love of others. She is a good model for my daughter."

In the case of unpleasant stories, we can use our resilience to understand what it is we dislike about them. What is it they say and how can we revise them so that they do support our growing resilience?

Martha, a woman who had used self-contained resilience and is now moving to modify this, told me,

When it comes to family histories, I've had a hard time accepting mine. We were weaned on tales of my great-great-grandfather selling healing potions at the county fair in the late 1800s, potions he'd cook up with whatever was around and then prayed over. A saving grace was my grandmother, who was a doctor in South America. But she couldn't pass the examination in the United States because of her limited English. So she worked for a doctor, tending women who were having what were then illegal abortions. Then there were the tales of my uncle being so good at selling home products in a pyramid scheme that eventually he was sent to jail for tax evasion.

When I was a little girl, I was so ashamed to think that most of my relatives were a pack of common criminals and charlatans. I told everyone my uncle was dead or that my mother was an only child.

As Martha grew up and had more experience in the world, her attitude about her relatives changed. She began to see her relatives' other qualities, such as their ability to live by their wits, their love of adventure, their interest in medicine.

I still abhor the lawlessness and willingness to victimize others demonstrated by the men in my family, but I also realize that they were independent people, even caring people, not afraid of taking risks for what they wanted. They liked living life on the edge. This appeals to me.

So I'm finding my own way of being true to my values. I need to, as a lesbian expecting my first baby. It's a risk, but my wife and I are thrilled. And so is my family. Now that I've made peace with myself and with my relatives' unconventional lives, it's easier to see, and enjoy, my connection to my heritage.

Part of our development comes from a very natural desire to stand outside our family system for a while so that we can see our family and ourselves more clearly. Finding our own way means using what works for us. Whether we accept or reject our family's stories and the lessons they convey, they can still play an important role. After all, rejecting a negative legacy may nevertheless point us in the right direction. If our own solution is prompted by our family's lack of one, then in a funny way we still have them to thank for our inspiration.

Resilience can help us look beyond what our family offers us to what we need in our lives. If we must, we can rewrite our legacy to champion new heroes and offer new understandings of old events. We can choose to adopt our family's beliefs as our own, or begin to take from them what we need for our roots or our wings. We are free to put to rest what we cannot or do not want to use.

Expanding Our Sense of Family: Choosing Our Friends

We are all born into a family composed of generations; none of us materialized out of nowhere. Whether we were raised by biological, adoptive, or foster parents, or a combination of all three, we are each a product of the generations that came before us. But just because we were born into a family of generations doesn't mean we cannot expand our sense of family to our friends, creating a family composed of horizontal relationships instead of just intergenerational vertical ones.

Doing this is a way of expanding our sense of connectedness and increasing the reach of the influences on our resilience. But to do this effectively means we need to have good boundaries and realize the limits that we have in all of our relationships.

Assessment Five: Decoding Your Family's Lessons

We are the hero of our own story.
—Mary McCarthy

We don't need to be rescued.
—Author Unknown

Think for a moment about stories you were told about yourself as a child. Allow your resilient voice to answer as you ask yourself what these stories told you. Write out your answers in your journal, and remember to work at your own pace and leave a few lines after each answer in case you want to add more later.

- What did your favorite childhood stories tell you about the resiliencies you showed?
- Can you better understand the origins of your *girly thoughts* through these stories?
- Can you find new, empowering meaning in these memories?

Think for a moment about an important family story. Perhaps it was a favorite one, perhaps it is one that you have struggled with. Pick one that has special meaning for you. Write it down.

Now look at your story and consider the following questions. Encourage your resilient voice to provide answers. Write down your responses in your journal, leaving a few lines after each response so you can go back and fill in more details if you remember them later. Remember to do this in your own time frame; do not let yourself feel anxious or rushed.

- How did you understand this story as a child, and what did it teach you?

- How do you understand this story now? Has your understanding
  of its message changed with time? If so what does the change
  tell you about your own growth?
- What does this story say about your *girly thoughts?*

Now, take a story that really bothers you. It doesn't matter why, just
that it does. Now change the way you think about the story. Look for the
hidden positive in this story.

- What strengths does it speak to, even if they are used in unusual
  or even painful ways?
- What is the message of the ending, the conclusion, that bothers
  you? Does it speak to your *girly thoughts?*
- How can you positively change the ending so that it becomes a
  story you can be proud of, in which you are the hero? For example,
  a story about the death of a beloved sibling due to an overdose
  can become one that also inspired your career to move into law
  enforcement and work with troubled kids.

Leave a few blank pages in your journal for now, and in your own
time, take another story, then another, and answer these same questions
for each one. Let this begin a process of your reinterpretation of your
family to see their strengths and to see the origins of your own. And
begin to have some fun by telling these updated stories at your next
family function!

For more about how family stories affect you, visit http://patri
ciaogorman.com.

PART THREE

Daily Action Steps to Develop Conscious Resilience

The minute you settle for less than you deserve, you get even less than you settled for.

—Maureen Dowd

Now that you have identified what resilience is, what pattern you are using today, and how the development of your resilience was influenced by your inner child and your family, you'll learn how to be consciously guided by the realization that you have the ability to make your crises *meaningful*, and you'll learn how to build your resilience into your daily life through understanding how to actually *listen* to this important part of yourself so you can challenge your *girly thoughts*. Finally, you will learn how to stay optimistic as you work with your resilience to resolve the long-standing issues that may involve trauma, and to develop gratitude for who you are as you set up clearer boundaries for your own resilient future.

SEVEN

Step One—Make Your Crises Meaningful: Choose to Develop Conscious Resilience

NOTHING EVER GOES AWAY UNTIL IT TEACHES US
WHAT WE NEED TO KNOW.

—*Pema Chodron*

My mother's essential wisdom was this: "If I'm going to have a crisis anyway, I may as well make it a good one and learn from it." I agree with her sentiment. Yes, life is tough. It isn't always fair. We know that. But life is also good. And part of how we can learn to focus on the goodness in life is by teaching ourselves to learn from the crises in which we find ourselves. By this simple decision, we begin to develop conscious resilience.

Yes, crisis is a part of life, too. It is not a part of life any of us like, nor is it a part of life that we choose. Unexpected things happen that are really difficult, and, even if we tell ourselves we should have "seen it coming," we are often blindsided by life's unexpected events. We find out our husband or partner has been having an affair, and we blame ourselves for not having been more vigilant, suspicious, not having asked more questions. Those are often our *girly thoughts* talking, when the truth is, we were distracted by work, children, an ill parent, a friend in trouble, or any of the other things outside of ourselves that form an important part of our lives.

Sometimes we can anticipate the crises heading toward us. We see the potential train wreck ahead; we know it will be tough, and we prepare ourselves. For example, if we need to change jobs, we know that will involve moving, putting the kids in a new school, making new friends, finding a new place to worship. So we begin to plan to ease our pain. Sometimes as we plan, we find things are worse than we thought, and they take more of our time, energy, and emotional resources than we thought were possible. A major health crisis can fall into this second category. For example, a friend of mine has a history of being called back for a second mammogram whenever she has her annual test. She braces herself for this, only to be told that she now also needs not only this second mammogram, but a sonogram, then a breast MRI, then a biopsy. She feels assaulted by her own body, and she's consumed by worry until the final test results are in.

Avoiding crisis is not an option for any of us, much as we would like it to be. But with practice, and with increasing resilience, we may learn to be able to get out of the way of the intensity and fallout of a major life challenge and just let it happen around us instead of letting it engulf us. We learn to become nimble, flexible, curious even, as to how we are going to handle this. In short, we turn our crises into opportunities to grow and become more resilient. We do this by trying the following strategies.

Give Meaning to Suffering

One way to change the way we handle crises is to give meaning to the inevitable suffering that comes from them. Learning from the intense challenges that life offers us, even those that come repeatedly, was the teaching of Viktor Frankl (2006), a psychiatrist who survived the Nazi death camps in World War II.

Suffering inevitably changes us. We often think that we will go through life unscathed, unaltered, that after a tragedy we will return to normal and resume our life the way it was. Instead, we need to realize that change is the constant that consumes our life. Whether it is the ceaseless change of our bodies from conception to birth through adolescence and old age, or the expansion and changes in our thinking, or the changes in our family through dating, marriages, births, and deaths, change surrounds us, and we embody change. So when great challenges come our way, they leave their mark on us, either visibly or invisibly. It is not a question in life of how to avoid this, but how to embrace it.

Accept that change is a part of living. Certain goals no longer may be attainable as a result of adverse situations. Accepting circumstances that can't be changed can help you focus on circumstances you can affect. These are the moments of change that call on us to use and expand our resilience.

Appreciate Life's Grand Design

So how do we determine what it is we are supposed to learn? Part of developing resilience is learning how to take hold of crises and not have them take hold of us. To accomplish this, I invite you to reframe how you feel during times of crisis; begin to think of your life in a broad way, as having many parts, rather than the incredibly narrow focus that crisis tends to create. Avoid seeing crises as insurmountable problems. Remember, you can't prevent stressful events from happening, but you can change how you interpret and respond to these events, as you'll see in the next strategy. This is how your resilience helps you.

And it's very important to keep a long-term perspective. In thinking of your life's many parts, think of them as connected to each other and existing within a structure. In fact, think of this structure as a grand design, a master plan if you will, for your life. And within this master plan there are goals for you. There are certain things you need to learn, certain challenges that appear again and again, that give you opportunities to master them and learn certain key lessons in the process. No, I am not a fatalist. I'm not saying that we cannot make major differences in our life. What I am offering is that if you think of your life as a design, a tempo, a rhythm, then it may be easier to make the changes to alter the direction you may want to take in your life. And to do this means becoming more conscious of one of your most valuable resources, your resilience, as a way to do this.

Einstein said that repeating the same thing and expecting a different result is the definition of insanity, but that doesn't stop many of us from trying it anyway. And we end up feeling a bit crazy, mainly because we feel trapped. So rather than feeling trapped and maybe even feeling condemned to live the same pattern, it may be helpful to reframe this and understand that these themes in your life are challenging you to make major changes. And the challenge to grow in this area, to gain resilience, is part of the grand design for your life. So what gets in the way of making a conscious choice to make our crises meaningful and our resilience conscious?

The Beginning of *Girly Thoughts*

As strange as it sounds, this strategy of forging solutions is one we have been using our whole life, albeit often not consciously. As an adult we search for an understanding of how the world works; we also did so as a child. We not only wanted to master tying our shoes but we also wanted to figure out what it was going to be like to be an adult. Growing up was so exciting. Some of us couldn't wait to see how we would look, what we would do. We were impatient to get there. We would sneak our mother's makeup, walk around in her high heels, play dress-up in her clothes, even spray on some perfume.

To figure out this journey we asked questions, seemingly endless questions that hopefully were answered. We carefully observed the adults in our lives, on TV, and in the movies. And we imitated what we saw. We used our imagination and played house or school, acting like the adults we saw, often using the same words to resolve the same dramas we saw played out in our life. As a result, we came to conclusions about ourselves, about how girls and women should act, what to expect when they acted differently, what was allowed, what was not, what worked and what didn't. It actually was pretty simple and straightforward. If we were lucky, we kept growing and developing and expanding our understanding, and we moved beyond the assumptions we forged in childhood about our role as women.

However, if this process of growth was interrupted through trauma of any kind, or not encouraged due to our family's view of women, or in some way interfered with, then our understanding of ourselves in the world was truncated. The reality we understood as a child is now what we carry forward into adulthood (and this reality is sometimes seen in our *girly thoughts*). As a result of this, as adults we now run the risk of seeing options for how to live and develop solutions to the myriad of conflicts that life offers us through the restricted lens of our three- or six-year-old self. We interpret the adult world based upon the beliefs of childhood and the reasoning of our inner child.

When we do this, we end up acting in ways that are familiar and based on our childhood understanding of life, based on our *girly thoughts*. We act in ways we believe are in line with what is expected of us as women, even if those beliefs are not currently productive and do not generate real solutions to the dilemmas in which we find ourselves.

Motivate Change by Identifying the Pain You Know

We usually know when things are not working well; after all, we've been there before, numerous times. We can predict what will fall apart and how. We can anticipate our own disappointments; we know how we will feel. And yet we go forth bravely doing what we've done in the past, setting ourselves up for the same pain we have felt before. This is the pain we know, the hard pain of the past (Oliver-Diaz and O'Gorman 1988). And as surprising as it may be, we set about making the same things happen again and again to keep away a greater pain, the pain of the unknown, so we can prevent the crises of change.

For Cherish, a woman with stellar resilience, hard pain came out in a different manner. She kept picking the same type of man.

God knows I've spent enough time working on myself in therapy and self-help groups like Adult Children of Alcoholics. But with men I'm hopeless. Somehow I keep making the same choices. I guess I just fall for those good-looking, hunky, outgoing, charming types, with plenty of energy, smart, with lots of funny stories. But it seems to always end the same way. They say they're committed, but there's always someone else, and eventually I find out. Like Rashawn. He said he didn't want to change his Facebook status because of work. "I work for a conservative investment firm, and, when I go public on Facebook, everyone will know, clients included," he said. And I thought this made sense. It turns out it wasn't work, but a particular analyst at work, who he was also dating, that required he not change his status and declare that we were boyfriend and girlfriend.

The pain we know can make us feel destined to do the same thing over and over again, even if we are not aware of what we are doing to contribute to this outcome. The result feels the same to us. We feel trapped or destined or doomed to not have something in our life that we desire; for Cherish, that was a committed relationship. For others, the desire might be maintaining a weight that is better for their bodies, or having a career that is fulfilling, or acquiring friends who also take care of us, or being a mother. This is the pain we know, and we need to challenge it so we can grow beyond it. So make conscious what you feel you are *destined* to do. In Cherish's case, it was not being able to find a man who could commit to her. "It's like I'm hardwired or something to keep finding the same type of loser guy."

We come by the pain we know honestly. And we invite in the pain we know to keep away new pain, the pain of the unknown. These are the commitments we knowingly make that are too much for us to handle, such as being in charge of the travel for our daughter's gymnastic team competitions because we are organized; saying yes to hosting our family's Thanksgiving because we love to cook; being the go-to person when our friends' lives fall apart because we have a degree in counseling; or, as in Cherish's case, the pain we know is staying in the same type of relationships. This type of pain can take many forms, but the key element is that it keeps us where we are, however uncomfortable that might be for us. Hard pain is the pain of the *known*.

The Challenge of the Unknown and the Thrill of Growth

Soft pain is the pain of the unknown: having that adventure we always wanted to have but couldn't because of too many obligations; wanting to climb the high peaks of the Adirondacks but having too many excuses about getting in shape for it; taking a weekend away to New York City or New Orleans with girlfriends; completing a degree; or taking that course in car repair. Soft pain is the pain of discomfort that comes from growth. As teenagers, we experienced growing pains: aches as our bones grew in spurts, pimples as our hormones changed; now we feel growing pains as we develop a vision of what is possible for us and begin to experiment with new ways of being in the world.

Edging Out of Our Comfort Zone

What leads us to change can be dramatic or subtle. Often things need to get bad enough to edge us out of the pain we know. We change due to a crisis that forces us to conclude that the same ol' same ol' is just a disaster, as we saw Cherish do.

Or sometimes we need to get sick and tired of being sick and tired before we figure out we need to change. Kelley, a woman whose resilience was overwhelmed, was exhausted.

I had no energy. Every day felt like the same well-choreographed disaster. At work, I'd get yelled at by my supervisor who thinks that if she speaks louder than you then she is right, and if she informs you of the error of your actions in a high-pitch shrill that it is for your growth and benefit. I'd come home and get yelled at by my kids, who seem to think that they can just dump their day's frustrations on me. And then my husband would start, yelling at me that this was a crazy house and that he couldn't get any peace and he was going to the bar. I realized one day that either I was the biggest screwup on the face of the earth, or somehow I was contributing to this mess with everyone being angry with me. Whatever the reason, I decided I couldn't take it any more, and that I didn't need to. I deserved better.

The third way that leads to change, and perhaps the most intriguing, is that the status quo gets boring. We know our own drama, and we decide it is just too limiting—it's gotten old—so we venture forth, take what feel like enormous risks, and begin to create new patterns that we hope can become familiar in time. And then we feel less like stepping off a cliff.

Erin, a woman with self-contained resilience, found herself tired of complaining, and she felt she was running out of friends who would listen.

I felt I was boxed in. Even I didn't want to listen any more. My list of things that had gone wrong in my life was getting old, and quick. So what if I went from being single and traveling for most vacations to being tethered to my home. So my father has Alzheimer's and I've stopped having a life since he's come to live with me. I don't date, I have to rush home from work so I'm not late for his day care, and I feel lucky enough to have even this support. Dinners are picked up already cooked, or delivered. I've no time to exercise and I'm getting fat. As the sibling with no obligations since I didn't have children, I was elected to do this caretaking, but it isn't working. So, I'm going to change and put some demands on some others, and just see what happens. In my worst moments I feel like I'm stepping into thin air, but I'm actually getting excited about what might happen.

The problem with telling yourself to "think outside the box" is that there is a box. You need to ask yourself, *What if there was no box?* What limitations would disappear, what anxieties would vanish? Where would you be if you didn't limit yourself to the comfortable next step? Your resilience can help you get there.

Your Resilience Journal: Documenting Your Growth

As part of this section of the book, you'll find opportunities to write in your journal about your interaction with the concepts discussed. Take a minute and note in your journal your responses to these questions:

- What is the *hard pain* of your childhood that you are still experiencing? In what areas are you feeling anguish, a sign that you may still resist changing your childhood beliefs?
- Where is your *soft pain* of current challenge and growth?
- Where is your current edge? What new challenges are you about to take on and step out of your comfort zone?

Get Curious About YOU!

Yes, get curious about yourself. You are probably already curious about those around you. You probably already spend lots of time trying to figure out *their* motivation: the intentions behind your boss's words, what your boyfriend is really thinking, how your parents can make that decision. And now, it's time to figure out what makes you *you*. Time to connect to this important part of who you are so you can put effort into trying to determine what makes you tick. You can develop the resilience skills of insight and self-awareness and begin to have more fun in your life.

As adults, we seem to easily forget that our curiosity is part of who we are. We become so problem-focused that we forget to relax, to explore, to have fun in our adult world, whether this is coming up with different solutions at work, or exploring new hobbies, or experimenting sexually with our partner.

As children, we lived in a world full of curiosity. We poked the cat or hit our brother just to see what would happen, just because we wanted to. We were very willing to experiment to see what would happen. We didn't second-guess ourselves. We didn't predetermine that it wasn't going to work, we didn't give up trying new things. We weren't full of assumptions about what we could do and what others couldn't do. We naturally explored, and explored some more, until we were satisfied. And if our experiment didn't work, or if our experimentation was greeted with annoyance from another, then we learned from this. We used the responses we received to grow, and we used our curiosity to explore new realms. Our curiosity so excited us that we would even giggle.

How can you reclaim your curiosity? There are two different avenues for doing this: speak to your inner child, and experiment.

Speak to Your Inner Child

Your inner child is naturally alive and curious and much more accessible than you may think. By reaching within and allowing this part of yourself to speak to you, you can begin to explore the world around you more spontaneously, with more of your senses firing and with less judgment. For some of you, this is like waking up and relaxing to be more in yourself.

Martha, a woman who had walled herself off with work for most of her life and had practiced more of a self-contained resilience, looked at me like I was crazy when I suggested this.

"This is so counter to who I am," she declared, "and you should know this."

Yes, I did, which is why I was recommending the opposite stance in her trying to develop an approach as to what to do after retirement.

"So, I'm supposed to figure out how I'd like to play, like when I was a child?" she yelled in her full CEO voice.

"Yes," I answered quietly.

Martha took an incredible leap of faith to try an area that she did not go into in a power position:

I felt like I was stepping into thin air. But I clutched that part of me that was terrified. I was also a little curious. So I screwed my eyes shut, held my inner child's hand, and jumped. At least that's how it felt.

Martha went to a seminar on aging and signed up for the creative arts section, "Just to prove you wrong," she blared at me, but I detected a twinkle in her eyes. She admitted it was painful at first: "I felt like an idiot. No, more like a klutzy child." Which *not* feeling, of course, was part of her motivation to become so proficient at work. This was in many ways a resilient response to childhood fears; she did something very positive with them and became very competent. There was a vulnerable side that was about to resurface now that she was retired and didn't have the structure of work to keep it at bay. So I helped her nurture it head-on.

> I surprised myself by actually liking my attempt to be creative with art. It wasn't as overwhelming as I thought it would be, just uncomfortable at first . . . I played with finger paints, just like I did as a child. I'm clearly no artist, but it was fun. I enjoyed the people who came, and I really liked the staff who were leading the various tracks, particularly the artists. They were so full of heart. I also realized that the whole effort, although worthwhile, was poorly organized. So I volunteered to help them organize it. This is what I do best. Organize. And I can do it on my own time, and be with these interesting, creative women, and maybe gradually learn how to play more myself.

Experiment

The second avenue is to give yourself permission to experiment. Yes, experiment like you did in high school science classes. This means setting out to try something new, within clear bounds, just to see what happens. It means keeping an objective eye on your actions so you can note if they are working to your liking or not. This is something I recommend that women do, and it is always greeted in the same way: with surprise and then curiosity.

Realize that our patterns are important. They tell us how we solve problems. They inform us concerning how we try to protect ourselves, how we try to control our environment, the type of influence we wish to have on our world. Our patterns also tell us a great deal about our past and how we made sense of events as a child, as so many of our patterns (particularly those that appear not to work for us as an adult) were developed in childhood. For example, do we wait for someone else to have the answer? Do we wait to see what is right? Do we volunteer because that seems to be our role wherever we are? Do we state our opinion because we really understand more than most? Do we prioritize the needs of others over our own needs because we know how to wait? Do we feel the pain of others and act quickly to relieve this pain without thinking through what it will cost us emotionally, even financially? Do we not ask for help because we know it will not be given?

Our patterns speak to an internal logic that we have, one built over many trials and many years. Our patterns form a road map that makes sense to us, one that lets us know that if we start here we have these paths to follow. Frequently, our internal map is not conscious, which is why we can feel stuck in always making the same choices. We can feel what we're supposed to do, but we don't see it clearly, and we may not be able to see options.

Sammie, a woman with stellar resilience, found herself always trying to figure out why her father, who abandoned Sammie at birth to live with her abusive and mentally ill mother, kept Sammie's two older sisters with him. Her father only reappeared in her life when Sammie was an adult, and he was ready to start over and have a good father/daughter relationship.

Sammie struggled to make sense of this relationship. She'd retrieve her old journals, cards her father had randomly sent her through the years, and pictures she drew as a child. She'd pour over these looking for clues as to why her father had done what he did. Sammie would read and reread letters and e-mails from her father, analyze them, send back her analyses to her father (and these were sometimes epic tomes) as a way to try to make sense of her hurt. Sammie kept asking her father to help her understand.

Her father would periodically disappear from her life again, only to reappear, and he would try to engage Sammie's adult sons and daughters. He would tell them, not so subtly, that Sammie had problems and they shouldn't take what she said about her own father too seriously. Sammie would respond by writing another "book" and sending it off to her father, as she began to feel her father was undermining her role as a mother with her own children. Sammie went into therapy, speaking again about trying to make sense of her relationship with her father.

Sammie's therapist asked her to explain her goal for the communication. In thinking about the answer, Sammie became curious about herself. She started to think less about why her father had abandoned her and what she had done to contribute to her own abandonment, and more about what she wanted from her father. She realized that she was trying to engage her father and bring him closer to repair the past. But no matter how much she wrote, how hard she tried, it wasn't working.

Sammie's curiosity about her own motivation led her to an important conclusion. She had to accept that this was her father. As an adult, her father, who was now in his late sixties, was essentially repeating the same pattern of abandonment. And Sammie realized that she, too, was following well-established patterns. If something was to change, it had to be something Sammie was doing. Maybe she had to stop expecting her father to be the father Sammie had always wanted and, instead, accept him as he was, a man who had many ghosts in his own life.

When you find yourself repeating a pattern you feel you don't like, or one that isn't helpful, don't get disgusted, don't feel hopeless—get *curious.* Be eager to learn more about this part of you. Make a commitment to spend time with the part of you that this pattern feeds. You may have been following this pattern for a long time, and you keep drawing attention to this need you have by spending so much time in its service. Let this part of you deserve attention, respect, and curiosity so you can learn to move on and change.

Your Resilience Journal: Determine the WHY in Your Less-Than-Helpful Patterns

You are a puzzle worth working on. Get curious. Begin by looking at your patterns. In your journal, in your own time, describe in detail a pattern you keep repeating. Pick one that is particularly irksome. It is a curiosity that demands attention. Use your considerable skills to analyze yourself.

- How did you come by using *this* pattern? Was it modeled by family or friends? Did it seem fun?
- What are you protecting yourself from by following this pattern?
- What would happen if you did something else? What else could you do that would be different, even if it is a stretch?

Curiosity . . . the Opposite of Shame

Don't judge yourself for whatever you're doing that isn't working. In judging ourselves, we tend to become angry, maybe beat ourselves up, which often leads to feeling shame and hopelessness. In fact, the root of feelings of shame—*girly thoughts*—are the very judgments we make of ourselves concerning what we see as our failings, our inadequacies, our blame. With shame, we see ourselves as the problem.

And shame doesn't feel good no matter how we package it. It traps us, sucks our energy, and, most important, shame keeps us stuck, which keeps us from accessing resilience. By disempowering us, shame facilitates us doing the same things over and over again. It keeps us in the same patterns that we know do not work for us.

The opposite of shame and critical self-judgment is curiosity. Curiosity invites an openness to understand, a willingness to dare to take the risk to explore. In fact, curiosity can actually be quite exciting! Experiment with changing some small things in your life to see if the earth falls out from under you. When you find out it doesn't, you, too, can feel this exhilaration.

Dare to Be Curious:
Set Up an Experiment in Your Life

Be curious enough to begin to consciously develop your resilience by testing it with an experiment. The fun thing about an experiment is that you do not have to be committed to the outcome. You can just do it and see what happens. Then you can decide if you want to continue it or not.

Begin simply enough by:

- deciding what to explore and deciding on a hypothesis—that is what you want to find out about you
- developing a plan involving small, measurable steps—baby steps that are totally in your control
- executing your plan
- noting your results

In your journal, write your answers to the following questions:

- What happened?
- Has this opened up a new avenue for your thinking? Your actions?
- And—very important—how does it feel?

Your Resilience Journal: Shame Versus Curiosity

You can use your emerging conscious resilience to help heal yourself—even your long-standing issues of shame. You can see shame as an oddity that again deserves your attention. It becomes something outside you and not who you are. Begin to transform your shame by using your resilience.

To understand what sparks your shame, ask yourself the following questions and journal your answers. This is part journaling, part visualization, so make yourself comfortable and work at your own pace:

- How do you judge yourself and find yourself wanting?

- Are you willing to free yourself to see an alternative and be curious about a new way of handling this?
- What would be helpful for you to do? What would you like to transform your shame into? Perhaps love for yourself? Or a new respect for the origins of what now can be your resilience?

Summary

Using your resilience is a decision on a basic level, particularly as you move toward developing conscious resilience. The crises that occur in your life can help you in this pursuit, for they are opportunities to act differently; crises do tend to shake things up and get our attention, and in this way they can be empowering. As such they present opportunities for us to step back and determine how we want to handle these immediate challenges, how we can use our new, more conscious resilience, and how we can discover a meaning in these painful moments that makes us more confident in ourselves.

EIGHT

Step Two—Uncover Your Hidden Resilient Voice: Use Your Own Wisdom to Determine What Is Right for You

H EAR THE STILL, SMALL VOICE THAT SO SELDOM LEADS
US WRONG, AND NEVER INTO FOLLY.

—Madame Du Defand

When we don't know how to listen to ourselves, all sorts of strange and unusual things can happen. The problem is that we don't know what to do about them. We have a tendency to either trust and to accept them or blame ourselves. This step will help you learn to listen to a new voice—that most important person: you!

Make Space in Your Life

I spoke recently to a conference organizer about hosting a training in the New York metropolitan area. I told her I believed the trick to having a large attendance was to get through the media saturation. *Much like my brain*, I thought ruefully.

We are all so very busy. We have our actual lives, our virtual lives on Facebook and in video games, and our other continual electronic connections. Our modern, high-tech world allows us to be on-call and online 24/7 if we wish. And in that 24/7 world, making space to do anything is an accomplishment, let alone making space to be connected to ourselves. When we do finally find a way to make this inner connection, there we will find the voice of our resilience.

But we need to make space to listen. Accomplishing this means making room in our lives for ourselves. Yes, we do have pressing demands. And we seem to find a way to make room for the children in our lives, for our partner, for our work, for our family with all their quirks, definitely for our friends. But to do this, we tend to crowd out room for ourselves, our emotions, our sexual feelings, our desires—our needs. And this is where we begin to pay the big price for being disconnected from our own wisdom.

So, do you want to make space in your life for yourself? My guess is that since you've made it this far in the book, the answer is *yes*.

The process of beginning to make space in your own life for you is both deceptively simple and very complicated. It is simple because it involves a very direct action on your part—making a decision to ask yourself what is best for you. It is very complicated because once you begin to factor in what is best for you—what it is you need, want, and, heaven help us, desire—then you need to determine not just what to do for everyone else, but also for you. This simple process begins through learning to listen to yourself.

Our Resilient Voice

We may come to know of our resilience in many ways: through intuitive reasoning, a spontaneous action that saves the day, an insight that points us in a new direction or validates dimly perceived feelings, our inner musings, a physical sensation that sparks us into thinking in a new direction, even our dreams. We may notice a "sixth sense" of which we were not previously aware. Yet when we do become aware of it, we can learn to use its counsel to help us decide what is right for us. Learning to use resilience is a matter of just learning to listen.

Several days after her family reunion, Anne told me this story:

I walked around smiling during my parents' forty-fifth wedding anniversary, but inwardly I was furious—an old, familiar feeling I'd never named before. All these hidden agendas! My mother, sister, and aunts fawning over all the men in the family and then cutting them down as soon as they were out of earshot—even Grandma! They boast to one another about how they have tricked their husbands into doing things for them, buying them things. They do it all the time. How could I have not noticed it before? What a female tradition!

This time, as they were talking, I realized how much I dislike this part of my family. I literally felt ill. I thought it was too much coffee. Now I realize it was just too much duplicity. When I tried to talk about some of the changes going on in our lives, no one wanted to listen. Talk about something real? Something to do with feelings? Never. I am so tired of being invisible, and I am so angry.

So there I was, caught up in the same trap I get into every time I see my family. I always forget how it works, or I think it will be different. But this time, I stopped to ask myself, *What's going on?* I took a little time to step back and get a better perspective. I could see myself playing along with a game I'd never liked. I said to myself, *I can't put up with this any more.* Then I thought, *I don't have to. I can leave!*

Anne told her family she and her husband had to leave early and would have to miss the family brunch the next day. She told me, "Maybe I'm learning to protect myself, to establish some limits about how much I can do for my family and how much I need to do for myself. It felt great. Finally, I was standing up for myself and taking care of me!"

Anne had begun to separate from her old patterns and listen to her needs. Realizing her feelings about her family instead of suppressing them, Anne took an important step toward drawing on her resilience to discover options to protect herself and what belongs to her.

This one act led her to establish more realistic and satisfying boundaries. In fact, it was a turning point in her life. "I began to feel that there was more of me," Anne said. "Now I pay attention to the physical clues I get when something is wrong. I realize that this is my personal early warning system that alerts me to situations that I need to change, whether it's with my children, on the job, or whatever. I'm more tuned into myself, and, as a result, I don't put up with as much as I did before. And I'm a lot happier for it."

Our Resilient Voice . . . *and*
Our *Girly Thoughts*

At first blush, our resilient voice and our *girly thoughts* might seem to be the same thing. After all, our *girly thoughts* do look after us. They tell us how to look and how to act, and they help us look out for how to not make fools of ourselves. So in this way it seems like they are protecting us. But the question is, protecting us from what? For some women *girly thoughts* are the loudest voice heard. They serve to keep us focused on the holy grail of the fantasy of the *ideal,* and they are among the earliest voices we hear in childhood.

Your *girly thoughts* keep you focused on *out there,* not what is in you, not what is right for you. They keep you focused on how you will be judged if you do not:

- look a certain way
- feel a certain way
- act a certain way
- have certain beliefs that keep *you* at fault and responsible

Girly thoughts represent *antiresilience.* They are not about what is strong in us, they are about the price we will pay for what is *wrong* with us. The way to counter our *girly thoughts* is to really turn up the volume on the resilient voice within us. Then we can moderate between what society is telling us and what we know is right for us. When we do, we may not choose to go with the shorter skirt length because we do have heavy thighs. Or we may embrace being full figured and show those curves without feeling bad. Our resilient voice is about determining what is our truth for what we should do!

How We Perceive Our Resilience

There are numerous ways in which we may perceive our resilience. Like Anne in the previous story, we may actually hear a voice speak to us in seemingly random thoughts. Or we may experience our resilience in the images of dreams or fantasies, as a narrative voice in writing, or as a presence. The first step, then, is to learn how our resilience "speaks" to us and how to create a dialogue with it.

Brooke was a participant in a retreat I led. She told me:

As we began to work with the concept of our resilient voice, a part of me was skeptical. But another part of me thought, *this is right, this is familiar*. It was when I invited this part of me to write a letter that I suddenly knew that I'd had conversations with this presence before.

As a teenager and young adult, I was a journal writer. I would write and write about how I felt about things. Everyday things. Many times it seemed as if there were two voices: after I'd written something, another voice would come in to comment on it. I used to be surprised when that second voice seemed to be a little smarter, as if it had an answer or information I didn't.

I vividly remember one such dialogue on my forty-ninth birthday. My husband had a rare cancer, and, after a lingering illness, he passed away leaving me with our teenagers. My life was in shambles, and I was a widow before I was fifty, but I recall my journal entry: life is for the living, even though I couldn't get my mind around it then.

This happened more than once. Throughout my life, this voice said, "Hey, what about *you*?" This voice was not always good news. I can't always say that the voice was a comfort, but it was always on my side, sometimes more than I was!

An Inner Presence

Jennifer's discovery of her resilient voice was less direct. She first acknowledged this part of herself in a recovery group for incest survivors.

> Through all my years of counseling and working on the trauma of incest, I somehow always blamed myself. Not intellectually. I knew enough to say, "I was only a child. How was a child to know?" But emotionally, I just couldn't forgive myself. I couldn't accept that I had not been strong enough to make the incest stop. I kept beating myself up for my innocence, my vulnerability, my stupidity.
>
> I was sitting in the group listening to another member share her feelings of shame—feelings that I know so well—when I felt an opening inside. My resilient voice wasn't so much a voice as a presence, like a guardian angel. Somehow I felt full in a place where I had always felt empty. I felt protected, understood, loved, and, perhaps most of all, pride for what I'd had the courage to endure. This allowed me to *feel* for the first time that the incest *wasn't* my fault. This presence had a special wisdom that I trusted.
>
> I have this feeling today, like a place within me, a centering. I know my resilience more through feelings than words. I feel as though my vulnerability is surrounded by love. I sense a capacity to love, accept, even nurture myself that I have never felt before. I feel safe for the first time in my life. I am learning to make an inner home by connecting to my resilient voice.

Jennifer's experience is common among women who have experienced childhood trauma. At first their resilience is less accessible, more obscured, but still available if they seek it. It can serve to give these women the perspective and self-compassion they need.

Jennifer quickly learned to draw on this inner resource. She said, "Strangely, this part of me never felt new. It always felt familiar, like an old friend I'd just gotten in touch with. I realized that my resilience had always been with me, guiding me, loving me. But when the incest began it was too painful, too confusing to listen to this inner love and wisdom and still do what I was told to do, to be a 'good daughter.' So I closed down part of me and lived to survive. Now I can use this part of me to heal."

Dreaming Our Resilience

The first awareness of their resilient voice for some women is through an unusual dream that points a new way, demonstrates new feelings, or clarifies an ongoing problem. Krista told me that she had had a disturbing dream that awakened her, but without the usual fear that had accompanied such dreams in the past.

> In the dream I am on an old train and have just given birth to a baby. The baby begins to nurse. It is a little painful. I wince but enjoy the moment. I am falling in love with my child. All of a sudden, my baby is wrenched from my arms by an older woman. I can't or don't move. The woman is dressed like a gypsy and is leading a band of men and women. They kidnap my child, and I never see her again.
>
> I woke up not afraid, but confused. I kept thinking, *You see, you did have a baby!* when I know I have never had a child. Why didn't I move? In waking life when something threatening happens to me I fight back, but in the dream I was so sapped of strength I couldn't move.

The dream stayed with me. Over the next few weeks, it was just around the edge of my consciousness, waiting for me, and my thoughts drifted there often. Along with this dream came a dialogue—me to me, or rather, my unconscious to my conscious mind—about what had and hadn't happened in the dream. This dialogue has been so helpful. For the first time, I'm spending time and energy on myself in a special way. I give myself time to think, reflect, feel. It is almost as if I have given birth to a part of myself, a nurturing, questioning self that is able to go deeper into what I need. I've realized that this is an inner guide, what you call my resilience.

Krista's dream allowed her to begin exploring parts of herself that she had not consciously focused on before. In heeding the inner tension generated by her dream, Krista recognized a viewpoint, other than her waking knowledge, that was still very much her own. As she questioned the meaning of the dream, she made some discoveries that surprised her.

In our ensuing sessions together, Krista began to understand the coping strategies she had adopted as a child. Her mother was an invalid whose needs dominated the household. Krista was not really allowed to be a child, as the neediness of her mother forced her to become self-sufficient at an early age. Hence, in the dream she sees her baby, her own childhood, taken from her by her mother, the gypsy, whom Krista experienced in the dream as she had as a child—not as a frail person, but as an all-powerful force.

What began as a troubling dream became, in fact, a new avenue of inquiry that unlocked many previously closed doors. Krista began to examine the new childhood memories kindled by her dream. As she spent more time with the images, feelings, and thoughts evoked by her resilience, Krista found her resilience grew stronger and more accessible. She began to work with it in other ways as well, to explore feelings and decisions in her life.

Literally Feeling Our Resilience

One "constant" women have in life is the changing ways our bodies feel. Many women can literally tell where they are in their menstrual cycle, not by checking a calendar but by paying attention to how their body feels. *Am I bloated? Having cramps? Feeling an increase in sexual desire?* Within a relatively short period of twenty-eight to thirty-five days, our bodies are in a constant dialogue with us, sending the same messages, in the same way, each month. How we hear these messages and how we heed them is part of how we build our resilience.

Many women become very uncomfortable for a certain amount of time: for days or weeks every month they feel betrayed by their body, even cursed by being a woman. Some women respond by feeling they must overcome and overpower their discomfort, instead of working with it and deriving the energy that can come from taking this monthly signal that they must take care of themselves. In this way, our body speaks to us of our needs, our vulnerability, and our power and reminds us to slow down, to dip into ourselves, to get to know ourselves, to take care of ourselves as well as we take care of everything else in our life. And this may be the gift that our body gives us in developing our resilience.

Margeaux has a very uncomfortable PMS that lasts almost two weeks.

It would make me so very angry. I felt like I'd gain two dress sizes; I'd get constipated and feel so bloated. I was miserable. My doctor suggested medication, but that made me angry as well. Did I mention that I also became very irritable? I decided I had to so something, and I decided to go alternative. I experimented with changing my diet, hating every moment of it, and began doing quick meditations throughout the day and exercising. It took time (which I didn't have), concentration, and a willingness to experiment and try to figure out what would work. Interestingly, I learned to make myself a priority. What a novel idea! And it worked.

Working with myself and my PMS began to be a metaphor for how I began to live my life, figuring out what I needed to do to take care of myself so I'd have the concentration and energy to take care of my priorities. I guess in this way my resilience spoke to me. And I plan to keep hearing the clarion call that is my body, especially as I age. I encourage myself that it's got to get easier to do this self-care if you keep practicing.

Visualizing Our Resilient Voice

For some women, their resilient voice appears as an image or a fantasy of what they would like to do or how they would like to handle a particular situation. They may actually envision themselves responding in a certain way, and this visual fantasy can be their guide for how to respond.

Taylor had often found herself blocked when making decisions about what she needed and wanted. "Usually I'd say, 'Oh, I don't care,' when in reality I just couldn't figure out what I wanted to do," she mused. She found that when she needed to make a decision, whether it was what to order for dinner or whether or not to continue swimming laps in the pool, the easiest way for her to decide was to stop, picture the choice in her mind, and see which way her visual fantasy took it.

> I've been surprised what happens when I see myself in a situation I am trying to make a decision about. One time when a friend asked me if I wanted to join her for lunch, I paused for a moment and saw myself running out of a restaurant. I said no to that invitation. Another time my son asked me if I would read him a story. I felt tired and inclined to say no, but when I pictured myself in the moment, I saw myself relaxed and cuddling my little boy. And so I said yes.

Over time, Taylor has become more skilled at tuning into this part of who she is. "It's like there is a private me that I rather enjoy. And the pleasure or confidence that I feel when I imagine enjoying myself or solving a problem gives me the permission to ask for what I want."

This sense of permission to ask for and arrange for what we need and want is the hallmark of our resilient voice. In learning to listen to ourselves, in learning to hear our own answers about our needs and wants, we strengthen our understanding of the part of us that knows what we need to take care of ourselves. We are no longer kept apart from what nourishes us. The more we use this part of who we are, the easier and quicker it becomes to access it.

Your Resilience Journal:
Using Your Resilient Voice

Listen to the voice or image in your mind the next time you need to make a decision—whether you want another cookie, need to work late, or want to set a limit with your child.

Pause for a moment. Ask yourself how to proceed and listen to the answers that come. Weigh which one feels right. Perhaps you'll hear an internal verbal response or feel a drop in tension as you consider a new option. Or perhaps you'll see yourself doing what you would really like to do.

Practice calling on this part of yourself—your resilient voice—on a regular basis. Consider the following, and journal your responses in your own time. Find out which of these three different avenues you use to perceive your resilient voice:

1. Are you primarily auditory, and you hear the right answer?
2. Are you primarily visual, and you see yourself?
3. Are you primarily kinesthetic, and you literally feel the right answers in your body?

Do your dreams or daydreams provide clues? For many people, resilience speaks through their unconscious, which is why making this process conscious is such a priority.

Continue to cultivate your resilience by using it frequently. Use it throughout your day. Ask yourself what you need, and see which answer is the right one. Play with this, and enjoy getting to know you.

Other Voices

Childhood is a time of taking in, of observing and imitating, of listening to parents, teachers, peers, and the media. From all these sources we internalize various beliefs and attitudes. These, too, often take the form of internal voices.

"Why is it so tough for me to make a decision?" Scarlett asked me. "Every time I take a step forward, I feel that I sabotage myself. I am so full of conflicting feelings and desires."

Scarlett was an intelligent woman who had recently completed her sophomore year at college but had difficulty deciding what to major in. Overprotected as a child by her blue-collar family, she had been trained to look to stronger adults for the answers, not to look inward for *her* own counsel.

I encouraged her to listen to the opinions that were warring inside her and to write them out. In our next session she told me excitedly,

I took your advice and started writing out the dialogue just as I heard it inside my head. As I did, I realized that I could make out at least several distinct voices. I recognized my older sister's, my mother's, and my father's voices; they were the ones telling me I couldn't succeed. My father's voice was telling me not to take chances, to go back to my old job at the supermarket, not to put myself in danger of failing. My mother's was telling me I was so pretty and I should just get married. My sister's would chime in, saying who did I think I was anyway, trying to do something better? And there was this other voice telling me what to do with my hair, how I was dressing badly, and so on. I know, those were my *girly thoughts.*

But then I was aware of another voice debating with these stronger, critical voices. I sensed that this softer, more compassionate voice was my own, expressing my side of the story—my opinions, my values, my dreams, my plans. *There it is*, I thought to myself. *That's my resilient voice!*

Identify the Dialogues

Pleased with this first discovery, Scarlett continued to use this technique of writing out the dialogues and gradually found that she moved through the criticism and fears that kept her from making a decision. "Although it seemed gentler at first, my resilient voice was more sure, more convincing than the other voices, which were really only reflecting my fears and doubts." She followed the counsel of her resilient voice to major in math and art. The last time I saw her, she had just accepted a position as a game designer.

As Scarlett discovered, learning to listen to our resilient voice is not always an easy task. For as we try to isolate this one voice, we begin to hear the many other voices we have heard over the years— the voices of our parents, family members, or close friends, perhaps social or religious authorities, the media, even our inner child—the voice of ourselves at an earlier age. In thinking through a course of action or response to a given situation, we may first encounter these other viewpoints. Until we learn to recognize them for what they are, they vie for our attention with our own voice, and we may give in to doing what others expect of us rather than acting according to our own needs.

The process of understanding our resilient voice involves our ability to identify these other voices that inhabit the maze of our often conflicting opinions and attitudes. In this way, we can more effectively override their less helpful aspects and begin to focus more clearly on who we are and what is best in our lives for our fulfillment and happiness.

Your Resilience Journal: Distinguishing the Dialogue Within

In your journal, write out a question you have about an event or incident that puzzles you or a course of action you have been unable to decide upon. For example:

- Why does seeing my mother always make me so mad?
- Why can't I make a commitment to my boyfriend?
- What is it that is keeping me from getting started on an exercise program?

Then write out every response that comes to mind without censoring your ideas, without stopping to think. Continue to write for ten to fifteen minutes without a break.

Read over all your answers. Do you recognize your resilient voice? Do you recognize the source of the other voices you recorded? Most people are amazed to see how internal voices represent actual people, such as a parent, sibling, or other important person in their lives.

Practice this exercise on a daily basis if possible. The more often you do this exercise, the more readily you will be able to access *your* resilient voice.

Why We May Not Want to Listen

Listening inward will cause us also to confront our less familiar aspects, those qualities or memories that we judge as not living up to the external standards we have imposed upon ourselves, our *girly thoughts,* so we prefer to keep these hidden from the world, perhaps even from ourselves. This is our tender side, our vulnerable inner self that houses what we find too painful, unsafe, or unacceptable to acknowledge. This may be our anger, rage, or neediness that we fear will alienate others, especially if we have already convinced ourselves that we need to care for others to the exclusion of caring for ourselves. This is our codependency.

This may be the part of us that we feel is *too* big to be acceptable. It may be parts of ourselves that make us uncomfortable, such as our jealousy, insecurity, or inflexibility, or even our competency, or a role we played at a particular time in our lives that makes us cringe now, such as the *good* girl. For many, it is the part of us that does not conform to the expectations of those we love or those whose opinion we value, and we feel their judgment before they even render it.

This side has to do with less-than-positive feelings and beliefs we have about ourselves; these are the sometimes harsh judgments we make about ourselves. We realize early on that we do not always behave as we would like to. We are not always even-tempered, loving, and strong; at times we are angry, anxious, want to be right, and even vulnerable. Here we need to forgive ourselves for being so very human, and we must come to understand and embrace those vulnerabilities. We all have limits to what we can do. Although this realization comes with age, I believe it is important for all women to learn that it is not shameful to have limits. It is an essential lesson we learn through our resilience.

While we instinctively distrust our vulnerable side, this very part of us often contains our most powerful elements, those that are most uniquely our own. In suppressing these parts, we not only keep ourselves from using this personal power but also expend psychic and emotional energy in doing so—energy that can be used more productively in our daily lives to accomplish the tasks before us.

If we are to be free to draw on our resilience, we need to develop the ability to speak about our vulnerabilities, to acknowledge and integrate these elements into our identity. In doing so, painful feelings and traumatic memories begin to be reframed and resolved. We can begin to see unacceptable parts, not as wrong or shameful, but as pieces of the puzzle of who we are. We can use the insight and skills we gain from our experiences—good and bad—to better understand what we need to do for ourselves, now and in the future.

As we transform these negative aspects, they lose their hold over us; we are no longer held back by the pain or the discomfort of being who we are or being less than we would like; our codependency and *girly thoughts* loosen their grip on us. We gain a new power, a new control over our lives. We claim the power hidden in our vulnerabilities and our desires.

Redefining Our Vulnerable Side

For many of us, our vulnerable side holds our rebellious side. This is the secret part of our self that houses the nonconforming thoughts and feelings that challenge the less-than-helpful messages we experience from our family and the greater society around us, and reacts to how we internalize these—our *girly thoughts.* This sense of difference has the potential to fuel our beliefs about our unworthiness or lack of desirability and leads to feelings of self-hate and rejection.

And these feelings can be reframed when we come to look at them through the perspective of our resilience. Once we look past our discomfort and other people's judgment of us, we can gain the courage to explore other choices and beliefs about ourselves. Once free of other people's narrow definitions of what is right and wrong, we can come to a new appreciation of our own needs, desires, and capacities.

When Cynthia married Tom, she felt pulled in two directions. She hadn't realized until then how different the life Tom wanted was from that of her family.

Her family had lived in Ohio since the 1850s, building careers in public service: the ministry, education, social work, and municipal government. They were generous, hardworking, career-oriented people. Cynthia was proud of her family's contributions and planned to follow in their path. Like her grandmother, she had earned a degree in early childhood education.

Tom was a writer. Midway to his master's degree in English literature, he decided it was more important to concentrate on his novel. He quit school and worked part-time while Cynthia finished her degree. After graduation, they moved to central Washington where the cost of living was far lower. Tom found a job as a reporter for the local newspaper, and Cynthia took a job at an elementary school.

My parents tolerated our move to Washington as part of our need to "find ourselves," as my mother said. Once the baby was born, however, the questions began: When are you going to grow up, take a real job, take your place in society? They dropped broad hints that they expected a visit soon. Were we planning to move? Didn't we want to be closer to our families, who could help with the baby?

I began to see myself in a different way, too. Before, I loved the life we'd made in Washington. The town itself was quiet and clean. The sense of community was strong, and I felt blessed to be part of it. We didn't have much in the way of possessions, and we didn't really miss them on a day-to-day basis. But suddenly I found myself thinking, *What am I doing with my life?* My sister just received a promotion in hospital administration. My brother, who worked in telecommunications, boasted a very good salary and terrific benefits. Tom and I had none of this.

It wasn't anything I could put my finger on, but I began to feel that everything around us was small, unimportant. I regretted being so far from home. The fact is, I had never given much thought to doing things any differently from my family until then.

Actually, I wasn't even aware of this running dialogue in my mind until one day while on summer break I sat on the front step in the sun with my daughter. I told her, "Aren't we lucky? My mom and I couldn't do this when I was a girl." Suddenly everything fell into place: I was living in a way that I had never been able to as a child. No wonder it felt so strange at times. My mother wasn't home with me; she had a career that involved travel and long office hours. While we were close and I was always provided for, my mother and I never had time to sit out on a summer afternoon. In Ohio, my family didn't know the neighbors very well or have time to participate in community events the way Tom and I do. Here, there was none of the pollution or crime and violence my sister contends with in Boston.

I realized Tom and I have made a life that isn't based on money, public works, or prestige, but on different values. It's a simpler, quieter life. Sure, it was hard to give up my old dreams of living in Ohio in my grandfather's house. But I see now that's all they were: dreams. It wasn't what I wanted for my life.

In recognizing our uniqueness we can step outside the definitions others have given to us. We begin to see our fundamental expressions of personality and choice in new ways. Cynthia's choice of lifestyle became a source of personal pride and happiness. Once removed from the context of "right" and "wrong" behavior, we see that what we thought of as "wrong" is actually only different. Recognizing that difference can be a turning point in the validation of our own individuality.

The Anger in Our Reaction to Our *Girly Thoughts*

Most women experience difficulty feeling and expressing anger without realizing that their anger can also be part of their resilience. Our society teaches us that women should be pliant, accepting, nurturing, and positive. Feelings of anger are not appropriate. Many women feel this pressure and work to fulfill the expectation at the expense of their true feelings. They begin to deny not only their needs but also the very expressions of hurt and anger when their needs are not met.

At times these feelings make women feel unworthy or ashamed because their emotions are not congruent with their identity or experiences. They begin to assume blame for being different. This tension between inner reality and outer expectation frequently results in displaced anger that protects others but depresses a woman's ability to access her resilience. This is how our *girly thoughts* combine with our codependency to silence our needs and our desires, and foster depression.

Anger is part of life and part of the human experience. When we recognize and channel it, anger can give us the power to change a situation, meet challenges, or try new possibilities. Whether this anger inspires us to leave a dead-end job, break off a bad friendship, recognize that we are too stressed, or challenge the existing status quo, it tells us change is needed. We gain power from our emerging understanding that there are alternatives to the present situation that we can pursue.

In the mid-1960s, Linda wanted to major in geology, a most unusual choice for a young woman, she was told. But Linda could see many old ways crumbling and the beginning of a new era. She demonstrated against the Vietnam War, stopped wearing a bra, and rebelled in many other personal ways, such as experimenting in the free-love movement.

I was furious with the discrimination against women I encountered in trying to get into a so-called man's field. Patronizing professors who would call me "Miss" while refusing to take me seriously enraged me. The more I tried to play by their rules and still get an education, the harder it became for me to contain my anger.

I finally was forced to recognize the futility of it when a professor scoffed at my question during a class discussion and refused to answer it. And this is after he kept "accidently" grabbing my ass during a field trip. I was so angry that I stood up right then and there and told him what I thought of him. I reminded him none too nicely that my tuition paid his salary. Once he recovered from his shock, he ordered me to leave the class and gave me a two-week suspension. Despite my excellent course work, I received a barely passing grade.

Some of Linda's friends told her to organize a boycott of the professor's classes. Linda thought about how much fun it would be to ridicule him the way he had her.

Then I thought, *What will it get me? Why waste all that energy when it won't get me any closer to my career goals?*

I realized that if I tried to stay with geology, I would spend all my energy just fighting to be heard. It wasn't a battle I was interested in, and perhaps wasn't one I could win.

This realization led Linda to pursue a new path. She reevaluated her goals and switched her major to political science. Her personal interest in change and revolution were right in line with the subject. She went on to become an environmental activist, a profession that would benefit from both her interest in the natural sciences and her natural temper as a fighter.

Today I spend my anger in more constructive ways. I've taught another generation to give voice to their outrage about our environmental policies. Rather than fighting small, futile battles, I use my energy to accomplish something, to speak out and rally others to important issues.

I realize now that I have befriended the anger that used to get me into so much trouble. It's as if the more I tried to conceal it, the more unpredictable and uncontrollable it became. I know now how to use it to accomplish what's important to me. It no longer rules me.

Like all emotions, anger is a clue to what is going on inside. As we recognize our anger and the situations in which it arises, we can learn about ourselves. Resilience gives us the courage to acknowledge and claim our anger and turn it to our advantage.

Your Resilience Journal:
Anger at Your *Girly Thoughts*

Take a moment and consider what your anger at your *girly thoughts* has propelled you to do. In your journal, write your thoughtful answers to the following questions:

- What areas of growth has it encouraged?
- What barriers have you confronted as a result of these thoughts?
- What limitations would you like to confront? And how?

For more exercises for tuning into your resilient voice, go to http://patriciaogorman.com.

Summary

Sometimes the most powerful act we can do, the most disruptive stance we can take, is an inner one. This is the significance of learning to literally have a conversation with yourself to listen to your own inner wisdom, your resilience.

NINE

Step Three—
Create Helpful Boundaries:
Take Charge and Stop
Setting Yourself Up

NOBODY CAN MAKE YOU FEEL INFERIOR WITHOUT
YOUR PERMISSION.

—*Eleanor Roosevelt*

For many women, *girly thoughts* very much represent how we see ourselves, how we describe ourselves, and importantly, how we see others seeing us and commenting on us. This is true whether the comments are to our face, behind our backs, in texts, or on Facebook. In short, these thoughts form part of our inner and interpersonal conversations, and they can profoundly influence our identity.

Many of you have probably come to the conclusion that defining yourself by your *girly thoughts* is less than helpful; in fact it is a major way that we set ourselves up. But if we reject this rather pervasive cultural definition of who we are, this raises the question: Who are we, if we are not bound by our *girly thoughts*? As easy as it might seem to answer this question, the process is a bit complicated. Part of challenging the idea that we're not what our greater culture says we are requires us to get to know who we really are.

We began this process in earnest in the last step by beginning to turn up the volume on our resilient voice, that part of us that knows the right answer for us, even when the answer is really going to complicate our lives. The next piece of our process is to begin to understand the positive parts of ourself; we need to identify the parts we want to share with others, how we want to represent ourselves to others, and what we want others to notice about us. We also need to learn how to speak about our strengths, then begin to test all of this by setting up some fun boundaries. Fun? Yes, because we can play with this. Of course, we don't usually live our lives *thinking so rationally,* but these are not bad questions to consider when we want to change. Because considering all aspects of what is right for us begins to form the basis of developing *conscious resilience,* even if in the beginning we can't see how to connect the dots.

Be Careful What You Say, *You* May Be Listening

As children, we were told to watch our language. We were informed, sometimes not too gently, that "that" word wasn't allowed in our home. We may have even been punished for our language, even if we apologized for it. Our language was considered important, not just for us, but also as a representation of our family.

Fast forward to adulthood. The way we speak about ourselves is just as important as how we speak about others. Our words can encourage a sports team we are rooting for, but our words can disempower us as well. Many times, and in many subtle and not so subtle ways, I've heard women take away their own power by their words.

When we begin to step into using our language as an extension of our resilience, we have begun to own our personal power. And having power can be fun!

NO as a Complete Sentence

Some words are very powerful, but these tend to be the words that we learned to edit out all too well. *No* is one prime example. For women, a word that naturally rolled off our lips at age two all too often becomes totally unacceptable by the time we reach our early teens. The reasons are complex, but they boil down to our desires to be socially acceptable, liked by others, and seen as sweet as well as desirable by those we desire. We begin explaining more and stating our exact thoughts and feelings less.

In her classic book, *No Is a Complete Sentence* (1995), Megan LeBoutillier explores this theme, picked up more recently by Lisa Frankfort, PhD, and Patrick Fanning in their 2005 book, *How to Stop Backing Down and Start Talking Back,* about why we have such a struggle with setting verbal limits. Why it is so difficult to say *no* to something that you know you will later resent doing, like another work assignment, feeding a friend's dog for the weekend, watching another football game on TV, or making a big pan of your special brownies for the high school band concert?

Neurologist Richard Cytowic speaks in a *Psychology Today* blog (2012) about the fact that we are hardwired to help others. Add to this our *girly thoughts* that come from all the social pressure women feel to be pleasing and acceptable, throw in a little codependency for good measure, and it is no wonder that saying *no* becomes such a challenge. But there are simple guidelines that can help you:

Ask Yourself if You Want to Do What Is Being Asked. Yes, it can be that simple: your desire versus your capacity. Yes, you can do it, but do you want to? This type of decision-making comes up frequently when women feel pressured into having sex when they really don't want to. Yes, they can. They are physically capable. But, no, they are not into this guy, or woman, they're tired, crampy, just not turned on.

"NO," coupled with your disarming smile (or not), is a complete sentence. Our responses can be simple. And a no can be as direct as a yes, even if it is unexpected.

Understand That Giving a Reason for Your NO Is a Mistake in Most Situations. By offering explanations, we offer more ammunition for the other to use to try to get his or her way. For example, in many sexual encounters an explanation for why you said no is perceived as an objection to be overcome, and that offers the other person an opening to try to persuade you against your will.

Stop Apologizing. Women frequently apologize for things that are clearly not in their control and for which they therefore have no responsibility. In this case, there is no need to apologize. It is almost bizarre that we feel we have to make nice, make things more comfortable for others, not make waves, not embarrass anyone, all at our own expense—those *girly thoughts* in action again.

When women speak in casual conversation or in a formal address, or when I read correspondence from women, they frequently begin with an apology: "I regret that I need to ask you…" or, "I'm sorry to bother you but you charged me too much for the latte," or "I know how busy you are, and I'm so sorry to have to add to your burdens, but if you could take a moment to . . ." and so on.

It is almost as if we feel we should be invisible, not make waves. So we begin by pulling back our power. "By taking responsibility for things that aren't your fault, you denigrate your self-esteem," says Linda Sapadin, PhD, author of *Master Your Fears: How to Triumph Over Your Worries and Get On with Your Life* (2004); this is the opposite of resilience.

Don't Explain Away Your Power. One of my favorite pet peeves is when I hear a woman say that she is an *overachiever*. Recently I was speaking to a woman who used this phase in a story about how she took over a project that wasn't going well.

Melody, a woman with self-contained resilience, worked as an accountant in a small, family-run firm. She was a numbers person, but her favorite part of being an accountant was working directly with her customers and helping them solve their financial problems. She liked people, and her firm had enough employees that there were some personnel issues that needed some development. Melody volunteered for the task.

Together with two other staff members, Melody began to tackle how to draft some personnel procedures. It seemed to her that no one knew how to begin, so she took it upon herself to take the weekend and draft out what she thought was needed. She presented it at the next ad hoc meeting of the committee to the great astonishment of her coworkers.

"They seemed surprised. I told them that I'm just an overachiever."

I took issue with that statement. "Why did you say that?" I asked.

"It seemed to calm them down," she answered. "I guess I feel a need for others to be comfortable with me."

I pushed. "How can you achieve more than you can achieve?"

"I've never thought about this before," Melody said thoughtfully. "I guess it doesn't make any sense. I use that term because I feel I'm just such a big package." And here she teared up. "Not just that I'm tall and big-boned, but I tend to get things done faster than others, and maybe I'm a little impatient."

I pointed out that rather than seeing her ability to solve problems quickly as a strength, she had lived her life seeing her competencies as problems because they made others uncomfortable.

I asked her to try that on, to see her strengths as assets, not as liabilities; as she sat there and thought about it, a smile slowly spread across her face. "I like this," she said.

Eva told me recently she was "anal," as she described receiving a superb evaluation. "Anal?" I asked. "How about describing yourself as having developed a great attention to detail?" She jerked back and then smiled as the thought set in.

So often we give away our strengths. Instead of owning them, we do the opposite and try to get others to not notice them, or to see them as the opposite of what they are. And we do this so subtly that we may not even be aware that we are doing so. Over time we may lose conscious contact with these fundamental parts of who we are. The way to counteract this is to begin to claim your strengths.

Describe Yourself . . . Differently. As verbal as women tend to be, it is sometimes a challenge for women to find the right words to describe themselves. A friend of mine who was heavier than she is now (and not feeling particularly good about herself) was shocked when one of her sons gave her the movie *Real Women Have Curves* as a Christmas present. She was shocked. "Curves? Overweight, yes, but curves? Curves almost sound positive."

She took the real gift her son gave her—a different way to look at herself—and she began to see herself as curvaceous. At first she played with this idea of being *curvy*, then she embraced it. She liked it. It fit her. For the New Year's Eve party she hosted, she bought a low-cut blouse and a pair of form-fitting pants that showed off her *curves*. Later she shared with me over coffee, "That word set my whole world on end. It opened the door that I ran through."

Become Your Own Heroine. "Big breasts, hot pants, and a gun in your hands aren't what makes you a heroine," said Sigourney Weaver. Look to your own heroism. What odds have you defied? What strengths are uniquely yours? Others notice these amazing things, so why not you?

New Definitions of Who You Are

Sometimes we hear others describe us in ways that seem a little alien to us. Good, in a nice way, but strange, as in unfamiliar. We may have a tendency to push that comment away, almost as if we're afraid it will get too close and tempt us; yet we're more likely to hold on to a random negative comment and try to figure out what it is saying about us.

The reason we do this is because we often don't fully understand ourselves. After all, we live inside ourselves. Everything makes sense, more or less, especially with our *girly thoughts* there to provide instant rationale. We take the person we are for granted. It is often a challenge to see something that may be an everyday accomplishment for us as something extraordinary. This is a struggle that those who have stellar resilience frequently find themselves in. What others see as remarkable is just another coping skill for them. But that doesn't make their skills any less stunning.

Gianna is a woman with stellar resilience. She grew up in East Texas as the oldest of five children. She was happy when she was accepted into the National Guard; she had recently married and life felt good.

Three years later, Gianna was separated and was in a contentious custody battle for her toddler. Her husband was as rigid in the custody arrangements as he had been in their marriage. The judge was not at all supportive about her need to juggle weekends due to her guard duty; Gianna felt the judge believed that women should not be in the Guard and perhaps shouldn't work at all. But Gianna was about to be deployed, and she was determined to make it all work.

Because Gianna kept sharing with her fellow Guardsmen that she felt blessed and was sure there was a way that this would all work out, she earned the nickname "Miss Sunshine," and this was something novel for her. It seemed the others liked being around her because she was so optimistic—this was also new for her. She tried to tell a friend that her optimism was just something that motherhood gave her, but her friend countered with, "I didn't get that from motherhood. I worried myself sick about deployment."

So when someone comments on something positive they see in you, consider it. It may be something that you can add to your conscious repertoire of strengths.

Your Resilience Journal:
Stepping into Your Strengths

It is important to develop a language that you are comfortable with, to assert yourself while setting limits. But claiming our strengths is more difficult without a vocabulary for our strengths. We need to have a way of naming and thus claiming these important qualities we have.

In your journal, make a list of the words that best describe your strengths. Take your time with this.

Make your list following these steps, and, remember, there is no hurry—you can compile this list in your own time:

- See what comes naturally without prompting, and don't do any editing yet—just write everything you can think of. If you need help, go to my *Strength Thesaurus* online (at http://patriciaogorman.com), but note the new ones you found there by putting a star next to them.

- Now group your strengths to see which ones you use in which areas of your life.

- Next, challenge yourself to see what you've missed. Are there certain areas of your life that you have considered your strengths, but not others? For example, is it easier to focus on your strengths at work, but not in your marriage? With your children, but not your friends? On your intellect, but not on your looks?

Have some fun with this, and use this exercise to try on some new ways of describing yourself; like trying on a new style of pants, try some new adjectives that describe you, and see how they feel. This is an important thing to do, as next we will address how to rethink your body in a more positive light.

Fighting Our *Girly Thoughts*: Accepting Our Bodies

No truer *fighting* words have ever been said for many women than the notion that they should accept their bodies. If there is one place that our *girly thoughts* reside, it is in how we see ourselves. We have been socialized by our western society to measure our desirability, our self-worth as women by our perceived attractiveness (Tiggemann and Williams 2012). This represents a very real challenge for many women; they struggle not to internalize how they are seen (Fredrickson and Roberts 1997), and not take to heart comments from people they may not particularly respect.

Judgmental looks and comments impact the developing child and adolescent. Some women grow up feeling repeatedly violated by the responses they encounter, and this can lead to feelings of shame. Others try to make sense of the sexual responses they elicit and the feelings these responses spark in others by exploring their sexuality earlier than perhaps they are ready for emotionally. Some adolescents and adults realize that their sexuality could be a source of power and begin to exploit this important part of themselves. Whatever the emotional response, the cumulative effect of such responses leads women to move away from internal validation and become more dependent on how others see them.

"I remember walking a really circuitous route to the subway, as I didn't want to pass any construction sites and get all the catcalls. I hated those guys," Jackie recalls, "and yet they affected how I'd feel about myself all day. Their comments about my boobs, or my tight ass, just made me want to run home and shower and dress really differently, like in lots of layers, no matter how hot it was."

Learning to accept our bodies, feeling delight in what our bodies can do, not just how they look, becomes more important to women with each generation. This need may help explain why recently so many women are becoming involved in yoga, or walking daily. Because when we do get in touch with our physical selves, this can offer new information about who we are and how we operate, creating not only ways for us to take care of ourselves but also opening up new areas that we can explore using our resilience—marathon training, anyone?

Accepting Your Body
Means Accepting Your Weight

Numbers vary widely about *how* dissatisfied we are with our bodies. But one thing is certain: we begin to stress about our bodies early in life, and we continue for many years after that. According to a study of how women see their bodies reported by Dr. Carolyn C. Ross, currently 80 percent of women in the United States are dissatisfied with their appearance (2012). Quite frankly, when you have that many people doing or feeling anything, you have defined a "new" normal. So why is it "normal" for women to feel that their body size is abnormal and undesirable? And more than 10 million of these women suffer from eating disorders; this is a staggering number! In Chapter 1, we spoke about how the unattainable *ideal* is held up as a goal for all of us to follow, and the impact of this attitude is just now being understood.

In 2009, *Glamour* magazine conducted a twenty-five-year follow-up to a study completed in 1987 on how women feel about their bodies. Sadly, more than 40 percent of the respondents still feel dissatisfied with their bodies; this number is virtually unchanged from twenty-five years ago. The good news is that women are developing some resilient strategies for dealing with this major issue, even if the end results haven't changed much. Women may still feel dissatisfaction, but today they see themselves as more than just striving to achieve the perfect body.

As we examine these ideas, let's first begin by looking at what we're not doing. Significantly fewer women are using diet pills today than in the past; significantly fewer women are starving or purging themselves. From this we can draw the conclusion that we are being less mean to ourselves than in the past, and we are looking to other areas to gain confidence and self-esteem rather than just relying upon body ideal. While we may still be dissatisfied with our bodies, we are becoming more satisfied with other parts of our lives.

There are several areas that women are using today to increase their self-esteem:

- **Work.** Professional achievements help women feel better about themselves.
- **Exercise.** Chemicals (endorphins) from cardio exercise produce a feeling of well-being, as do the meditative aspects of

yoga. The benefit is there even if your dress size doesn't go down.

- **Sex.** Being sexual helps you feel better about your body by literally getting you in touch with yourself and by the powerful hormones released during orgasm (Lee et al. 2009). Women are becoming freer in discussing, and exploring, this most private part of who they are.
- **Healthy eating.** The focus women had on food restriction is being replaced by one on healthy eating.
- **Compliments.** Women value being seen by other women in a way that makes them feel more admired.

Research shows that our dissatisfaction with our weight begins early in life. It is not unusual for girls in elementary school to be concerned about their weight (Smolak, Levine, and Striegel-Moore 1996). By adolescence, this concern is in full swing (Barker and Galambos 2003). And this is not just a problem in the United States. A recent study of twenty-four countries from all around the world found that body-weight dissatisfaction was higher in girls than boys and was (interestingly) correlated with an inability of girls to speak to their mothers about their concerns. A study about body-weight dissatisfaction and a teen's communication with her parents, by researchers Haleama Al Sabbah and associates, emphasizes the importance of female traditions in the shaping of *girly thoughts* (Al Sabbah, Vereecken, Elgar et al. 2009).

Making Friends with Menopause

Menopause?#! Yes, growing older does present us with a new array of challenges. And as many of us know, our *girly thoughts* are not just the product of our youth. They continue with us throughout our lifetime. Our *girly thoughts* are one of the reasons why women have such difficulty aging and are spoken of (somewhat disparagingly) as *clinging to their youth.*

We live in a youth-oriented culture where we continue to judge ourselves against the cultural standard (meaning young and attractive), and as oppressive as that standard is when we are young, it is much more elusive as we age. But does this dissuade us? Well, perhaps some of us wake up, but many women keep chasing the ideal and end up feeling less and less attractive.

At menopause, many women experience some depression, and not all of it is hormonal. For many women this life transition signifies the end of an *identity* as a woman, for they can no longer bear children. And our western society does not have a new identity for women to transition into, like Native American cultures do where women become elders. A woman, no longer young, no longer able to birth a child, perhaps heading toward retirement and the end of her identity as a productive worker, needs to create a new identity. And here even our *girly thoughts* do not offer much guidance, which may be a blessing. As Germaine Greer points out in her book *The Change: Women, Aging and the Menopause,* "A grown woman should not have to masquerade as a girl in order to remain in the land of the living" (1993).

No wonder humorist Erma Bombeck offered, "Menopause will be good for you. It will take your mind off your problems" (1979), because as we age, menopause is just one of the many challenges we face. And yet the debunking of many of the myths surrounding menopause do not seem to be reaching women. Research has shown, for example, that a woman can continue to lead a satisfying sexual life if she has a partner she is connected to emotionally (Wise et al. 2001). This research reinforced a study done in 2007 of more than 3,000 fifty-seven- to seventy-five-year-olds that found a satisfying sex life can continue for as long as one desires; both studies emphasize the importance for women of not just hormones but of an emotional connection.

Menopause is a time to take stock of one's life. It is a time to acquire serenity and personal power. To achieve this, we need to begin to shift our focus from so much energy focused upon our body as a key component of our identity to an understanding of our soul. It is in middle age that we move from a reproductive being to a reflective being and truly begin to relish our resilience and all that it has taught us.

As they age, some women actually feel freed from the pressure of society to focus so very much on their looks, and they speak about challenging those *girly thoughts*. Psychologist Susan Nolen-Hoeksema of Yale reported on research that shows that women in menopause had a more positive body image, felt less lonely, were more satisfied in life, and had increased marital satisfaction (2010).

Why We Don't Confront

With all of this evidence about the unfairness of how women are portrayed in the media, it is amazing we do not have the equivalent of the *Arab Spring* or the *Occupy Wall Street* movements. But that is not what we find happening. Women tend to be very economical in their decision-making about whether or not to confront discrimination of others or of themselves. Researchers Good, Moss-Racusin, and Sanchez found that women tend to weigh perceived costs of such actions against the perceived benefits (2012). What makes a difference for women is if they feel optimistic about the results of their actions; that is, whether they feel empowered and believe their action will produce the result they desire. If they do, they are more easily able to overcome perceived risks of anxiety and creating displeasure in the other, and push forward and confront what is making them or another feel uncomfortable. But if they don't feel that confrontation will make a difference, they are more likely to appear outwardly to accept or try to ignore the discrimination. How they feel inside is a different story.

Germaine Greer has a different take on our silence. In her book on menopause, *The Change*, Greer speaks to the need for women, particularly as they age, to *tell their story*, to share their strength, their wisdom, and not to keep silent because we all need role models. She points out that there are few voices for older women and reflects that our feelings about aging will only happen as women tell their own stories through novels, biographies, and blogs, and not just to each other (1993).

Your Resilience Journal: Our Bodies, Our Selves

In your journal, describe how you think you hold your body, both literally and figuratively. Jot down your thoughts about this major part of who you are. If you're artistic, you can even sketch yourself.

Now think about what you can say to yourself or do when you are feeling uncomfortable with your body. Get in touch with your body through:

- Exercise, even if it is limited.
- Make or buy healthy foods that you like to eat.
- Taking time to pick out clothes and colors that work for you.
- Be sexually active.
- Give yourself a compliment. Write it in your journal as an affirmation.
- Put on some music and dancing. Do it! Feel it! And then write about it.
- Sing a favorite song. Sing away! Feel those words inside. And then describe what happened: Did the dog howl along? Did the birds sing, too? Did you keep humming the same tune for days?

Take action about how you feel about your body:

- Put up favorite pictures of yourself at different ages around your home. Even post some on Facebook or Instagram; celebrate yourself at the different seasons of your life.
- Speak to a friend about how she handles her body-image issues and share yours with her. After your conversation, write about how you felt after the conversation.
- Vent your anger. Write a letter to an advertiser whose ad utilizing a woman is just ridiculous.

Playing with Boundaries

Boundaries do not have to be rigid. We can explore moving them, even playing with them. We can be creative in how we exercise our power to change this part of our lives, and we can do that by setting up *helpful* boundaries that are good for us. This tends to be an area where many women struggle. Yes, we are very aware of what is good for others, what they need, how they feel, the pressure they are under, but what is good for us, helpful for us? And I say *helpful* and not *healthy*, because we need to focus on aligning our actions as being helpful in serving our needs, our desires. So it would be a good idea to ask ourselves what is helpful for us to do, or to think, to see ourselves as taking care of who we are. *Healthy*, I find, is often seen by women as a value judgment. Something is healthy or it is not, but *helpful* is more gray, more nuanced, drawing more upon the subtler aspects of our coming to know ourselves as we search for how to give to ourselves, even in the midst of caring for others.

Boundaries with Family—Challenging Toxic Loyalty

Most of us feel bound to our families. We feel the connections, we know the stories, we are well aware of the conflicts. Some wise person once said: "Families: Can't live with them, can't live without them." We learn much about how to be strong in the world through our families, and we also learn so much about how not to approach things, about what is wrong in life, from our families.

Loving families allow us to take the best and leave the rest. Families with considerable trauma aren't always so able to be generous. This can be a trap for the resilient child. For in order to be resilient, a child needs to learn to be adaptable, to find a way to ride some rough waves while still staying connected to those she loves. And a hallmark of a family in trouble is that it often cannot be very flexible, and it relies on fewer and fewer solutions to solving the challenges it faces. Loyalty to a family that is not functioning very well creates a conflict, particularly for the resilient child who is beginning to develop skills beyond those shown by her family.

How does the developing child, and later the adult, stay connected to the family she loves as she grows beyond them and their solutions to life's challenges? Growing beyond one's family often results in at least a transitional period of feeling lonely, rejected, perhaps angry, and grieving the loss of these close bonds. But this is a normal development. A resilient adult needs to move beyond those ways of functioning that were modeled by her challenging family. But when an adult cannot do this, we speak about *toxic* loyalty, which is loyalty that is hampering the adult developing her resilience.

Kim, a woman who used her resilience paradoxically, always felt torn between how she should act at home and how she should act with her mother and her aunt, who lived together in a poor urban area. When Kim visited at their home, or took them to their various medical appointments, she was meek, very quiet, and confused. At work, and with her husband and two children, she was no-nonsense, loving but tough.

> I think my life has forced me into this. In college I was date-raped as a virgin, and of course I became pregnant. I wanted to talk to my mother about how to handle my pregnancy, but anytime I came near to bringing it up, she'd look terrified. So I had an abortion, alone. I began to realize that she needed me more than I needed her. And that continues today.

As Kim's life became more stressful, she began to not want to visit her mother and aunt. But she felt she had to make sure they were safe, so she would make the journey, even if it meant her own life was put on hold. Many times, she skipped having dinner, would need to stay up all night to meet a work deadline, or she'd miss one of her children's games or concerts. Her concern for her mother and aunt began to eat at her. And her husband and children became increasingly stressed whenever they visited her family because she would act so "weird," so not like herself, both during the visit and after they left.

Kim was loyal to staying in the role of the dutiful daughter, which caused her significant stress in her life. Eventually she realized such loyalty was toxic to her own well-being and increasingly toxic to her family's, and it was eroding her feeling of sanity in her life. "I just can't be doing whatever they want and then kick ass in my job. I'm operating like I'm two different people." She began to put some limits on her availability.

Boundaries at Work: Bosses and Peers

It is important to have your resilient self in charge at work. And most women do, most of the time, until they become upset and turn to their peers. For many women, this is a variation of looking for love in all the wrong places. They are looking to be taken care of, to be understood, yet end up feeling like they've been stabbed in the back by someone they have to compete with, give direction to, and work with the next day.

What happens? There is so much pressure on women today—to establish a career, to have a family, to work out—that time for friends is at a premium. And as women, we really need our friends!

As a result, many women see their work peers as friends, often confusing two very different relationships. And then when there is work conflict (as there will be at any job), over a difference of opinion, between who is doing more, who is doing less, who is the favorite, who is more competent, the "friendship" is put on the line.

When this situation occurs, many women then feel compromised, because, as their *friend*, their coworker knows a great deal of personal information about them, which they hope will be kept in confidence. When it is not . . . well, then, feeling betrayed is not uncommon.

Sometimes women compound this by treating their boss as someone who is a variation on the loving parent—maybe the loving parent they had, or maybe the one they wished they had. This leads them to approach their supervisor not as the strong resilient women they are, but more like someone who is asking a parent for a favor or a special treat. These women lead with their inner child as opposed to their adult, as we explored in Assessment 4 (see page 119). A cue that you may be doing this is if you feel something akin to rage when your supervisor doesn't approve your request, whether this is for time off, the need to switch a project, or to move your workstation.

I recently recommended to Trina, a woman with stellar resilience who I saw clinically, that she consider working less than full-time at her primary job, if possible. She was quick, smart, and actually was able to do her job in much less than the allocated hours. But she had been having a number of workplace dramas: an affair with a married coworker that some of her *friends* at work knew about and conflict with her supervisor, who she considered stupid. And she was outspoken about decisions within the department, so much so that she had gone on several occasions to the supervisor of her supervisor's supervisor.

But this was Trina's "bread and butter" job; her passion was in being an artist. She was beginning to sell, and she had a big show looming; the stress was getting to her. Between her job and her passion, she was working around the clock and becoming ill. She thought working less than full-time was a great idea and announced that she was going to ask her supervisor about it the next day.

"No!" I almost shouted. Trina looked surprised.

"What's your plan?" I asked.

"Plan?"

"Yes, your plan. You need to figure out if this is a good idea for you, if you can afford it, what the ramifications are for your pension, for time off. You need to consider all this before you go to your boss. She's not there to necessarily protect you; she's there to run the department. You don't want your suggestion to play into her agenda, whatever it is, before you have thought it through. You need a clear plan about what is best for you."

"Oops," Trina said, "guess I had my inner child in charge again. She just wanted this over. And she'd be really angry if this didn't work out." With that, Trina smiled as she started speaking from her resilient self. "Okay, I'll make a plan and figure out what it is I need."

Summary

Consciously challenging our *girly thoughts,* as opposed to being exhausted by them, is an important step in our development of conscious resilience. And challenging our *girly thoughts* is a vital part of embracing our life's complexities and our transitions. One way we can effectively challenge our *girly thoughts* is to set helpful boundaries on everything, from dealing with our looks (particularly our weight), to realizing that menopause is just one of the many natural transitions we have already mastered. Developing boundaries that support us can be a freeing way to develop our resilience, allowing us to experiment, and to even play with, what works for us and what does not.

For more on techniques for challenging *girly thoughts*, visit http://patriciaogorman.com.

TEN

Step Four—Protect Your Heart: Love Resiliently

I HAVE YET TO HEAR A MAN ASK FOR ADVICE ON HOW
TO COMBINE MARRIAGE AND A CAREER. . . .

—Gloria Steinem

So much of life is about how we connect to others. The poet Rainer Maria Rilke described love as the embracing of two solitudes. This means two whole beings who come together but do not lose who they are individually. This is the opposite of loving codependently, which is loving another instead of loving yourself. Ideally, in loving another we continue to love ourselves. We do not give everything to the other, and, even while we care deeply for our partner, we keep some of our energy, our caring, and our desires centered on ourselves. This is balanced love.

The sustainability of love depends upon our ability to achieve this balance between independence—our wholeness—and vulnerability—

our willingness to embrace. As we have seen, this is what resilience is all about, the balance of self-regard and regard for others. We need to decide how much of ourselves to yield in a relationship and how much to retain, how much to give and how much to ask that others give us. And this is a dynamic equation that changes according to our needs and wants.

Using Resilience to Find Love

This may sound a little like a puzzle, but how can we use our strengths to find someone who is safe to be vulnerable with? Someone who will elicit and return our deep feelings of tender affection and connection, someone with whom we have a desire to be with and for whom we have a passionate attraction? The answer is that it actually becomes easier to find someone who will fit when we lead with our strengths, focus on what is right for us, what it is we need in another, what it is we can offer, and how we deserve to be treated. And yes, that does mean there will be many who don't fit. But isn't it easier to understand who isn't right rather than picking a partner with the hope that he or she will change?

How often have we heard family or friends speaking about molding or shaping their men, only to become disappointed when the man decides he has an opinion about that? How often have we heard from women that they "can make it work," yet we see the stress and strain this is creating for them? And be truthful: have you ever seen this and asked yourself, *How she could think this is love?*

Women sometimes choose a partner for reasons other than love, even though they may not be clear about this within themselves. I hear from many women that they don't want to be alone, and so they pick someone, sometimes quickly, and hope they can make it work.

So in speaking about love we need to understand some basics of what drives us to connect with another, and picking someone because you don't want to be alone is often a reason that women come to regret.

There is a great difference between aloneness, loneliness, and love. Being alone is just that: You are without another. Some women find they enjoy their alone time; after all, if they know themselves, then they know how to entertain themselves. Remember you are the only person you will spend your whole life with, which is why learning to feel comfortable with *you* is so very important. Being lonely is different; this is a need for another person. This is a longing for companionship. Loneliness can lead to isolation, and, for those with a trauma history, it can trigger memories of rejection. But loneliness can be resolved through having friends, a pet, peers at work, or volunteer activities. Resolving your loneliness through deciding to partner with someone, or even deciding that you love someone, is a rather radical decision, one in which you are giving a certain amount of power over to the other. If that other person decides to create more distance between you . . . well . . . remember, again, what the poet Ranier Maria Rilke said: "Love consists in this, that two solitudes protect and touch and greet each other." To love we must be whole. We must love ourselves in order to truly love another. It is unfair to ask someone to compensate for parts of ourselves that we struggle with. It is unfair to ourselves. This is our work.

This is not to say that we should pick someone who is a "perfect match" for us. Hopefully we will change, as will our partner, so again our flexibility, our resilience, needs to be in play with our decisions, for we each need someone with whom we can grow and with whom we can negotiate. A relationship and love are not always smooth sailing. But neither is a relationship, or love, just about work. Yes, there are things to negotiate, compromises we must live with, but this should only be around those issues that you are comfortable in compromising. A good relationship is about balance. The important question is, are we getting enough to offset what we need to give? And answering this question just for the present is not enough. Any of us can go through a challenging time of needing more, or of more being required of us. The answer to this question is, overall, how are you being cared for? Because in a fundamental way, in a good relationship, your needs—from emotional, to financial, to sexual, and others—are taken care of. For a relationship to last, we need to be satisfied; our partner's satisfaction isn't everything. Some women feel this approach is selfish, as if they shouldn't have a self in play in this decision-making about love; they feel that somehow love is all emotion. Yes, emotion is a part, a big part, but not the whole, as we will see.

Your Resilience Journal:
Are You Using Your Resilience to Find Love?

Find the time to take out your journal and ask yourself the following questions. Leave space between your answers, as you'll want to go back and further elaborate on these:

- Do you feel you love your partner, and that you are loved in return?
- Do you both understand your relationship in a similar way? For example, is this a committed relationship, an exclusive one?

- Have you used your resilience voice to articulate your needs in your present relationship? Are your needs being met?
- Have you picked someone you can grow with? Do you dream together? Do you have the same goals? For example, is marriage a goal for both of you?

If you answer yes to these questions, then you are using your resilience to inform your feelings about your loved one. If you answer no to many or most of them, then there is a space between the two of you that you need to negotiate— and you must protect your heart as you do.

Or do you:

- pick a partner because you think you can shape him or her and make the relationship work;
- compromise in the hope that you will get what you want or need because you are a *good girl*;
- fear voicing your needs or concerns because they will be rejected or not understood; and
- spend lots of time in the dreams of the future because the present is too painful?

If you answer yes to these questions, then you need to begin to use your resiliency in your relationship and face what is really occurring between you and the one you love; right now you are reacting to what you wish was happening.

Love and Resilience Styles

Jean was startled by the sense of excitement and well-being she felt as she contemplated living alone for the first time in seven years.

> By letting Mark take care of me, I allowed myself to be held hostage to his whims without realizing it. I lost myself. Once I planned to leave, I began to feel alive again. I realized I had been so tense trying to hold onto something that was not real. Now I had to take care of myself instead of depending on someone else to do this for me. Framing the situation this way, I suddenly began to feel strong enough to do it.

Many women with underdeveloped resilience experience a similar dilemma when they fall in love. Like Jean, they tend to be reluctant to take charge of their lives. They look for relationships that will provide them a sense of definition, seeking fulfillment from their partner. When we consider ourselves to be someone's "other half," we can never feel whole.

Women of underdeveloped resilience often enjoy traditional roles as the loyal helpmate of their partner, continuing their childhood pattern of turning power over to others. To correct this, they need to begin to listen to their own resilient voice, as quiet as it may be, to develop their own self-definition and self-worth. Doing this allows them to begin to both see and believe in their power and ability to decode their own needs.

A woman with balanced resilience, by contrast, who is already adept at recognizing both her strengths and neediness, will be better able to ride the ebb and flow of relationships. She knows that finding what she really wants may require her to take chances and that she has the resilience to risk being vulnerable. More than women of other resilience patterns, she is liable to be successful at the give-and-take relationships require. She tends to have the wisdom to look for love in places where it is likely to be fulfilled, while also understanding the need to care for herself. When women are balanced in love, it is often due to tuning into their own needs and giving their needs a voice—in short, using their resilience to care for themselves in this vulnerable aspect of life.

Women of self-contained resilience styles frequently spend so much time and energy on their careers that they may believe they have no time for relationships. That is their excuse, at any rate. It is more often true that they experience inner conflicts in relationships and so minimize the role intimate relationships play in their lives. Just as they used their competence to shield their vulnerability in childhood and to survive difficult circumstances, now they continue to distance themselves from the vulnerability of deep relationships.

Women of self-contained resilience can benefit from the recognition that risk-taking and mastery are part of who they are, and that they can draw on these qualities in all areas of their lives. This appreciation of their strengths may allow them to use this skill on their own behalf in risking intimacy.

Moriah was a successful insurance adjuster who worked at the same agency as her husband. In many ways they had the perfect relationship, as each fully supported the other's career. Sometimes this meant that they lived in different cities for months at a time, seeing each other only on weekends. This carefully maintained balance was upset when Moriah realized she was pregnant. She came to counseling to work out her feelings about the situation.

I have always wanted children at some point in my life, but this has always been an abstract desire. I'm not ready to be a mother. And it's not only the idea that I would have to take on such a new and foreign role, but that I would need to depend on Stan in so many new ways. That is the terrifying part for me. Stan and I are companions, good friends, but always independent of each other. A child would change all this.

This, she said, was the reason she was planning to arrange an abortion. The difficulty was that her pregnancy had made her very aware of how much she wanted to have a child.

We talked about her fear and about the other times she had been afraid of important changes in her life. "How did you deal with those?" I asked.

"Sheer moxie," Moriah said, smiling proudly. "I've taken risks all my life. The more afraid I was, the more determined I was to see it through."

"And now?"

"I guess I'm terrified enough to talk to Stan about having the baby and what I'll need from him."

As it turned out, Moriah was amazed at her husband's response. Later she reported, "Stan said he would support my motherhood as strongly as he had supported my career. And he's been true to his word. We became even closer during my pregnancy. We began sharing the more personal sphere of hopes and fantasies that there never seemed time or reason to share before. And since our baby was born, we've become closer in ways I never thought was possible."

Women who have stellar resilience also have trouble letting down their guard. It is hard for them to believe that love can be different from what they experienced as a child. They have been betrayed before and have learned that trust is not to be given lightly. For this reason, a woman with stellar resilience may unwittingly test anyone who proclaims love for her. This testing can take many forms, from distancing to see if he comes after her, to accusations of infidelity, to hurling charges that her partner doesn't truly love her, taunting the partner to prove it.

Brittany had a difficult time feeling loved, so she kept setting up situations for her husband to prove his feelings.

Somehow I've always had difficulty believing that someone could love me, even though I love him. So I'm always looking for ways to judge my partner's love. It's no surprise that Roger and I had problems, all of which I seemed to blame on myself.

The worst is that Roger travels extensively on business. I feel so rejected by his not being home. I get so lonely I spend time with my friends in clubs, meeting guys, dancing. Not hooking up, just having some fun. But I still feel empty. He comes home and we argue.

The last fight we had, Roger yelled, "You won't *let* me love you!" Something clicked when he said this. I realized he was right. I was afraid to let him love me. Instead of looking for his love, I kept searching for his rejection. It's started some fundamental changes in the way I understand our relationship, and my reactions in particular.

When they love, women like Brittany need to learn to use their resilience to give them the guidance and the courage to love without the expectation of pain. In doing this, they will be able to trust intimacy enough to allow others to get closer to them, reminding themselves that they are resilient; they can take care of themselves. Learning to love themselves while they love another is another step in their already defined path of growth.

Paradoxically resilient women are unable to achieve a balance between their vulnerability and their strengths. They may section off their ability to love, keeping it apart from their self-identity; if so, they will fail to derive satisfaction and personal meaning from it, perhaps seeing it as more sacrifice than nurturing. Or they may feel very confident in their ability to love another but not in their own lovability. These women need to learn to embrace the two halves of loving—the giving and receiving—and trust that they can learn to do both. Here an inner dialogue can help to remind them of their many different needs and abilities, including their ability to take a risk, and help them achieve a better balance in their resilience.

Women of overwhelmed resilience will tend to carry on a tradition of the unhappy love experienced as children. These women have learned that love involves pain and that being in love may involve rejection, abandonment, humiliation, and the intensity of "making up." They need to learn how to love and give while protecting themselves and risking only what they can afford to lose.

And women whose resilience has been very overwhelmed by recent crises need the reassurance of loved ones that they are cared about as they seek to regain their balance in the aftermath of the tragedy they have experienced.

Falling in Lust

Lust is all about emotion. It can be a part of love, but it isn't the same as love. Sexual feelings evoke many complex and deep emotions that we may not even be aware of. They may be based on beliefs taught years ago, such as "women do not enjoy sex," or "having sexual relations outside the context of a long-term (if not lifelong) relationship is wrong." These beliefs may be at odds with the times in which we live or our values in other areas of life. In today's atmosphere of sexual freedom, we may find it difficult to know how to recognize what we want, or how to ask for it once we do. More important, we may feel shy or may not know how to speak up about issues of safety in intimate relationships.

Despite the so-called sexual revolution, many women have difficulty in relationships because they have been taught that it is wrong for a woman to have strong sexual feelings. While strong feelings of affection are permissible, strong sexual feelings are not—even in marriage. To compensate for this, some women decide that they are in love when all they have is a strong physical attraction to another. This confusion is compounded by the hormones released during sex that can lead to a woman feeling emotionally bonded to her partner (Lee et al. 2009).

Marissa was telling her brother excitedly about the new love of her life. He responded by asking her a devastating question: "When *haven't* you been in love with the person you're dating?" Marissa was surprised.

> I realized I didn't have a good answer for him. I usually feel that I'm in love with whomever I'm seeing. I could say I always pick winners who are easy to love, but I know this is not true. The truth is, I feel so empty inside that I need someone to fill me up. I do this through sex. And I convince myself that I'm in love with whomever I'm dating, so it's okay. I know I'm not committed to them.

When we don't understand our sexual feelings, we may seek satisfaction in self-defeating ways. Consider the situation of two women competing for the same man. Both may try to bed him, avowing their commitment and love to him, while he remains detached and seemingly ambivalent about whom he prefers. Yet if either woman could step outside the situation for a moment, she might wonder whether someone so unavailable is truly desirable. If honest, she might admit that it is the quest that excites her and not the man.

Other women feel they must block off their feelings if they are to adhere to societal and familial norms and mores. They may suppress their sexuality or seek to be punished or hurt because of it. They may unconsciously seek out partners who are judgmental of their sexual needs or uninterested in them sexually.

Ginger's husband would withdraw whenever she initiated any sexual activity, whether kissing or lovemaking. "It was devastating for me," said Ginger. "I needed sex. And just when it seemed that we would make love, Max would close down and turn away. I would be left hanging, and so I'd masturbate. But that felt empty."

Still others seek only to pleasure their partner without receiving pleasure themselves. They deny this part of themselves. Mandy found receiving pleasure difficult and married someone who had difficulty in encouraging her sexually.

"Our sex life is perfunctory," she said. "Somehow we've managed to have three children, but sex doesn't mean much to me."

Your sexual self is an integral part of who you are. Use your inner voice to discover and keep up a dialogue about this very important part of you. The more you know about yourself sexually, the more you will be able to share with your partner and the more enjoyable your sexual encounters will be. You deserve this. Claim your sexuality by becoming friendlier with this part of you.

Audrey, whose resilience was underdeveloped as a child, found that taking responsibility for herself as a sexual adult allowed her to grow.

I had been brought up in a very traditional and religious family. I somehow always felt that life for me would be just the same as for my mother.

Then I graduated from college and found myself living away from home in a strange city. I'd meet men who were attractive, but I didn't have a clue how to date. I didn't have my church or my family to give me guidelines, only myself. So I became the resident expert on what I needed. I learned to trust myself, and most of all to listen to what my impulses were telling me was right. So after dating men, I realized that I was attracted to women. The added benefit is that I can be very clear with my partner about all aspects of our relationship, including sex. She appreciates this and has learned to respond in kind. I think it's made the relationship much stronger.

Keeping Sex Safe

Being safe while being sexual is a major challenge today. It requires women to be assertive and to take responsibility for their own well-being. This means learning to do things that would have been considered unnecessary a few years ago, such as carrying condoms or using vaginal condoms to protect themselves from both unwanted pregnancy and sexually transmitted diseases. Being safe also means learning to insist that a potential lover take HIV and STD tests before the relationship becomes sexual. This requires planning and alters the level of spontaneity in the relationship. These steps are difficult for some women to take, particularly if they have trouble speaking up or if they have abdicated most of their power to their partner. But making a decision to keep yourself safe is so very important and is a concrete indication of your resilience.

Your Resilience Journal: Speaking Up

Think about how to use your resilient voice to speak up for yourself and to make your concerns known, particularly in terms of what will protect you from unsafe sex. Think about how you use your resilience in your life to keep you safe. When you are ready, take out your journal. Be sure to leave space after each response so you can go back later and add to your responses. If this is difficult at first, consider using your journal to rehearse broaching difficult topics, such as requesting that your partner use a condom every time you have intercourse. Here are some techniques that might be helpful.

- Try writing out what you would like to say. When you are comfortable with the words, you can send your partner a note or text, saying you want to talk, but please don't post the details on Facebook!
- Practice talking into a recorder to hear your voice acknowledging what it is you need from your partner.
- Talk to friends about how they discuss sexual subjects with their partners. Note which points would be helpful for you.

- Talk to your partner and write down what happens.
  Remember to try to fight your awkwardness, embar-
  rassment, or annoyance, and find the words that
  convey your feelings.

Find the method that works for you, and use it until you
are more comfortable. Realize that you are entitled to bring
up the topic of safe sex more than once. Your life depends
on it.

Protecting Yourself in Love and Lust

Anita always came back glowing from her regional sales meetings. She would inevitably find the perfect man, a star-crossed lover
who was perfectly suited for her but who, tragically, was married to
someone else. The affair would begin intensely and then gradually
wind down as some tragic flaw was discovered, such as the fact that
his wife was pregnant, or that he was also seeing someone else.

I'm compulsive about everything else, why not how I fall in
love? Maybe I'm just an intensity junkie.

But something is changing. Just this last trip I heard myself
thinking, *I'm getting too old for this. I need to settle down and
find a man that's real—read available.*

In the past I used to hear a voice saying, "Take what you can
get. You can cultivate your garden later. You're in a hurry now."
For the last ten years, this has been fine. But this time, I realized, now *is* later. I'm almost thirty-five and haven't had a serious
relationship with an available partner since leaving college.

I recognized my father's voice as the one telling me I was in a hurry. In many ways I'm very much like him, the son he never had. I'm aggressive and take what I want. Like me, he was in sales, always making a deal, never home, always traveling.

Anita realized that this style of love was no longer satisfying to her. She wanted more from a relationship than just excitement and intensity, and her inner voice let her know that it was time for a change. But how was she supposed to change? Anita saw that she was afraid to make a commitment to a partner, something she had no problem doing in her career. "It's time to shift gears and bring some of my strengths to work for me in relationships," she said.

As we explored in Step 2, in the process of finding your own voice on the issue of love, you may hear other voices within you. You may hear a voice that says women are there to please their husband, or women can never love their mate as much as they love their children. There may be voices that state your inherent unlovability. Allowing yourself to hear and identify these different viewpoints allows you to move beyond them and no longer be trapped by self-defeating beliefs.

Setting Boundaries: When Love Hurts

While commitment can give us our wings by defining our hope for what our love relationship can give us, commitment alone does not prevent serious problems, such as those that occur in abusive relationships. Physically and verbally abusive relationships are often about power and control. Even average women can be swept up in this cycle when they begin to give their power to another. They begin to hear only the voice of their partner and tune out their own inner voice.

In a typical scenario, women are attracted to partners who sweep them off their feet. "Ed and I had a whirlwind courtship. He was the most romantic man I ever met," said Courtney.

So two weeks after we were married, when he beat me for changing the TV channel, I really thought I had done something wrong. Especially when he later apologized for it. But gradually the beatings came more often. I blamed myself. There was always a good reason, it seemed.

When I got a promotion that caused us to move, Ed took a cut in pay and blamed me for it. He became even more jealous and possessive. The beatings continued. Finally came the moment of truth. One morning I sat crying in the bathroom after an all-night battle. I caught a glimpse of myself; my face was red and contorted, a bruise forming on my chin. I said out loud to my reflection, "What in the world are you doing here?"

In that moment, I realized that I had been taking care of the relationship as if it was some third entity and not composed of just Ed and me, at the expense of my own well-being. Now it was time to begin taking care of myself. I found an apartment and told Ed I was going. I still see him on weekends so he won't get too angry, and I pay for his apartment. But I am finding the strength to separate and just take care of myself.

Whatever your resilience pattern, your own emerging voice contains an inner wisdom. It can help you decide when what you have is enough or too little, when you need protection, or when you can trust your partner enough to risk intimacy. In the end, your ability to love your partner and to build a fulfilling relationship will always depend on your ability to love yourself and maintain a healthy and fulfilling relationship with your resilient self.

Your Resilience Journal: Love and Resilience

If you and your partner are experiencing serious problems, don't avoid them or pretend they don't exist. Use your resilient voice to help you answer the following questions in your journal.

- What keeps you in the relationship? Are you more guided by love and commitment to your partner, or by fear of being on your own or fear of your partner?
- Have you grown in this relationship? Do you feel there is potential for you to continue to grow if you stay with your partner?
- If you are in a challenging space in your relationship, what has worked for you in the past? What do you need to do now?
- What is the nature of the compromises you have made or need to make to continue the relationship? Are they balanced against the quality and satisfaction you derive from the relationship?

Please note: If you are involved in an abusive relationship, seek professional help. Every year thousands of women suffer serious injury or death as a result of domestic violence. There are many organizations and therapists who specialize in domestic violence and can offer both emergency and long-term help. Nothing can be accomplished in a relationship as long as you are unsafe. For more information about domestic violence please go to http://patriciaogorman.com.

Summary

Being resilient in love is about allowing enough space around you to take care of your self, your needs, your sexual desires. It is not about codependency, which is just focusing on the person you love. Resilient love allows for both parties to have needs, and keeps self-love as a very worthy goal.

ELEVEN

Step Five—Become Strong in the Hurt Places: Heal Your Wounded Self

ROCK BOTTOM BECAME THE SOLID FOUNDATION
UPON WHICH I RE-BUILT MY LIFE.

—J. K. Rowlins

There are two main challenges to your developing resilience: your *girly thoughts,* which you come by honestly as a woman living in the western world, and your personal traumas in all of their forms, which can reinforce your tendency to develop a victim mentality. This step will focus on offering strategies for building strength at the points in which you are the most vulnerable when you have been really hurt.

When Anger Is a Friend:
Be *Angry* at Being Seen as a Victim

Let's face it: sometimes you do feel like a victim. You feel one down, without power, at the mercy of others . . . , yuck. This is a feeling we come by honestly, one wrought by the near impossible (that many women take as normal) set of tasks to be accomplished in their normal day. We were all raised to fairy tales of the helpless princess needing Prince Charming to rescue her; the depiction of women as vulnerable and in need of rescue was a major influence in our development of our *girly thoughts*.

In the classic book *The Cinderella Complex* (a book I still highly recommend), author Charlotte Dowling speaks to the price that women pay when they buy into this myth. The need to be rescued keeps women stuck and at risk of seeing circumstances as victimizing and disempowering them. The alternative, of course, is for women to see and exercise their own power—their resilience—to accomplish their personal goals in life, and use the injustices of life to fuel them to fight back, using their anger as a source of strength.

But to do this means addressing what has been a reality for many women: experiencing the many unfortunate circumstances in life that may have enraged them, even traumatized them, from bullying, to rape, to sexual abuse and sexual harassment, any of which left them feeling wounded and vulnerable. As a result of their trauma and its aftermath, they may feel like a victim, and trauma in the present has the ability to rekindle trauma of the past, resurrecting earlier painful memories.

Angela experienced this as she was trying to reestablish her life after a divorce.

I met one mother and she seemed fun. I thought maybe even we could go out together and look to meet some guys. Before I knew it, I was involved in her really messed up life and I was trying to help her. Fun she was not. Crazy maybe. But not fun. I'd actually leave her home crying sometimes, I'd be so upset. She was like so many of my friends in the past, takers, all into themselves, totally narcissistic, just like my mother. I couldn't take it any more.

Clearly, Angela's new friend was triggering her. She realized it and ended the so-called friendship. In doing this, she decided to no longer be the victim. "I realized that if I had the guts to end a marriage that wasn't working, I could start looking for new friends who would have my back occasionally."

Our resilience is based in part on overcoming the traumas in our life. It isn't as much about *what* we experienced as it is about how we *handle* the trauma that makes the difference. Riley, a beautiful, vibrant woman with balanced resilience, was twenty when she was diagnosed with cancer. By the time she was twenty-two, she'd lost one year of school and her fourth cancer site was found.

"I get angry when people feel sorry for me," she says. "I really don't need anyone's pity. And I'm not a victim. I'm a healthy young woman who has cancer! It's not that my cancer doesn't affect me. It does. I really don't like it. But I'm determined to finish my semester at school and not loose it again to the yucky C. And then I'll have my fourth operation."

Riley is determined to live a life—despite the fatigue, despite the recurrences in different parts of her body.

"I'm young, I'm dating, and I'm working part-time. I have goals, friends, and my family. I'm good!"

Your Resilience Journal: Your Trauma Legacy

In your journal, take some time to write about the ways trauma functions in your life. As you review your experience, journal the answers to these questions:

- What traumas have you experienced?
- How do you see yourself taking the lessons from your trauma and using them constructively in your life?
- How have you used your trauma to create your resilience?

For more information on the different forms of trauma go to http://patriciaogorman.com.

Reframing Your Negative Experiences— From Pain to Gain

Many women suffer shame or unresolved pain because of traumatic events in the past. We are reluctant to reexamine the memories of difficult or traumatic experiences because we know we will also recall the negative feelings and messages associated with them. When we focus on our resilience in surviving them, when we reframe these experiences and focus not just on the pain but what this pain has taught us and what we have gained, we can change these feelings and messages. This new perspective can help us to look at our experiences from the inside out as sources of strength and insight rather than vulnerability and shame. We have new options to explore.

Asli was a young woman who came to see me for depression. One session, she told me of the Thanksgiving when she was eleven. Her mother was a hidden alcoholic, as drinking was forbidden in her culture. Her parents had invited relatives over to celebrate this American tradition, but her mother was unable to prepare the holiday meal. Rather than have her mother face the recriminations of their visiting relatives, Asli took it upon herself to prepare a complete Thanksgiving dinner for her family. I was struck by the resourcefulness and courage of this feat.

The pain of this memory was evident as Asli recounted it. Yet rather than asking her about this aspect of the event, I asked, "How did you know how to cook a turkey and make stuffing at eleven years old?" Asli looked at me blankly.

I went on, "That took quite a bit of planning, skill, and perseverance. How did you know how to do it?"

She faintly smiled and said, "I guess I was pretty smart."

It was clear she had never considered this incident in such a way. In Asli's memory, the shame and fear that had motivated her at the time remained uppermost in her mind. The positive and worthy aspects of the event had been lost beneath these negative emotions.

As we talked about this incident, Asli realized that even at that early age she had possessed the wisdom to keep her family together and create a Thanksgiving dinner that corresponded to her image of what it should be. She had recognized her needs and learned the skills necessary to take care of herself and her family.

This opened up a new avenue of exploration for Asli. Without denying the hardship of her early experiences, she began to see the choices she had made that had brought her safely through those painful years.

"I'm beginning to see myself no longer as the victim of my childhood, but as a survivor, maybe even a thriver," said Asli. "For the first time, I recognize the strengths and abilities I have developed along the way."

Viewed from that perspective, this experience and others began to take on a new meaning for her. She saw the other choices she had made that had consistently brought her closer to what she needed, and she began to see the pattern of control she had unconsciously exerted on her life. Her sense of powerlessness, a major factor in her depression, no longer seemed overwhelming.

If we have come to see ourselves as victims who were damaged by the circumstances of our lives, recognizing our resilience can help us to see instead that we are survivors, and even that we learned to thrive amid the pain. Like Asli, we can use our resilience to review the past and see, perhaps for the first time, the unique blend of opportunity and challenge we experienced and the value we have made from it. For many of us, moving from being a victim to becoming the person we want to be involves learning to forgive ourselves. There may be many areas that we need to forgive ourselves in, but, in terms of identifying the sources of our resilience development, an important one is around our vulnerability. As women, we tend to have different vulnerabilities than men; most women are not as strong as men and, as a result, can be more easily overpowered physically. This is a fact of nature. And in love relationships, women tend to lead with their hearts. This is a common *learned* behavior, one where you can use your resilience to help protect your heart.

Your Resilience Journal: Understanding How You Make Sense of Negative Experiences

Recall one or more negative or traumatic experiences that you had. As you review your experiences, journal the answers to these questions:

- What traumas have you experienced?
- How did you respond to them?
- What messages did you take away concerning yourself?
- Were there *girly thoughts* or codependency involved?

Now look at this experience through your resilience. Let your resilient voice guide you as you answer these questions:

- How have you used your trauma to create your resilience? What did this experience teach you about yourself?
- Are you still using these lessons?
- If not, can you make them more conscious, so they can be more available to you?

Trauma Triggers

Life is full of moments that evoke the past. Sometimes these are positive memories, moments that bring back the promise of our youth or remind us of a favorite activity or food. Sometimes the memories are of unpleasant, perhaps even horrific, events. Trauma triggers are situations, events, or feelings that trigger a memory of previous trauma. Or the trigger may be the actions of another. We feel that we are being picked upon, not heard, ignored, not supported, and our response to this is major. Our inner child is incited to action, and we respond from this deep, early part of who we are, ignoring the cues in the present, responding to only those familiar ones from the past.

Memories can also be called to consciousness by our senses. We smell something that we can't quite place, but it makes us uncomfortable. Smell is a very strong sense that we tend to ignore in our adult life, unless it comes to choosing a favorite scent, but it is powerful and evocative of often preverbal memories, memories so early that we had no words yet to hold them. Or the light plays across our eyes and we begin to feel anxious. But no actual visual memory arises, we just feel like running, closing down, striking out, we can't breath, our heart is racing. We are having a body memory, a nonverbal sensory memory (O'Gorman and Diaz 2012).

Loretta had an old-fashioned name that suited her, for that was what she wanted to be: an old fashioned girl. But she was a young engineer who used self-contained resilience, and who was plagued by her looks. Even when she dressed in layers, she felt that men were only noticing her body and not paying attention to what she said. While she knew that some women got off on that type of attention and found it fun, for Loretta, it was a confirmation that, well, she just wasn't that smart. So she would try harder. She put in extra hours at work, took work home, all so she could prove herself. And then she went into work wearing no makeup, a boxy suit, her long black hair pulled back, only to be met with a leer from a senior manager, or a comment from a peer about how she made that suit look good, and she'd just feel like she was worth nothing.

All the attention to her looks triggered lingering memories of the sexual abuse she had sustained as a very young teenager. The perpetrator was a neighbor, an older man who would make cookies for the neighborhood kids; when her mother was late to meet the bus, she'd call on him to meet Loretta. He would tell Loretta how beautiful she was as he would touch her, and those memories haunted her. Thoughts of him made her skin crawl and made her feel that being beautiful wasn't exactly a safe thing. She remembers arguing with him, telling him she wasn't beautiful, and he'd say, "With a body like yours, you'll never need brains." But she wanted to have brains. Somehow, she thought if she was smart, she'd be safe. Because being beautiful meant she'd be a victim.

Trauma Reenactment

The term *trauma reenactment* sounds more like something you'd expect to see acted on a stage than something unconsciously acted out in your very own life, but it is most often seen when we find ourselves reliving (because we have re-created) a trauma from the past in our current life.

When we are involved in a trauma reenactment we choose the people we let in our lives because they elicit a specific type of response in us; we know how to deal with this type of person—so much like our experience of *letting in the pain we know* that we discussed in Chapter 7. This may be a type of boyfriend that we keep finding ourselves attracted to because, for example, he is emotionally unavailable and will eventually leave us. Or we may choose friends who all tend to treat us the same way—for example, expecting us to take care of them. Or we choose jobs with supervisors that draw on certain parts of who we know ourselves to be—for example, hardworking, able to get the job done. Or we may treat our own children in ways that we experienced as a child, even though we swore we would never repeat that behavior.

Sometimes we reenact trauma by the type of situations we put ourselves in: painful, perhaps, but familiar. Yes, we do this to keep away the challenge of the pain we don't know that we discussed in Chapter 7, but it is more complicated than this. We sometimes put ourselves in challenging situations because we are acting courageously and are trying to forge a different outcome than we experienced previously as a child, a teen, or a young, vulnerable woman.

All of these choices serve to confirm certain beliefs we have about ourselves, usually limiting beliefs that keep us stuck in the past. And all of these choices place us in certain scenarios in which we are a major player, scenarios that are as painful as they are familiar. These are the situations in our life which make us feel *trapped,* in which we may hear ourselves saying, "This is all I'm good for," which is depressing because we feel that there are no alternatives for us.

Why We Re-Create Past Traumas

Yes, life is complicated. Yes, if we have trauma, there are probably many potential triggers available. Still, when we re-create trauma and bring past triggers into the present—by the choices we make—

could it be because we still have something to learn from what happened in the past? And just what *do* we have to learn?

The lesson to be learned varies by person and is thorny, but it has to do with owning the resilience we developed to deal with our past hurts and building on that. That is one of the reasons why the development of *conscious* resilience is so important. The consciousness part of us needs to realize we are still reacting to something that is in the past, and that we do not need to keep bringing it into the present. And sometimes when we re-create past traumas it is because the situation, no matter how painful, is so compelling precisely because we do know how to deal with it. So we set in play a series of events that, although painful, allow us to feel competent, even powerful, even if it is a very expensive way to feel this.

Some women reenact trauma with the men they choose. They pick the same type of charming man who can't or won't commit, or who is oblivious of their needs. In a women's group, Marie shared, "I find myself playing the 'look at me game,' imported directly from my childhood."

Leitscha nodded knowingly. She shared how using her resilience allowed her to change her behavior.

> I've been there, but I've learned to decide whether or not to pursue a guy based on new criteria. I learned to "tough out" a first date, even if the guy wasn't scintillating, hunky, or drop-dead gorgeous, just to see what he was really about. It was hard, but that's how I met Evyon. He's a bit nerdy, but once I took the time to get to know him . . . and now we're engaged!

Others reenact their trauma in more subtle ways over an extended period of time, at work. Take Eloise, for example. She grew up in a physically abusive home and survived by blocking out most of it, shutting down her emotions, and learning in the process to tolerate high levels of violence and confusion around her. But she was far from passive: she learned to push back, and hard, when she felt there were threats around her or to her siblings, even those who lived with their different mothers. Eloise left the ghetto of her birth and went to college, knowing she was a survivor, and she used her stellar resilience as a badge of personal honor.

She chose to become a case worker at a residential treatment center for boys. There was something about the physicality of the boys, especially when they "lost it," that was familiar, and she knew how to handle it by calming "her boys" down as she worked to soothe staff. Her problem wasn't with the kids; it was with her boss, the chief of social work. She felt he was abusive of her personally in his tone and manner, was more than mildly flirtatious with her, and expected her to do more than the others because she was "so good at her job." This led to huge arguments during her supervision appointments, and sometimes even in the hall. Eloise told me, "I vowed to myself growing up that I'd never let anyone abuse me again. And I'm for sure not going to let Mr. 'I'm–so–caring–full–of–you–know–what' do that to me." And so she quit.

Her next position was with the county's department of social services, also as a caseworker in the Medicaid department. Here again, Eloise worked with the disenfranchised and did a great job with her clients. Again, her conflicts came with the administration. Her caseload was huge, their expectations were unreasonable, and she wouldn't reduce herself to treating people as just numbers. After a while, she left there as well.

I first saw Eloise two jobs later when she was referred by her employee assistance program coordinator because of her attitude problems. By then, she had a state position, and she was still in conflict with the administration.

We began to work on how she re-created her family in her work environment. This was where her trauma re-enactments were the clearest. Eloise acutely felt the abuses of power that can exist in a work environment, and she responded to them with a vengeance in a highly personal manner. After we worked together to have her manage her triggers, Eloise came to understand why she kept having the same altercations with her superiors. "I realized that I wanted to take them out. I wasn't a kid anymore. I could take care of myself. But what I didn't see is that as an adult, I had other tools to use, like my verbal skills. I didn't just need to fantasize about decking them. That was my inner child demanding a piece of their you-know-what."

If you have had trauma, consider if some of the patterns that are interfering in your life are trauma reenactments. For a more intensive analysis of personal trauma and trauma reenactments, go to http://patriciaogorman.com for exercises to help you determine this.

Codependency Traps: When the Familiar Is False

Codependency traps are a type of trauma reenactment in which the major issue being reenacted is caring for others, while simultaneously not caring for yourself (O'Gorman and Diaz 2012). This has some cultural power behind it as it reinforces the codependency cultural stereotype that women are supposed to care for others. As one friend of mine described it, "For a traumatized woman, this is looking for recognition and reward in all the wrong places."

A codependency trap can have many variations. Ella grew up as the oldest of seven girls and was "mother's little helper," a term she loved as a child and eventually grew to hate. She assisted her mother in all aspects of raising her sisters, even though she was only a child herself. She knew how to change a diaper, bathe her sisters, even use the food processor to grind up their food. Ella equated her self-worth with what she could do for others. She received lots of praise for being so very helpful but also had very high demands put on her. When she was a teenager, her friends thought it was weird that she was never available because she needed to work, and eventually they stopped asking her to join them.

Ella grew more withdrawn. She loved art but hardly had any time to pursue the art club after school. For college, she only applied to those schools near her home so she could continue to "help out" at home. After graduation, she applied on a whim to be an administrative assistant for a famous artist who lived not too far from her home.

Ella learned that the job was more akin to what she did for her mother than how it had been advertised. She felt she was on call to the artist 24/7. Her boss was talented but also enormously self-centered. And very demanding, just like her mother.

Alexis, a forty-year-old woman with stellar resilience grew up with a single parent, her mother, who Alexis felt had bipolar illness. As an adult she was still often surprised that things she thought were one way turned out to be another.

> I would feel that I had this connection with someone, like a potential supervisor on a job interview. I'd feel very comfortable with what they were saying and feel like we connected and could work together, only to get the job and hate it because I'd feel taken advantage of. I'd be asked to actually work while others

would only focus on their Facebook and texting. Yes, being new, you need to earn your place, but this was ridiculous. So I'd quit this job, find another, only to be taken advantage of again.

Camille, a woman with paradoxical resilience, would meet other mothers at her children's sporting events.

We'd bond over kids the same age and share the fun and boredom of endless soccer practices or the stress of hockey travel. And if you're going to spend this much time at these events, you need to have friends there as well, so I'd try to get to know them.

I became close to this one mother, and she began to ask me to pick up her son for hockey practice. She'd say she was on the way, sort of, as she was tired after work, and her husband was often drunk. And I foolishly said yes, even though I also work full-time. The kicker for me, no pun intended, was when she asked me if I'd take him to an away tournament since she needed to rest, and my two were going anyway even though this meant that we needed two rooms. Then she gave him no spending money. I began to steam, but I felt really sorry for her kid, and I felt I had a third son.

Glynnis, also a woman of paradoxical resilience, began to see a pattern she didn't like with the guys she dated.

I'd meet a great-looking guy and begin dating, only to find out he was in the middle of a really bad divorce, and his psycho-ex would begin to see me as a threat. If this happened once, you'd say it was bad luck. But this kept happening. With the last guy, I felt like calling his ex and saying, "Look, I just met him. He seems like a really nice guy, a little easily intimidated maybe, but sweet. Maybe you should stop stalking him and try to work things

out." But I felt like I was now moving from caretaking him, a
bad enough deal, to being their therapist, and since I'm a social
worker, I thought this really was mixing pleasure with business.
Thank goodness I caught myself and stopped. I realized that I
really didn't need to rescue him, I needed to extricate myself.

All four women were in my women's resiliency group. Camille
summed up their collective dilemma: "I think I'm just a good person. I like to help people. But I always begin to feel that I have 'den
mother' tattooed over my forehead, and I'm the only one who
couldn't see it. Somehow everyone expected me to take care of them.
And inevitably, I would."

What's going on here? The term *codependency trap* sums it up.
There are familiar cues—so subtle as to not even be conscious, and
so familiar as to be almost effortless to react to. But they pull on old
patterns, where strength is derived from giving to others, where a
sense of self-concept is shaped from one's capacity to give, to endure,
not from a self-loving, resilient concept of self that is based on taking care of one's own needs. It is a trap because we frequently do not
see the *option* of acting differently, let alone feel we can struggle to
actually act differently.

What each of these four women needed to do was somewhat different, as their use of their strengths and resilience varied. Ella and
Alexis, who predominately used stellar resilience, needed to edge out
of the comfort zone of being such *survivors* and begin to use their
strengths to expand their identity, realize that they have some vulnerabilities, and begin to grow their strengths to protect themselves
in these areas. Camille and Glynnis, both of whom tended to use
their strengths in work but not in their personal lives, have paradoxical resilience. They need to stretch the use of their strengths and use

these assets consciously in their personal lives. Their goal is to take better care of themselves by making different choices—Camille with her friends, and Glynnis with the men she chooses.

Your Resilience Journal: Codependency Traps

Ask yourself the following questions and journal your answers:

- What codependency traps are you in? What familiar caretaking roles have you assumed that are not working for you? That are keeping you from growing? That are choking the life out of you?
- What options do you have? Perhaps these options have consequences, but as you consider them, no matter how far-fetched they seem, you might think of others that are more palatable.

Compulsive Self-Reliance

Self-reliance is a good thing. From the time we are born we are searching for autonomy and the corresponding ability to do things on our own: from learning to sit up to tying our own shoes, from getting our own apartment to rehabbing after a hip replacement. Our search for independence in our lives is ongoing. Beginning in childhood, we push ourselves, over incredible obstacles, to master skills like crawling, where we are literally on our hands and knees and willing ourselves to make this work, to walking; even though we fall many times, we keep going. We have a goal. And we're going to make it. And we do. Each of us has been through this in life. We have mastered many things. This is the gritty path of resilience.

However, compulsive self-reliance is another issue altogether. This is not just a quest for mastery; this is that quest on steroids because it is propelled by a lack of trust in those around us due to trauma that we have experienced (O'Gorman and Diaz 2012). Compulsive self-reliance is often seen in those who develop self-contained resilience (the type of more brittle resilience in which the person is more isolated), and sometimes in those with paradoxical resilience, where they use their resilience in certain areas to compensate for those areas in which they have almost admitted defeat.

When we are compulsively self-reliant, we are not just propelling ourselves toward a goal. We are also running from our past, a past in which we have usually been victimized, abused, or in some other fashion had our self-concept so compromised that we feel we must continually prove ourselves to those around us. And we must *at all costs* protect ourselves. The only safe way to do this is to accomplish whatever is needed by ourselves. Our lack of trust and/or confidence in those around us is so pervasive that it has influenced our problem-solving style. Rather than ask anyone else, we'd rather do it ourselves. While using our strength and skill is admirable, our inability to ask others for help isn't helpful to us.

And yes, it does look good to others, especially others who don't have to work as hard because the work is done by the person who has compulsive self-reliance. If that is you, you may think you are so very resilient because you are so very strong. It is true that you are strong, not true that you are resilient. Remember, resilience also involves flexibility and the ability to take risks, including the risk to learn to take care of yourself. That is the dilemma for anyone with compulsive self-reliance: she thinks she is taking care of herself by playing keep-away with everyone else. By being in such constant motion she keeps others from getting too close as she accomplishes everything that needs doing.

Your Resilience Journal: Identifying Compulsive Self-Reliance in Your Life

Reflect for a moment on how you handle things in your life and then ask yourself the following questions:

- Do you have a tendency to just take on projects?
- Would you rather do it yourself than ask for help?
- Do you feel it is shameful to ask for help?
- Do you become angry if someone hasn't performed a task as well as you would have?

If you find yourself answering yes to these questions, consider the role of compulsive self-reliance in your life and use the steps outlined here to begin to build your resilience to also take care of yourself.

Use Your Pain and Trauma to Grow

We can transform our trauma. Transformation is the essence of resilience. It's what we do with the pain we've experienced. Trauma is a heightened pain, a psychological and perhaps physical insult that we have endured in our life, and is no different from any other pain. We can do something with this "thing" we wished we never had to endure, and make it—transform it—into something that can enrich us, and perhaps even others.

Jasmine grew up in a solidly middle-class family. When her father lost his job and the family needed to move, she remembers the many changes that occurred within her family, but somehow the hurt and shame that came from not being able to go to her senior prom because there was no extra money is a memory that epitomized this wrenching time.

As an adult, Jasmine found a way to use this painful memory to take powerful, constructive action. She joined a local women's club and started a program to collect gently used prom dresses that were cleaned and given out to inner-city youth for their "big" night. She also volunteered to do hair and makeup. "I still love dressing up and am so grateful that I can give this to these young women, not only for what it gives them, but also for how it helps heal me."

We can find a way to make sense of our pain and trauma, to redefine it, to make it a portal into the suffering of others that we can perhaps uniquely understand, and, through our understanding, we can take action. In this way, we can begin to use the resiliency skills we developed in living and learning through our previous pain and traumas to grow through a conscious application of our strengths.

Summary

Trauma hurts, but pain is not all that it sparks. Trauma can also be the most stimulating reason for why we develop resilience. Resilience allows us to become strong in precisely the places where we are hurt. And as we have seen, those who have experienced trauma and learned to take care of themselves realize a deeper connection, not only to themselves, but to others.

TWELVE

Step Six—Think Positively: It's the Best Revenge

LAUGH AND THE WORLD LAUGHS WITH YOU.
CRY AND YOU CRY WITH YOUR GIRLFRIENDS.

—Laurie Kuslansky

M*aintaining a hopeful outlook* in a crisis is the very essence of resilience. An optimistic outlook enables you to expect good things to happen in your life. Imagine that: expecting good things as opposed to waiting for the next shoe to drop! What an incredible shift in energy that would be. And the good news is that positive thinking is something you can practice and get much better at doing. This step will provide you with tools you can use to shift your attitude in a more positive direction, by offering you specific strategies to increase your optimism, including learning how to present the best that is in you.

Walk on the Wild Side—
Change the Way You Think

Thinking positively is one way out of the victim trap, and you can even have fun doing it. You can control your thinking by challenging the negative thoughts that arise and beginning to deal with why those thoughts are there in the first place. This two-step process begins with asking yourself a simple question, one that can literally change your life:

What do I want to think?

As you saw in Step Two, you can focus on your resilient inner voice. You can turn up on the volume on this part of who you are and then make a decision to focus on the positives in your life, even if these are somewhat hidden. This is different from running away from problems or putting your head in the sand. It means focusing on your power to determine your inner reality. Do you smell the flowers, or just focus on the exhaust? Yes, you *can* control what you think, not what pops into your mind but what you allow to stay there rent free. Here are some easy ways to do so.

STOP Thinking

I don't mean literally! The first thing is to challenge your thinking. If you find yourself dwelling on a negative thought, situation, or possible outcome that you know won't go anywhere because you've traveled down this road, many, many times, then you can challenge yourself to literally not think the thought. You can do this simply enough by saying *STOP* to yourself when these rather hopeless thoughts arise.

Everything in life is easier when you practice, and this is no exception. Begin by finding a safe place, a quiet place where you can *yell* and no one will hear you. Yes, yell. Practice shouting STOP so you have it on your inner mental track. And make this a good STOP, one yelled from *hara*, your belly button, the part of you that was connected to your birth mother. Don't croak it from your throat; that tends to sound wimpy. Make it a STOP that gets your attention, that makes the hairs on your arms stand up, one that give you goose pimples, one that commands your thinking to STOP and change direction. Once you've practiced shouting out loud, you can call on that power wherever you are, whenever you need it. Starting now, every time this negative thought comes up, think your powerful STOP.

Cultivate Positive Inner Thoughts

Focus on the positive thoughts that abound in your mind, purposefully creating an inner garden. Consciously create positive thoughts through pulling up pleasant memories of the past and focusing on helpful images of favorite foods, flowers, people, or blue-skying where you'd like to go for the weekend or for your next vacation. And you can focus on the positive in front of you, even when you're having a really bad day.

Keisha decided early in life that she would only think good thoughts. As a child, she wasn't aware how revolutionary this was. But her grandma DeeDee, a loving woman with such severe arthritis that she was using canes in her early life, told Keisha in many ways to "focus on keeping the good ones. You are what you think. Think good thoughts. That's where the power is." Keisha grew up with an incredibly positive attitude that sustained her as she struggled with learning disabilities in school. When a classmate laughed at her writing,

Keisha was overheard saying, "You write frontwards, and I write the other way. So what?" And that positive attitude sustained her through single motherhood, an abortion, even Hurricane Katrina, where she lost her home, her dog, and her beloved grandma.

Positive Inner Song

Another tactic for focusing on the positive is to sing to yourself; you can do so in your mind or even out loud. You can pull up an inner song, something designed to bring you out of your unpleasant musings. But make it a positive song. There are plenty of songs out there that speak to a broken heart, songs that trash women. Those won't help you stay positive. Pick songs with positive lyrics. "I think of the silly grace we sing before meals," one of my clients told me. "It makes me smile." A positive song will bring you back to a positive frame of mind when you've moved into other territories. And it will keep you entertained.

Affirmations

Noticing and affirming what is right about you is a way to create positive energy in your life. Some of us tend to speak negatively to ourselves and complain to others about our perceived deficits, which only increase our negative focus. Affirmations are a way of claiming and proclaiming what is right about you. They are a powerful way to change your thinking and very simple to do as you go through your day; you can repeat them to yourself, and no one will even notice. (See Your Resilience Journal in this chapter for suggestions.)

Meditation

Meditation is about creating an opening inside ourselves, taking our mind off the immediate, and creating peace within. And it's possible to do the cultivation of mindfulness approaches in one-minute segments on the go. By giving yourself four to five minutes of peace a day, all in one-minute intervals, you can cut the buildup of your inner tension and create an oasis within, one you can dip into regularly. Surely you can make time for these one-minute moments, and you'll come out refreshed. (See Your Resilience Journal in this chapter for suggestions.)

Prayer

Prayer is an offering up, a making of a request of our God. Prayer can be comforting and allow us to feel connected to a force greater than ourselves, decreasing our sense of isolation and providing consolation. Prayer is a way of lifting ourselves above the immediate and transcending it, even transforming it.

Nourishing Food, Exercise, and Rest

I know that this has been recommended so many times, by so many people, for so many things that it is almost hackneyed. But the reason why it is so often recommended is because it works! On one level, our bodies are biochemical machines. They need sustenance to function properly. A good meal, a nice workout, even if it is just going up and down the stairs instead of using the elevator, and a good night's rest (or even a power nap) can make you feel replenished and—yes, you get it—more positive.

When All Else Fails, Act as If . . .

I was raised with a saying that may surprise you, for it addresses how we develop positive thinking in perhaps an unorthodox way: "Sometimes we need to *fake it until we make it*." Sometimes our patterns are so ingrained and come so very easily that we need to *act as if* until we can makes the changes we desire in our own thinking. So acting as if you are more positive can actually help you get there.

A recent patient taught this to me in a very poignant way. Annabel came to see me because she had problems with organization and conflict in her few close personal relationships. Articulate, bright, and witty, she worked as a union organizer and prided herself on keeping calm in the midst of very heated meetings, her ability to focus on her agenda, and usually being able to win the points she prioritized. As she began to describe her personal life, her sense of accomplishment shifted.

"I keep being criticized for not being more open with those I'm close to." She added that she had a sixteen-year-old son who she suspected might have Asperger's syndrome (an autism spectrum disorder), although he had not been formally diagnosed. She then looked at me and said, "I've been wondering if I also have this." She went on to describe how she indeed fit many of the hallmark characteristics, relating this to her inability to often express and share her feelings. "I think I have feelings. They are in here, somewhere, but I don't seem to get them out there."

Annabel added that her struggle had been lifelong. She went on to discuss other decisions in her life that had gone well. In college she'd majored in theater with a political science minor; she'd loved acting in campus plays and continued doing local community productions after graduation.

As we spoke, I shared with her how brilliant she had been in preparing herself to solve her communication challenges. Majoring in theatre and staying active in this had been so helpful to her, for in studying acting she had learned to portray feelings of all types. I encouraged her to use her acting skills in her next personal discussion with a friend. I suggested that when she sees a gap, when she senses the apparent disconnect between the reaction of the person she is with and what she is sensing on the inside (but perhaps not expressing on the outside), she should literally *act* this out.

Annabel loved this idea. During our next session she relayed that this was working much better. "I had a conversation with my son's father and he didn't get frustrated with my not sharing. I think I'm beginning to close this gap I have inside me, like I'm beginning to make others more comfortable with me." She smiled.

Annabel's resilience had been self-contained. She was an island unto herself out of necessity. But she decided to consciously expand her skill set in communicating with others. By experimenting with using her acting skills with those close to her, she began to expand her sense of self and was rewarded by others beginning to feel a little more comfortable with her. (See Your Resilience Journal in this chapter for more on "acting as if.")

Loving Ourselves Instead of "Should"-ing Ourselves

Let's face it, we spend a portion of at least every day daydreaming, thinking of our plans, blue-skying it, and thinking of the past. Our thoughts float through our minds, some settle, others move on. While none of us can control what comes into our minds, we can control what we allow to stay rent free.

When we think of the past, many of us have a tendency to be very critical of ourselves. We berate ourselves for how we "should" have handled certain situations. We don't allow ourselves to grow through a difficult experience, to gain in resilience. Instead we become angry with ourselves for having had the bad experience, feeling that if we were smarter, the insight we now feel in hindsight could have predicted the distress we currently feel and could have been avoided. In other words, "I should have seen it coming."

This is particularly compounded for those of us who are also mothers. We need to learn to love ourselves in order to teach our children to love themselves. Yes, we strive to be patient and accepting of them, loving them even in the midst of their mistakes and wrongdoing, but reaching self-love? This means making room for our own mistakes as we make room for theirs, and learning that progress, not perfection, is the goal. Modeling patience with ourselves teaches it to our children.

Casey was a bright and active six-year-old. When his tantrums at school became too disruptive, his mother, Kirsten, was called for a conference. His teacher explained that Casey had tantrums when his clay figures fell apart or he made a mistake in his drawings and couldn't erase them. "I'm so stupid! I can't do anything right!" he'd yell and knock the work materials to the floor.

When the teacher relayed this to Kirsten, she winced. "I know where he gets it," she said. "From me. I'm pretty hard on myself when I make a mistake." Kirsten realized that as much as she complimented her son and praised his efforts, he also heard her anger at her own mistakes. It wasn't how his mother acted toward him, but how she accepted her own frustrations that he had used as his model.

When we can accept ourselves—faults and all—with self-love and respect, we demonstrate an important aspect of our resilience. When we pick up and start again after a defeat, or acknowledge failure and make another attempt, we, as well as our children, gain a valuable lesson. And this lesson is so much more valuable than beating ourselves up for having made a mistake to begin with. (See the pages that follow for more about "should"-ing ourselves.)

Your Resilience Journal: Cultivating Positive Thoughts

To begin this journal entry, arbitrarily list as many positive things as you can think of. Now close your eyes and run your finger down the list and stop at random. Start with that one positive thing and think about it, about how you can focus on it consciously throughout your day. Put your focus on the positive! Next to your chosen trait, write how it feels to have this positive as a focus of your thinking. Tomorrow pick the next one. Keep adding to your list and make each positive the focus of a special meditative thought for each day.

The following are suggestions that are entertaining while helping you achieve your goal.

Positive Inner Songs: Make a list of upbeat songs that appeal to you such as "You Don't Own Me" by Leslie Gore, or "Rest of Me" by Erin Harkes. Load them onto your iPad, computer, or your Walkman if that's what you have—and listen to them.

Affirmations: This is a simple process, one I suggest you do several times a day. Write your affirmations in your journal, your calendar, on stickies posted on your bathroom mirror, or anyplace that ensures you will notice them. Make them simple, write clearly, and be sure they state what is right about you. For example:

I am grateful for the love that I have for myself.
I am worthy of my own best efforts.
I am perfectly imperfect.

Meditation: Meditation is a powerful practice that can change your thinking and your feelings. Meditation can take many forms, from a formal practice that you make time for each day to one you can practice on the go in one-minute intervals throughout your day.

Acting "As If": Think about where you are stuck, feel trapped, and are unable to be positive. Now consider how to *act as if* you were positive and having the kind of impact you would like to have. Write this down. Consider creating an affirmation that states this, and add it to a sticky on your bathroom mirror or at your desk at work. And experiment with acting it out.

Stopping "Should"-ing: Think about what you say to yourself that includes the word "should," then write down at least five examples in your journal, leaving a blank line after each one. How can you release yourself from this blame? With what positive thought of encouragement can you replace this blame? Write those new, positive thoughts below each "should" example, then consider adding these positive thoughts to your list of affirmations.

For more ideas, examples, and suggestions on ways to cultivate positive thoughts, visit http://patriciaogorman.com.

Fight Those *Girly Thoughts* and Focus on Your Preferred View

So how do you want to be noticed? Billions of marketing dollars are directed toward getting us to purchase an array of products, from longer lashes to sexier cars, cleaner kitchens, and thinner bodies, all so we'll be noticed for the qualities the product is enhancing. There are women who monitor fashion trends closely, and others who make their own fashion statement "going back to nature," getting numerous piercings, wearing vintage clothing, or (one of my favorites) acquiring the thrift-store glam look. We have all been sensitized to how we look to others and to ourselves. And as much fun as it is to play dress-up, even in our adult lives, we have to remember that this does not define all of who we are. When we do allow how we look to be a major definer of who we are, we are giving into our *girly thoughts.*

To combat *girly thoughts,* we need to remind ourselves that how we "look" goes beyond how we dress. The way others perceive us is often colored by the qualities that others notice about us, like our confidence, sense of humor, independence, or warmth. So it also stands to reason that we might also want to notice our inner qualities and want others to pay attention to them as well. Many of us do this but rarely think it through. As a result, we run the risk of defining ourselves based on what others notice, leading us in some ways to be more sensitive to what others see in us than what we see in ourselves. Another trap is falling for beliefs that tell us hidden "truths" about us, like an obsessive interest in our horoscope. Yes, there may be something there, but building your calendar around the stars, or only dating Aries men? What's this about? Here I think we need to ask ourselves what we are running away from. And so often, the answer is our power to define ourselves.

At Our Best—Our Preferred View

We dress carefully, spend tons of money on our makeup and hair (not to mention our shoes and clothes), so we'll be at our best. And many of us like doing this; we feel it is pampering ourselves, projecting an image of which we can be proud. But this isn't the only way we are at our best. We are our best when we think of ourselves and imagine that people in our lives see us as acting in alignment with our *preferred view.*

If this sounds awkward, just think of ads on TV: a gorgeous woman smiles at others who look at her admiringly, whether this is due to the yogurt she is buying, her figure, or the beverage she is drinking. This common theme in advertising is based on our very human needs for recognition and appreciation. We all look for these moments in our daily life because they signal approval, even if we are not conscious of this. We all want to be recognized for our positive qualities—our intellect, our looks, our smile, our sense of fun, our dedication, our generous acts—whatever is important to us and is unique to who we feel we really are. And as we go through our day we scan to see who is noticing us in these special ways.

The concept of *preferred view* was introduced by psychologists Joe Eron and Tom Lund in their groundbreaking book (1996). Preferred view embodies the qualities we wish others to notice about us and the discomfort and complications that can arise when we feel others are seeing us in a way that is not accurate, not really who we are. We begin our understanding of our preferred view by taking the time to understand the qualities we want others to notice about us, knowing that these tend to be different in different sectors of our life.

Early in my professional life I knew a female administrator who was very clear about how she wanted to be seen at work. She was tough, no-nonsense, not prone to any personal conversations, overly direct, and brief—some even said curt. One day my face must have registered my consternation at how she was speaking to me, because she remarked, "This may surprise you, but my children love me, I've been married to the same man for twenty-two years, and I go to church on Sunday and am at peace with my God." She was right: I was surprised; shocked was more like it. She was very clear about how she wanted to be seen at work, and she made no apologies about it.

But we are social creatures, and so we do care how others perceive us. Facebook is just the latest manifestation of this need. With Facebook and other social media, we carefully manage how others see us: *just so*. We post just the right pictures, staged or otherwise, we say just the right things. Many even devote a significant amount of time each day to their online persona. In real life, in real time, we notice how others see us, but, interestingly, we often devote less conscious time to managing our in-person persona.

Your Resilience Journal:
How Others See You

In your journal, list how others would describe you.
Leave space under each description to answer the following
questions:

- What do you hear from others that sounds good
  but unfamiliar?
- What descriptions have you heard that you'd like to be
  you, but you're not sure they are, yet.
- What strengths do others mention about you?

Now begin to think about yourself in terms of the strengths
you've listed. Use words describing your strengths to think
about yourself, to speak about yourself, then journal about
your feelings.

- How does this feel?
- What does doing this awaken in you? Ask yourself if
  you like this new emerging you. If so, keep going . . .
  if not, take a deep breath and focus just on how to
  describe yourself today.
- Are there strengths you would like to develop?
  What are they?

On the next page of your journal, make a list of these soon-to-be strengths, and follow the same three steps used before. When you get to the third step, ask yourself what you would like others to notice about you. Sometimes it's easier to see the changes we'd like to make from the outside in, rather than the inside out. Ask yourself how it would feel to be seen in this way. Know that you can build these new strengths. Plan out how you can begin to use them. And when you try them out, remember you can experiment, make a note of what happens in you and in those around you.

How You Want Others to Understand Your Actions

Other people see only your actions. No one can read your mind. Others do not see your inner motivation, your planning, not even your caring. They see what you *do* with those things. They see your dealings. When others misattribute your actions and you don't like their conclusions, then you need to consider what to change, even if your intentions are golden. An important question to ask yourself is: what do I want others to think or say about what I do?

Allegra was a young, brilliant guidance counselor who used her resilience in a stellar manner. As a child she was diagnosed as having juvenile diabetes; she also had a brother who was born with a significant birth defect and a single mother who valiantly kept the family together. Allegra was now happy that she could be a major financial contributor to her family.

She loved her job and was very good at it. And she had a particular knack for writing the perfect letter with the perfect timing that helped an unusually large number of her students be accepted at the more competitive colleges. Her students liked her; their parents appreciated her. But in case conferences within her department at the high school, she frequently broke down, crying as she discussed the stressors in the lives of the children she served.

Allegra liked to think of work as a safe place, where she could have her feelings. She felt she needed to be more guarded at home, and she realized that she couldn't share personal information with the kids she worked with. But she thought her peers were safe. Her colleagues, however, made other attributions about her outpourings. There began to be whispers that she was unstable; questions as to whether she should work with children. Her supervisor was someone who didn't like confrontation, and so he never spoke to her about his concerns and the growing concerns of others.

It took a conversation with the vice principal for her to realize that there was a problem. She was shocked and felt so betrayed that people spoke around her but no one spoke to her. In fact she found out that a fellow staffer had set up a Facebook page posting Allegra's "cry of the week." Her supervisor and her coworker were attributing her tearing up to negative qualities. Their vehemence stung. Not what she wanted. She was appalled. "And my name means happy," she lamented to a friend.

Understanding Our Hopes, Intentions, Desires, and Dreams

Allowing ourselves to be held hostage by what others may think, how they may feel, and how they may misinterpret our acts, doesn't work. We run a terrible risk of losing who *we* are when we base our actions solely on our obligations and the response of others. When we do this, we run the risk of living our lives based upon the findings of a committee instead of our own working knowledge of who we are and what is important to us: our hopes, intentions, desires, and dreams. These are the things that need to inform our actions.

Allegra's resolution to her challenge at work can help us see this. With all that was going on, Allegra realized that she really loved working with the kids and their families. But she understood she needed to get a better handle on working with her peers. She decided to see a job coach to figure out what she could do. Her decision surprised her supervisor, who thought for sure she'd see a therapist and probably end up on antidepressants. But Allegra didn't feel particularly depressed. In fact she felt a great many feelings. It was how to share her feelings that was a challenge for her, not her access to them. Job coaching it was.

The advice she received was helpful and direct: Consider your audience. Her reaction was immediate. "My audience. But these are my peers. I don't want to have to act around them." Allegra had a real dilemma.

She solved it by returning to her intention in taking this position to begin with. Her dream was to help kids, particularly to help this group of rural kids who had few supports get into college. Yes, she wanted to be able to work with a group of similarly educated peers, but that wasn't her primary motivation. As she clarified her hopes and intentions, she was able to arrive at a solution for handling her weekly case conference and to be seen by her colleagues as she wanted to be.

Your Resilience Journal:
Your Preferred View

Open a fresh page in your journal and begin a list titled "Wonderful Qualities I Possess That I Want Others to Notice." Remember, these do not have to be the traditional qualities we associate with being a woman. Break your list down into the different sectors of your life; you will probably detect some subtle differences. Take your time so you can be clear. Use these bullet points to help you get started.

- **Home**. What do you want your parents to notice, or your children, or your partner, or even your dog or cat? Your kindness? Your cooking? Your love? Your commitment to them? Your gratitude for their commitment to you?
- **School.** What do you want your teachers or professors to notice about you? The fact that you usually know the answer? How smart you are? How well you work with others?
- **Work.** What do you want your supervisor, executive director, or coworkers to notice about you? Your commitment? Your innovations? Your volunteering for extra projects? Your excellent work? Your teamwork?
- **House of worship.** What do you want your priest, pastor, rabbi, or iman to notice about you? How devout you are? Your attendance? Your good deeds?

- **Friends.** What do you want your friends to notice about you? Your love of fun? Your loyalty? Your willingness to be there no matter what?
- **Romantic interest.** What do you want this person to notice about you? Your attractiveness? Your sensuality? Your caring? Your commitment? Your sense of humor?
- **Community.** What do you want other members of your community to know about you? Your commitment, dedication, good ideas?

Next, look back at your list of strengths and plug them into the areas of your life listed above. Ask yourself which of them you want to be more prominent. Bookmark this exercise and go back periodically to update.

Dealing with How You Don't Want to Be Seen

Sometimes a series of circumstances calls forth the best in you, as we saw in Step Five. Perhaps you've just been hired by a new firm, or you're meeting the people you hope will be your in-laws, or you've just moved and are meeting your new neighbors. In many circumstances like these, we all have a tendency to put our best foot forward, to act in a way that shows us at our best. And we often do this consciously. We dress in a way we like, one that shows our assets and hides our flaws, we speak verbally and through our actions in a way that demonstrates our grasp of the situation. We are on our game.

Other times we need to make unpopular decisions. Our children, our supervisor, our partner may not like a decision we've made, but we feel it has to be done, so we understand why they're upset with us. That's not what we're talking about here. We are speaking about circumstances that induce the worst that is in us. Sometimes you find yourself feeling a way that is familiar, but not who you really know yourself to be; this might be an old you that you've moved beyond, or a new creature (and you're not sure where she came from). You start feeling like a victim and feel like you are crumbling, or you start lashing out, and later you feel truly horrible about how you acted. You have a confrontation with a coworker who is being mean, and you cry at work instead of being smart or strategic. You become angry with your children and come close to striking them. You work late for weeks and go into survival mode and find you're just too tired for sex at home, so you become cold, punishing, and withdrawn.

The problem is that this is what others see. And we have a tendency to become more uncomfortable as we see others seeing us in ways that are not really who we are, sometimes causing us to do more of what is not working, like yelling louder when we are not understood. This gives us three choices: We can notice how we are being seen and change our actions, argue that others are wrong in what they see, or do what some women unfortunately do, and eat or medicate our growing frustration. If you find yourself in this situation, don't be too hard on yourself. Sometimes, things have to get bad enough for us to get our own attention, so we can begin to act differently. As a result, those we are close to may see changes in us even before we are aware of them. But you have a choice: do you use those moments to grow, or do you fight them?

The Gap

The space between how we want to be seen and how we see others seeing us is known as *the gap*. As Eron and Lund wrote, the greater the gap, the greater the discomfort one feels (1996). This discomfort is a main reason why we have difficulty changing, for to change means entering the gap—taking the time to acknowledge what's going on, how we are being judged in a way that we feel is not accurate, and *plan* on how to have our *best* seen again. Yes, *plan* to make it different, plan to *close the gap*, not react to what's happening that is *so unfair,* or arguing that they are wrong about what they are seeing you do and you are right. This will take some guts, but here is an opportunity to use resilience again.

Your Resilience Journal: Closing the Gap Between How You Are Seen and the Real You

Notice how you are acting in a way that does not reflect your true self. Begin by describing *the gap* between how you want to be seen and how you are being seen. Journal the answers to the following questions:

- What do others notice?
- What are you doing that is causing others to notice and to react to you in a negative way?
- How does it make you feel to be seen in a way that is not you?

Closing *the gap*:

Close your eyes and see a way for you to close the gap between your true self and how you've been perceived. Journal the answers to these questions:

- How do want to be seen? What would this look like?
- What changes on your part can make this happen?
- What solutions have you used in the past that you could try again?
- What new strengths have you developed that could be applied here?
- How would it feel to be seen again as your best? Describe in detail in your journal.

Summary

Being positive is the lubricant for the development of your resilience. This involves daring to change your thinking. If you can see the upside to the downside, then you can more easily figure out what to do to take care of yourself. And you can do this very concretely by being aware of your best and how you want others to see you—your *preferred view*.

THIRTEEN

Step Seven—
Develop Gratitude for
Who You Are and
What You Have Learned

IF EVERYTHING IS OKAY ON THE INSIDE,
EVERYTHING WILL BE OKAY ON THE OUTSIDE.

—*Dr. Patricia O'Gorman*

Living with an open and grateful heart is a choice many of us would make. We truly do want to feel positive; we want to be optimistic about our future and relaxed in our present. We want to look forward to tomorrow and feel that we can be thankful for today. We'd like to feel less burdened. But unfortunately, many of us feel that there are just too many obstacles in our lives to adopt this attitude. There are too many struggles, too many things that are totally out of whack, too many altercations with people around whom we'd be able to relax if only they'd change. We feel there is an answer, but that it is outside ourselves.

There is a solution, a much simpler one than we imagine. It is a solution in which we are in total control. Sound too good to be true? Well, it isn't. A major, courageous way out of this trap of being overly focused on the challenges in our life is to adopt an attitude of gratitude. How do we begin to do this? We begin by focusing on our inner life and begin to appreciate and be thankful for what we find.

I know this sounds hokey, but indulge me. *You* are the master of your *now*. Try it on. Know that in many ways, you create the flow of life around you by how you respond to what is occurring. Yes, what is happening now is important. You can't deny it. Yes, when awful things occur, we all respond. How can we not? Yes, awful things may shake your confidence in yourself, make you feel threatened by others, by our political system, by events both natural and man-made. But the key is not what is happening outside you. The key is what is happening within you and what you do with it, because what you focus on determines much of the quality of your life. And it is your inner life that is the key to how you feel and respond.

Your inner life is, after all, a reservoir, a holding place for what you feel is important enough to retain. It is a part of you that you fill daily, and it speaks to you in every moment; you'll hear it if you are listening. Your inner life is what you cherish, what you prioritize, what you feel you need, and ultimately what defines you to a very important part of who you are: it defines you to yourself. It constitutes your beliefs about yourself and about others. It influences what you focus on and flavors how you see life around you. You add to it daily, perhaps not consciously, but by your actions and your thoughts. And in moving to become more resilient, deciding how to do this more consciously can be a very self-loving act.

Gratitude is a building block of resilience. To be truly grateful requires you to develop the ability to be flexible in your thinking, in your perceptions, in your responses. And as you've learned, flexibility is a hallmark of resilience. This raises some questions: Where do you direct your attention? Do you notice the beauty of the sky, or the gracefulness of the architecture of the buildings in your city, or the smile of the child you pass in the supermarket? Or does your mind replay constantly the insults you feel you have endured at work? The deadlines looming for projects? The argument you had last night with your partner? The latest Facebook posting that is critical of you? Striving to take control of your inner life is an important step in creating resilience. Begin by expanding the role of gratitude in your life.

Creating Gratitude

We need to challenge ourselves to realize that we have the power to create positive outcomes in our lives, but first we need to focus on where we invest our energies. The most popular test is the answer to this question: *Do I look at the glass as half-full or half-empty?* But things are rarely this black and white. Some look at the glass and try to predict if the contents are going up or going down. They don't want to commit until they determine this; they live in fear of being exposed, of being more vulnerable than they already are. In essence they are stuck, often due to trauma as we previously discussed. But there are ways that we can begin to move past our trauma, past our pain, past our indecision, and begin to create a different life—a more rewarding, more resilient life—by developing the ability we have to see and to be an instrument in generating the good around us.

Give to Others

Marilee was only nine years old the first time she volunteered with her church group to assemble food packages for children living through the Sub-Saharan drought.

> I remember feeling overwhelmed when I learned that children were starving. I asked my grandmother what I could do, and she invited me to go with her to our church's event. This started other kids going. It got to be quite the thing. I remember feeling so good that I could help others. Now I'm a mother. I work part-time in a clothing store, but I still volunteer at my church to help those much less fortunate.

Marilee learned the power of gratitude early in life.

The lessons about how to make good things happen in our lives to create gratitude come early, and they come often. Sometimes they are very subtle, like sharing a toy with a shy peer in school. Other times they are more dramatic like a friend of mine who gives a small amount of money to every panhandler she passes. "This way, not only do I thank my God for my fortune, but I also feel I walk straighter and take in my environment, as opposed to needing to block out parts of it such as those who are less fortunate and are asking for my help." These moments can often present themselves at the most awkward times, such as offering kindness by not taking personally a rant about your performance by a work peer, but helping him redirect his comments to speak about his child who was just in an accident.

See the Goodness in Others, Even When You Don't Want To

We've all had the experience of being very angry with someone and wishing them ill, only to find them doing very well. And most of us felt we had enemies at one time or another, people we felt were out to get us, or people who said (as one of my supervisors once said to me), "It's going to be either you or me, and it's not going to be me."

These experiences can be terrifying. They can bring out our worst childhood fears and give them a new face. They make us feel impotent, powerless, destined to be a victim and taken out by the other. My friend Penny taught me how to handle situations like this early in my career. She was pretty balanced in her resilience until she began to have a major political conflict at work, and that plagued her. She was a top county official and had been having an ongoing conflict with another commissioner. "This was going on and on and I couldn't see how it could end unless I left. It totally drained me. One day I even thought I was having a heart attack and was rushed to the ER. I just felt crappy about myself," Penny confided in me.

As an out-of-the-box-thinker, she used a strategy that I found remarkable. She decided to take *A Course in Miracles,* a self-study spiritual thought system (1976, 2007) that teaches the way to universal love and peace, and it changed her life.

> I had tried everything I could think of, so I thought I'd try something different. My anger at this man had turned into a black hole, consuming much of the energy I felt I had in my life. Even though I'm Jewish, I took the course. It changed my life. I learned to focus on the good in this person, not just seeing him as the undermining, conniving, royal pain you-know-where. This wasn't overnight, but I kept at it. And I began at some point to actually feel sorry for him and how lousy his life must be that he was devoting so much of his time and energy to trying to make me look terrible.

I remember passing him one day in the hall and giving him a genuine smile. I surprised myself. I no longer felt he had any power over me. He looked so shocked, and he actually stumbled. And I felt good, not because he stumbled but because I was beginning to act more like me, more direct, able to take him on, including the positives he offered, and less like the scurrying mouse I felt I was becoming. By seeing the good in him I had reclaimed my power to see what perhaps motivated him, freeing me up to figure out how to deal with him on my terms.

See the Good in Your Competitors

Part of how we can see the good in others, even those we are competing against, is by respecting their strengths. This is the essence of successful sport competition. Competitors study each other, not just for vulnerabilities, but also for what they can learn. Men appear to have an easier time doing this, perhaps because they tend to play highly competitive sports for much of their lives, but women are catching on. In either case, they study their competition; they plan their strategy to defeat their opponent by analyzing the competitor's strengths, their best plays, and their vulnerabilities. But they also celebrate them. There is a ritual at the conclusion of many sporting events where both teams meet on the field to celebrate a good game. In the locker room afterward, members of both teams relive the game, the good plays, how hard they played, and the errors they made. They speak about the fairness or lack thereof. But they are together, debriefing, enjoying, realizing it is just a game, whether they are on the winning team or the losing one. It is not who they are. It is how they *play*.

Annika, a young woman with balanced resilience, began to understand how to do this when she entered college. She had never been particularly athletic in high school except for playing some soccer, when she was commended for her footwork. But when she went to college she fell in love with rugby, which astonished her parents as she was planning to be a religion major, and they had a hard time seeing the two going together.

Annika loved the action, but mostly she loved the other players. This is what she focused upon. It didn't really matter to her if they won or not, as long as it was a good game. It was all about the adrenaline rush before and during the game. The contact. How well she played. How they all connected, even if she did get a split lip or two. It was great fun to really put herself out there, with friends, with support. That's what she was grateful for.

Laugh

There is a saying that laughter awakens your soul. Certainly there's nothing like a good laugh, even if it is at our expense, to help us feel better, good, even grateful.

Marje was hired to supervise a group of very talented women. The only thing she was told beforehand was that they were cliquish, but what she found was a mean-girl group, just like she had seen in high school. These women loved playing gotcha with others, and there was evident fear within the group that, if any of them crossed the leader in some way, she'd be the next target.

Marje did her own freak-out. How could she get these women to respond positively? Yes, she could notice and thank them for their best efforts. And she could notice and be grateful for her own efforts, even if they didn't work as well as she had wished, even if it felt like more and more of a stretch. She needed a radical approach that would drive home a positive attitude.

Marje implemented a mandated daily laughter club. Each day the members of her team assembled for a meeting that began with fifteen minutes of laughter. Of course, the team thought Marje was nuts; she was just happy she finally had their attention. And what they found is that laughter is actually contagious. What begins with forced laughter actually becomes real laughter, laughter at how ridiculous the situation is, how funny your coworkers look, how good it feels to just release in a positive way. In spite of themselves, the women began to enjoy their working environment, and Marje could begin to manage them and really use her strengths, and for this she was very grateful.

Gratitude Behind Change

We can alter our attitude about change, or we can develop gratitude for our ability to change. I suggest the latter, as change is an inevitable fact of life for women, and developing gratitude for who we are and the lessons we have learned along the way can help us enormously in refining our resilience.

In case you haven't noticed, not only do our bodies change pretty dramatically as we develop and age, but, for most of us, change also comes to our bodies each month with our menstrual cycles and the often accompanying feelings of bloating, discomfort, and fatigue. Pregnancy radically changes our bodies and our lives. We are always changing. Menopause brings about another major change to both our bodies and our spirits and is often a time when we make major changes in our personal lives as we become empty nesters, explore new relationships, discover new talents, and become more introspective.

Throughout our life cycle we experience change that occurs naturally within us and over which we have little or no control. Perhaps this is why we often change so much of ourselves, trying to stay one step ahead, trying to stay in control; it can be fun, and for this we can be grateful.

We constantly change how we look, and there can be great pleasure and freedom in doing this. Our wardrobe variations are influenced by what is in fashion—the colors that are in this season, the length of our skirts, the padding (or lack of) in our shoulders. We have our hair cut into a new style or add the newest highlights. Our nails are a fashion statement in terms of color and design. And it seems we are always fiddling with our makeup as we try the latest lip color or rouge, eyeliner and mascara colors, foundations with minerals or without, or additives to grow our lashes—or even the decision to add permanent liner or lashes. In fact, these are some of the easiest changes we can make, and they do positively affect our mood and our outlook. But deciding how to do this is, well, complicated.

As my hairdresser Shelly, an expert on women and change, says:

> Some women must have their hair the same every time they come in. This is the only control they feel they have in their lives. And to their credit, they take it. Others play this out differently. They keep trying new hairdos, new colors, new makeup. They feel they have control in this area, and they take it. I encourage women to make these changes. And I find that once women make a change that they like, they aren't worried what others think. If they like their hair, they leave feeling confident. I find the more they play with the possibilities and get comfortable with change, the less they worry about what "others" are thinking about them (2012).

The conundrum is this: if we can change how we look, if we can add purple highlights to our hair or wear green nail polish or make our lips bright red and not take personally the reactions of others to our new fashion statement, then why do we struggle so with the reactions of others when we change how we act? If we are ready to change, to notice our strengths, to walk with more self-confidence, then why do we set ourselves up to be hurt by their disapproval in the process?

The simple answer is that in being so focused on how others react to you, you are still taking care of them. Here is that codependency sneaking into your life again and taking some of the fun out of it. When you care more about what others think than you care about what you think, then you know you still have more work to do.

Gratitude Allows You to Not Take Things So Personally

No, it's not all about us. And for that we can be grateful. In fact, we can use our gratitude to help us develop a perspective that allows us to not take personally so much of the confusion, hurt, and pain that others fling around. In fact, doing this can allow us to develop compassion for the others in our lives who create such turmoil.

We can begin this by owning our power to create positive outcomes in our lives and seeing this as quite a considerable achievement, one that should not be taken lightly. We do this by looking for the positive in whatever is happening, as we learned in Step Six, and taking it further by actually realizing that we can be grateful for this inner muscle.

Realizing that we have power to change our perspective and not take others so personally can initially feel puzzling, and, as a result, some of us flee from it. Perhaps this is why feeling like a victim comes more easily to us women. Yes, we do have the fairy tales that portray us as needing to be rescued. From Cinderella to Rapunzel to Snow White and many others, we are somewhat brainwashed into feeling we need a Prince Charming to come to our rescue. But just because we have been told this for generations does not make it true. We actually have much more direct control over our lives than this. But it's sometimes a struggle to own this.

And sometimes the positive outcomes we need occur in a way that makes sense to us but may not quite be understandable to those who are not part of our lives. In these situations, it is our resilience that allows us to do what is right for us. This played out in my own childhood when I went to school for a time in the Deep South. There I met several young girls my age, and, as girls do, we discussed our futures and our weddings. I was surprised that many spoke of being sure that they "would faint" on their wedding day. This was important enough to be a topic of ongoing conversation, complete with stories of weddings they had attended and how the bride's fainting was greeted. It even seemed to be a source of pride for the bride's young friends and relatives—my classmates.

I was miffed that this was coming out of the mouths of these steel magnolias. Coming from New York, this was an entirely new concept to me, one I couldn't grasp, and it made me feel even more isolated. I just couldn't understand why brides would faint. It seemed to me to be a negative, not the positive that they giggled about. I remember being concerned about what would happen to their wedding dresses if they fell on the ground. I came to understand that this is how they would demonstrate their vulnerability, a reminder to their new husbands on this important day in their lives that they needed to be taken care of. This was the positive outcome *they* were looking to create. I came to realize that their need to talk about this wasn't about me and my northern ways, but about their need to soothe their entry into this new, very important part of their lives.

Develop Gratitude for Self-Awareness

An important way to see your gratitude in action is to use your resilient inner voice and create ways to soothe yourself. Yes, yourself, not everyone else. This involves taking the time to figure out what you need to do to be sweet to yourself, and, trust me, what you'll usually find is that you *will* have time to do it, and it will make you smile inside and feel grateful—to yourself!

Rituals are one way to do this. You already (perhaps unconsciously) create rituals in your day: Your morning ritual may involve a run, a shower, a cup of coffee, fruit, and yogurt; your evening routine includes how you take off your makeup and get ready for bed. Think about what you do on an ongoing basis that calms you, that prepares you for the next transition in your day, and take in how this is a gift you are giving yourself.

Self-soothing is one place where your *girly thoughts* can actually be put to good use! They provide some avenues by focusing on products that can be helpful; rubbing your face or even your feet with a soothing cream can be nourishing, even calming, and the idea of giving yourself a gift just because . . . is a treat to yourself and also acknowledges your specialness.

But you can expand on these and create additional rituals based on a combination of both things you need and that soothe you. This may involve taking a weekly yoga or exercise class, regular lunch dates with close friends, walking during lunch to get some fresh air, breathing deeply and walking at a slower pace on your way to the subway, or taking a couple of breaks throughout the day for the one-minute meditation that we mentioned in Step Six (pages 248–49), even if the ladies room is where you have to meditate. And you can extend your need for soothing to developing plans with your partner. As women, we need time to connect. An end-of-day "hello" can be expanded from the quick peck most couples use to something more elaborate. Tress and Jerome stand next to each other and take turns sharing about their day; one relates stories as the other says soothing things such as "Oh baby, poor you," or they just hug each other and rock gently back and forth in each other's arms. "I know this may look silly to others, but it works for us," Tress told me. And that is certainly the important thing: finding what works for you.

Meg and Tim have a different evening ritual for calming themselves down after their kids are in bed. When they finally get into bed together, they strip down and hug each other, not so much sexually as to feel the skin contact as they speak about what they need to share. "We may not have any other time during the day when we really connect emotionally, but we make sure that we do before we fall asleep. And it's great. Since we started doing this, I no longer need any sleep aides," Meg shared.

Being resilient doesn't involve just the heroic things we accomplish; it also involves the highly personal things we take care of daily that soothe our souls.

Gratitude for Expanding Our Capabilities

We take risks every day; risk is very much a part of life. Most of these are risks we are comfortable with, like crossing the street against the light, riding our bike along a country road, moving in with our boyfriend, planning a pregnancy, or going online to meet someone. But some risks take us way out of our comfort zone. In many ways, they show us what we are truly capable of doing. I call these our *personal best,* an example of our growth for which we can be grateful. Often these are things that others take for granted, but for us require tremendous courage. I remember when a friend of mine left New York City to move to the country with her boyfriend, to a charming two-hundred-year-old house in the middle of nowhere. It was idyllic; the only problem was my friend couldn't drive. "Who drives in the Big Apple?" she laughed. So at age thirty-two she took driving lessons. She was terrified, because at this point in her life she knew that cars weren't just a romantic means of transportation: cars could kill.

Another example: I worked with a woman who wanted to become sober.

> I thought getting sober was a risk. Yes, I do see life very differently. I'm still trying to figure how my relationship with my wife will work now that I'm not anesthetizing myself. But a challenge I didn't anticipate was where I'd go to AA meetings. I thought I'd be most comfortable going to meetings in my suburban neighborhood, but I find the best meetings are in a downtown women's halfway house. Here are incredible women with their tales of risk that I never really thought were real: imprisoned on gun charges, suffering abuse, having their kids taken away from them. This is the group that gives me strength. If they can risk being sober, well, quite frankly, what am I whining about?

Gratitude for Risk and Resilience

What constitutes a risk for one of us may not be a risk for another. So it is easy to dismiss a challenge that friends or colleagues may have without realizing that what they are struggling with is huge for them. This opens up the point that, as we become more comfortable in our resilience, we become more comfortable in seeing resilience in others. Andrea and Sierra illustrate this: Andrea risked changing her outside, and Sierra risked changing her inside.

Andrea wanted to have a facelift. As an almost fifty-five-year-old architect in a basically all-male department in a firm in Jacksonville, Florida, she felt attuned to all the "ism's": sexism, ageism, weightism, "If there is such a word," and felt she needed to battle against them all. As a woman with stellar resilience Andrea began to think that she needed to expand how she thought about herself. So she did, with her typical vengeance.

For her birthday she decided to become her ideal self. She used her skills to carefully plan. She went on a diet, lost the forty extra pounds she had been carrying about, researched a surgeon, and decided to have a breast reduction as well as the long-anticipated facelift. Two weeks after the operation, as she returned to work telling everyone she'd had a vacation, Andrea was surprised about the tightness and numbness she felt around her neck. In fact, it scared her. She confided her concerns to her friend Marcia, who lived in Philadelphia. "Why didn't you call me before you had it done?" Marcia queried. "You know I had a facelift last year. I could have told you what to expect."

Andrea was flabbergasted. *Why didn't I call?* she thought. *Why didn't I research postoperative concerns? I researched everything else.*

"Yes, it is a huge change," Marcia continued, but Andrea wasn't listening. She realized that she had really wanted to get the facelift, and, if she'd known it was going to be so uncomfortable, well, perhaps she'd been afraid that she'd chicken out if she had gathered more information.

"So not me," was Andrea's takeaway. "I really should have more confidence in my personal decision-making." And the personal epiphany she had helped her do just that.

While the movie *The 40-Year-Old Virgin* was a comedy hit, it is often not funny when men and women find themselves approaching birthday milestones without ever having had a significant relationship, not to mention a significant sexual relationship. This was the case with Sierra, who was approaching her thirtieth birthday and was still a virgin. As a star athlete playing competitive soccer in high school and college, Sierra was used to having male friends, many male friends. "I can talk the guy-speak of sport stats with the best of them," she boasted. But this comfort level has not so far extended itself to her having a romantic relationship. "I think I'm too demanding," she admitted. "I tend to break it off just before it gets started. If it doesn't feel right, I just end it. It's weird: everyone is getting engaged, married, having kids; I feel like such a freak because I've barely been kissed. I get so scared about being alone when I'm old."

Sierra was a computer programmer by profession, and she was used to problem-solving by using nonverbal and intuitive means. So she was not adverse to my suggestion to break dating down into a series of small scripts, each of which would fit into the larger piece of actually forming a relationship with someone.

She began by taking a deep breath when she met someone and telling herself that all she had to do was to talk to him. The next step was to get to know him, but only if she wanted to. And getting to know someone, she began to understand, was something she could do gradually, that it wasn't "all or nothing."

"I realized that in the past I would scare myself by getting so far ahead of where I was in a relationship. I had him judging me for being so inexperienced sexually, then rejecting me because I wasn't good enough. I'd have us married, then divorced. I'd get myself so mixed up and frightened, I'd just want to run away. So my way of handling this was to just shut *him* down, especially if I liked him, and look like the *bitch* that I'm really not."

Understanding the Price We Pay
When We Are Not Grateful

What happens when we do not practice gratitude? Adrienne is an example. As a woman of self-contained resilience, she spent her life in constant fight mode, criticizing those around her, picking on them, trying to point up their negative qualities and their poor decisions. And as someone who devoted much of her time to this effort, she of course found others who were less than perfect, and she succeeded in pushing them away from her. This included her husband (who divorced her), her children (who distanced themselves from her), and her colleagues (who couldn't wait for her to retire). But Adrienne's attitude was *I'll be damned if I let them see me as inconsequential as well.*

Adrienne was a teacher who devoted most of the free time she had in the summer to making life miserable for the CEO of the local residential treatment program for the mentally ill that she had knowingly moved next to twenty years before. Now that she was retired, she increased her efforts. She derived much of her self-worth from trying to shut down this program, and she was a very disgruntled neighbor who attempted to rally the other neighbors about all sorts of imagined problems. She found other malcontents who also had less purpose in their lives than they perhaps wished, and together they kept after this program.

Adrienne invested a great deal of time and energy in her cause. In addition to organizing others to write and distribute flyers, she made phone calls and held meetings that provided some level of social engagement; her life was essentially barren except for this effort.

One day Adrienne found out her oldest son was visiting her ex, who still lived in a nearby community. She confronted her son, demanding to know why he didn't make plans to see her. He finally exploded and called her a bitter old woman. Something clicked in Adrienne. She realized the accusation was true. In her anger about all of the unfairness that life heaped on her, she had become someone she didn't even recognize and wasn't even sure she liked. But she wasn't sure how to change the situation. She was so very angry, and the treatment program was her target (but she sensed it was not the cause) of the great unhappiness that was her life.

Adrienne went to her house of worship that weekend and was able to listen to the service with a more open heart. The teaching was on the psalms and gratitude. She began to wonder what she had to be grateful for.

Gratitude Is the Key

The CEO of the residential treatment program decided to try a new approach in dealing with "the situation." She began by feeling some sympathy for Adrienne, who, the CEO believed, was so obviously unhappy and angry. And the CEO used her own resilience to get in touch with her gratitude and humor, beginning with being grateful that she was not Adrienne. This was a strategy that worked for her: The flexibility in her resilience allowed her to begin seeing Adrienne from a different perspective. And in doing this she took away the power she had been giving Adrienne. The situation was still very difficult, but now she saw Adrienne more as a flawed human being than as the avenging angel she was portraying herself to be.

We take so much in life personally, when so much of what we receive is really not about us. It can be humbling, actually, to think about life this way. Gratitude allows us to focus inward, creating space to see others more objectively.

Creating Gratitude on the Road to Resilience

There are many ways to use our gratitude to help us in being resilient. Within ourselves we can realize the joy that comes from being grateful, which is such a simple, formidable pleasure, and understand that, when we experience gratitude, many times we are owning our ability to redefine a situation so it is now safe and no longer toxic; this is a powerful antidote to life's stressors. With others we can use our gratitude to keep us focused on ourselves where we have control instead of focusing on others where we may have only influence (and that's only on a good day). In addition, we can appreciate ourselves more and use our gratitude to value what there is to understand in others, leaving the rest behind.

Sometimes, understanding the creativity required to pull gratitude out of a situation can give us a good laugh. And there are other humorous ways of using gratitude to help us in situations that are fraught with conflict. Two of my personal favorites are being grateful for not being married to *him*, and being thankful for not having *her* as a mother.

There are many relationships that we need to make sense of, and others where we burden ourselves by taking to heart more than we need to. Using our resilience is a very helpful approach to dealing with other people as we figure it all out. And for this we can be grateful.

Your Resilience Journal: Develop Conscious Gratitude

Begin a *daily gratitude* section in your journal. I encourage you to make this a daily activity where you note how you have created gratitude in your life.

Begin to notice that for which you are grateful. This may take some energy. It may take a change in perspective. It seems that so often we are hardwired to notice, to comment, to fester on what is not working. This is an opportunity to appreciate what is working, even on the smallest, almost inconsequential level.

Ask yourself: What am I grateful for today? Remember that you can be grateful for the random, the most gentle of things and events. A bird flying, the first snow, a smile given to you totally unexpectedly, a thank-you from your teenager, recognition from a coworker or supervisor, a day relatively free of pain, the love of a friend, the love of God.

Ask yourself: How have I created gratitude today? What have you given to others? Who have you thanked? Who have you smiled at? Who have you held the door for, or gone out of your way to do a small moment of service for? Who have you helped today, even if they did not know you did it?

For additional exercises to help you develop gratitude, visit http://patriciaogorman.com.

Summary

Our gratitude is a potent force in our developing resiliency. Our gratitude allows us to change our experience, to look for the positive, to understand the lessons in the challenges we face, and to be thankful for our ability to learn from them. Our gratitude also can help us diffuse conflict with others by enabling us to see beyond the conflict, sometimes using humor, by helping us not take personally the nonsense that others dish out. And our being grateful helps us appreciate the world around us and deepens our positive connection to ourselves and to others.

Conclusion

Owning Your Personal Power

TELL ME, WHAT IS IT YOU PLAN TO DO WITH YOUR ONE WILD
AND PRECIOUS LIFE?

—*Mary Oliver, Pulitzer Prize–winning poet*

START BY STARTING.

—*Meryl Streep, Academy Award–winning actress*

YOU CAN FALL, BUT YOU CAN RISE ALSO.

—*Angelique Kidjo, Grammy Award–winning singer and songwriter*

W*hen read in sequence,* the three quotes above are the
essence of using your resilience consciously. Throughout
this book you've learned about making a deliberate decision to
use the challenges in your life for strengthening your resilience and
applying what you've learned to enrich your life.

The key is to keep your resilience as a focus in your life and to be
vigilant about identifying and confronting the antiresilience factors
in your life—those *girly thoughts.* Stay focused on your resilience

patterns, whether you are using your strengths in only one area or in all of them; whether you are dealing with a crisis or just need to stop crowding out other important parts of who you are.

You now have the seven steps to guide you. Practice at least one step a day; that's why there are seven. By using this system, you can allow your mind to focus on concrete actions, and those actions will keep strengthening your resilience as you work through the steps on an increasingly deeper level. Experiment with making this work for you at your own pace by:

- giving meaning to the crises you face,
- listening with greater clarity to your inner resilient voice,
- enjoying your power to create helpful boundaries,
- relishing being optimistic, even when it feels reckless,
- practicing loving enthusiastically as you protect your heart,
- combating your *girly thoughts* with humor and grit as you lose your victim mentality, and
- creating gratitude in your life for who you are and what you have learned.

See what exercises you may want to develop for yourself, what new experiments you may want to devise to tackle a new challenge or as you revisit an old one. Remember, you can do this one exercise at a time, one step at a time, all on a daily basis. This is what consciously developing your resilience is all about: having more control over your life as you enjoy the gifts of *your* personal power.

Bibliography

Al Sabbah, H., C. A. Vereecken, F. J. Elgar, T. Nansel, K. Aasvee, A. Abdeen, K. Ojala, N. Ahlu-walia, and L. Maes. 2009. "Body Weight Dissatisfaction and Communication with Parents among Adolescents in 24 Countries: International Cross-Sectional Survey." *BMC Public Health* 9(1): 52. Accessed September 8, 2012. doi:10.1186/1471-2458-9-52.

Barker, E. T. and N. L. Galambos. 2003. "Body Dissatisfaction of Adolescent Girls and Boys: Risk and Resource Factors." *Journal of Early Adolescence* 23:141-165.

Broverman, I. K., D. M. Broverman, F. E. Clarkson, P. S. Rosencrantz, and S. R. Vogel. 1970. "Sex-Role Stereotypes and Clinical Judgements of Mental Health." *Journal of Counselling and Clinical Psychology* 34(1):1-7. doi: 10.1037/h0028797.

Cawood, E. and J. Bancroft. 1996, 2009. "Steroid Hormones, the Menopause, Sexuality and Well-Being of Women." *Psychological Medicine* 25(5):925-936. doi:10.1017/S0033291700035261.

Cekelis, S. 1998. "The Influence of Second Wave Feminism on Applied Psychology." Retrieved July 11, 2012, from psybernetika.ca/issues/1998/spring/cekelis.htm.

Chareny, D. 2004. "Psychobiological Mechanisms of Resilience and Vulnerability: Implications for Successful Adaptation to Extreme Stress." Washington, DC: American Psychiatric Association.

CNCA (Cancer Nutrition Centers of America). 2012. "BUSTED! Health & Aging Myths that Every Woman Should Know." Retrieved September 23, 2012 from http://cncahealth.com/health-info/.../womens-health-aging-myths.htm.

Coy, P. and E. Dwoskin. 2012. "Shortchanged: Why Women Get Paid Less Than Men." Retrieved from http://businessweek.com/articles/2012-06-21/equal-pay-plaintiffs-burden-of-proof.

Conely, T. and L. Ramsey. 2011. "Killing Us Softly? Investigating Portrayals of Women and Men in Contemporary Magazine Advertisements." *Psychology of Women Quarterly* 35(4):469-478.

Cytowic, R. April 9, 2012. "No Is a Complete Sentence." Retrieved August 23, 2012, from http:// psychologytoday.com/blog/the-fallible-mind/201204/no-is-complete-sentence.

Dolnick, S. and D. Hakim. August 29, 2012. "Women Employed by Lawmaker Describe Sexually Hostile Office." *New York Times.*

"Do We Really Want Un-Photoshopped Pictures?" July 16, 2012. *The Great Fitness Experiment.*

Dowling, C. 1981. *The Cinderella Complex.* New York: Simon and Schuster.

Dreisbach, S. 2009. "Exclusive Body-Image Survey: 16,000 Women Tell Their Body Confidence Secrets." Retrieved September 18, 2012, from http://glamour.com/health-fitness/2009/03/women-tell-their-body-confidence-secrets#ixzz26reSArjy.

Engineer Your Life. 2012. http://engineeryourlife.org/.

Danoff, R. January 18, 2011. "Myths of Sex and Menopause." MSN Health (BreastCancer. org).

Eron, J. and T. Lund. 1996. *Narrative Solutions in Brief Psychotherapy.* New York: Guilford Press.

European Women's Lobby. 2012. "Women's Rights and Cosmetics Advertising."

Felitti, V., R. Anda, D. Norenberg, D. Williamson, A. Spitz, V. Edwards, M. Koss, and J. Marks. 1998. "Relationship of Childhood Abuse and Household Dysfunction to Many of the Leading Causes of Death in Adults: The Adverse Childhood Experiences (ACE) Study." *American Journal of Preventive Medicine* 14(4):245–258.

Foundation for Inner Peace. 1976, 1992, 2007. *A Course in Miracles.* New York: Random House.

Fanning, P. and L. Frankfort. 2005. *How to Stop Backing Down and Start Talking Back.* New York: New Harbinger Press.

Frankel, V. 2006. *Man's Search for Meaning.* New York: Beacon Press.

Fredrickson, B. L. and T. Roberts. 1997. "Objectification Theory: Toward Understanding Women's Lived Experiences and Mental Health Risks." *Psychology of Women Quarterly* 21:173–206.

Gere, J. and C. Helwig. 2012. Young Adults Attitudes and Reasoning about Gender Roles in the Family Context. *Psychology of Women Quarterly* 36:301–313.

Good, J., C. Moss-Racusin, and D. Sanchez. 2012. "When Do We Confront? Perceptions of Costs and Benefits Predict Confronting Discrimination on Behalf of Self and Others." *Psychology of Women Quarterly* 36(2):210–226.

Greer, G. 1993. *The Change: Women, Aging and the Menopause.* New York: Random House.

Hutchinson, S. 2012. Personal communication, August 17, 2012.

Jacks, D. 1993. *Silencing the Self: Women and Depression.* New York: William Morrow.

———. 2010. *Silencing the Self: Across Cultures: Depression and Gender in the Social World.* New York: Oxford University Press (USA).

———. 2011. "Reflections on the Silencing the Self Scale and Its Origins." *Psychology of Women Quarterly* 35:523-529.

LeBoutillier, M. 1995. *NO is a Complete Sentence.* New York: Ballantine Books.

Lee, H. J., A. H. Macbeth, J. H. Pagani, W. S. Young (June 2009). "Oxytocin: The Great Facilitator of Life." *Progress in Neurobiology* 88 (2): 127–51. doi:10.1016/j.pneurobio.2009.04.001. PMC 2689929. PMID 19482229

Levine, M. 2012. *Teach Your Children Well: Parenting for Authentic Success.* New York: HarperCollins.

Lund, T. 2008. Personal communication.

Nolen-Hoeksema, S. January 2010. "The Power of Women: Could Aging Be Good for Women?" *Psychology Today.*

O'Gorman, P. 1994. *Dancing Backwards in High Heels: How Wonen Master the Art of Resilence.* Center City, MN: Hazelden.

———. February 2009. "Dancing Backwards in High Heels: Women and Resilience." *Recovery Living.*

O'Gorman, P. and P. Diaz. 2012. *Healing Trauma Through Self-Parenting: The Codependency Connection.* Deerfield Beach, FL: Health Communications, Inc.

Oliver-Diaz, P. and P. O'Gorman. 1988. *12 Steps to Self-Parenting.* Deerfield Beach, FL: Health Communications, Inc.

Pesta, A. July 18, 2012. "The War on 'Teen Vogue': Young Readers Escalate Campaign for 'Real Girls.'" *The Daily Beast.*

Ross, C. 2012. "Why Do Women Hate Their Bodies?" *Psych Central.* Retrieved on September 18, 2012, from http://psychcentral.com/blog/archives/2012/06/02/why-do-women-hate-their-bodies/.

Salter, J. 2012. "Legitimate Rape" Uproar. http://mercurynews.com/elections/ci_21354432/legitimate-rape-controversy-congressman-akin-lies-low-amid. Accessed August 20, 2012.

Sapadin, L. 2004. *Master Your Fears: How to Triumph Over Your Worries and Get On with Your Life.* New York: Wiley.

Smolak, L., M. Levine, and R. Striegel-Moore. 1996. *The Developmental Psychology Of Eating Disorders.* Mahwah, New Jersey: LEA.

Sussman, A. L., *Beyond Ballgames, the Impact of Sports for Girls: Women in the World.* http://womenintheworld.org/stories/entry/beyond-ballgames-the-impact-of-sport-for-girls. Retrieved 10/20/12.

Tessler Lindau, S., L. P. Schumm, E. O. Laumann, W. Levinson, C. A. O'Muircheartaigh, and L. J. Waite. 2007. "A Study of Sexuality and Health Among Older Adults in the United States." *New England Journal of Medicine* 357:762–774. Retrieved September 23, 2012.

Tiggemann, M. and E. Williams. 2012. "The Role of Self-Objectification in Disordered Eating, Depressed Mood, and Sexual Functioning Among Women: A Comprehensive Test of Objectification Theory." *Psychology of Women Quarterly* 36(1):66–75.

Tough, P. 2012. *How Children Succeed: Grit, Curiosity, and the Hidden Power of Character.* New York: Houghton Mifflin Harcourt.

Whitman, M. 2012. *The Martian's Daughter: A Memoir.* Ann Arbor: University of Michigan Press.

Wise, P., D. Dubal, M. Wilson, S. Rau, and M. Bottner. 2001. "Minireview: Neuroprotective Effects of Estrogen—New Insights into Mechanisms of Action." *Endocrinology* 142(3):969–973. Accessed May 30, 1012. doi:10.1210/en.142.3.969.

Wolf, A. 2002. *Get Out of My Life, but First Could You Drive Me & Cheryl to the Mall: A Parent's Guide to the New Teenager, Revised and Updated.* New York: Farrar, Straus and Giroux.

Wolin, S. and S. Wolin. 1993. *The Resilient Self: How Survivors of Troubled Families Rise Above Adversity.* New York: Villard.

About the Author

Patricia O'Gorman, PhD, a psychologist in private practice in Albany, and Saranac Lake, New York, is noted for her work on women, trauma, and substance abuse and for her warm, inspiring, and funny presentations that make complex issues accessible and even fun. She has served as a consultant to organizations in preventative and clinical strategic planning. Dr. O'Gorman is a cofounder of the National Association for Children of Alcoholics, and she has held positions ranging from clinical director of a child welfare agency to interim director of a crime victims organization to director of the division of prevention for the National Institute on Alcohol Abuse and Alcoholism (NIAAA). She is a veteran of numerous television appearances, including *Good Morning America, Today*, and *AM Sunday*. She is the coauthor of *Healing Trauma Through Self-Parenting: The Codependency Connection, Dancing Backwards in High Heels, The Lowdown on Families Who Get High, 12 Steps to Self-Parenting for Adult Children, 12 Steps to Self-Parenting Workbook, Teaching About Alcohol*, and *Breaking the Cycle of Addiction*, as well as numerous articles in magazines, including *Addiction Today, Counselor*, and *Recovery*. To learn more, visit http://patriciaogorman.com.

Index